SALT SPRING ISLAND

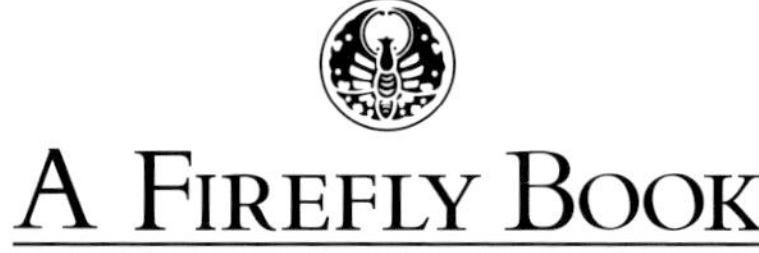

Published by Firefly Books Ltd. 2026

First Printing

Library and Archives Canada Cataloguing in Publication
Title: Salt Spring Island : a natural beauty / photography by J.A. Kraulis.
Names: Kraulis, J. A., photographer, author
Identifiers: Canadiana 20260153613 | ISBN 9780228106340 (softcover)
Subjects: LCSH: Saltspring Island (B.C.)—Pictorial works. | LCGFT: Photobooks.
Classification: LCC FC3845.S27 K73 2026 | DDC 971.1/28—dc23

Published in Canada by
Firefly Books Ltd.
50 Staples Avenue, Unit 1
Richmond Hill, Ontario
L4B 0A7

Published in the United States by
Firefly Books (U.S.) Inc.
P.O. Box 1338, Ellicott Station
Buffalo, New York
14205

Printed in China | E

We gratefully acknowledge the financial support of the Government of Canada for our publishing program.

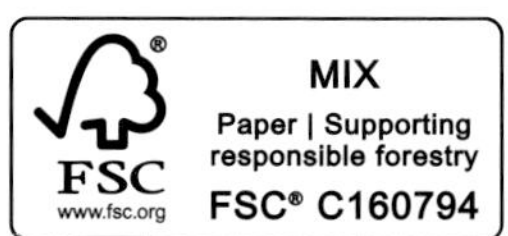

SALT SPRING ISLAND

A Natural Beauty

PHOTOGRAPHY BY

J.A. Kraulis

FIREFLY BOOKS

INTRODUCTION

IT IS A LATE MORNING in December on Salt Spring Island and stubborn clouds obscure all but the lowest portions of the island's rugged terrain. Outside, all is still. Not a twig on the leafless Garry oak by my window stirs, nor the slightest sway disturbs the long Douglas fir boughs that arch over the house. It has been like this for an hour, motionless, breezeless. Meanwhile, across the harbour shreds of floating mist drift, grow, dissolve, recompose, meandering slowly around the trees, evidence that air moves stealthily even when we can't feel it.

I am entranced by the languid, shifting loveliness of it. Such thoughts are what motivate my work. Photography involves memorializing a moment, a happenstance that will never repeat in exactly the same way again. And for the serious photographer it is about paying attention to beauty.

How to pay attention to Salt Spring Island? The island sits in the middle of the Salish Sea, the arm of the Pacific, all of which hooks around the southern end of Vancouver Island. It is the largest and most populous of the more than 200 Gulf Islands.

Every island is a territory uniquely identifiable, its natural boundary defined by water and water alone. The shape of Salt Spring is especially recognizable. It resembles a much-torn triangle, with numerous bays, coves, and long inlets among the bluffs and headlands.

Meanwhile many high points in the interior give grand vistas across the island-strewn sea towards major mountain ranges in all directions. To the north are the Coast Mountains; to the south, the Olympic Mountains; to the west and northwest, the Vancouver Island Ranges; to the east and trending southwards, the Cascades. Few places in North America offer such sweeping panoramas in the midst of such spectacular and varied geography.

Networks of hiking trails descend through forest that remains verdant year-round with abundant moss on the rocks and trees. It is especially lush and bright green during the wet weather. While almost all of Salt Spring was logged in the past, mature second growth makes the island densely treed again and there are still some surprises from the past in the woods: the occasional solitary old-growth Douglas fir with a two-to-three metre diameter trunk or a very stout western redcedar. Sitka spruce, grand fir, western hemlock and yellow cedar, round out the six largest species of trees in Canada, all of which grow on the island. Thriving amongst the conifers as well is the bigleaf maple, largest of all maples with the largest single leaves of any tree in the country, some of which have been measured to be half a metre wide.

Here in the rain shadow of the mountains, within the small region that is the only part of Canada which enjoys a Mediterranean climate, grows the Garry oak. Central to a threatened and rare savanna ecosystem, the younger trees are picturesque in their wildly free and gnarled growth. I often pause to admire the furrowed bark of the more shape-conforming older specimens which have progressed into a finely textured silvery grey. If bark is clothing, then the mature Garry oaks are dressed in elegant, well-tailored suits.

The most eye-catching tree on Salt Spring is the arbutus, unique both in kind and appearance. With dark glossy leaves year-round, it is Canada's only native broadleaf evergreen. The youngest trunks and branches are a sleek reddish orange, but as the tree grows the papery outer bark is regularly shed, revealing a skin-smooth yellow-green layer that is capable of photosynthesis. Clusters of small white flowers in the spring yield red berries in the fall, sometimes so profuse that at a distance the tree could be mistaken for having autumn foliage. With curving, twisting and turning limbs the arbutus can be sculpture as much as plant, and it is certainly the most frequently painted and photographed tree in British Columbia.

There is one arbutus at the end of a hill walk that I take regularly and which I have photographed dozens of times, accumulating over a hundred varied photos over the seasons. It is unremarkable in stature and most of it has died, with just two slender branches alive amidst the bulk of grey weathered bark-stripped limbs. But by studying the textures, forms and contrasts, the close details as well as the silhouettes from different sides, one can discover enough varied beauty in just a single tree to fill a book on its own.

In clearings in the woods and in the fields one encounters an abundance of flowers, which with their gorgeous colours and intricate geometry are the epitome of beauty. In the spring, most notably in Burgoyne Bay Provincial Park (Xwaaqw'um), daisies and buttercups gloriously carpet the meadows. But both species are invasive, crowding out the native plants, and restorative work seeks to redress the balance. Much worse are Scotch broom and gorse shrubs with a spectacular profusion of brilliant yellow blossoms but which residents are enjoined to extirpate wherever possible. As early as the beginning of February snowdrops and crocuses appear, then later in spring daffodils and foxglove, none of which are considered harmful but all of which also happen to be European in origin.

It is along the waterfront where one best experiences the nature of an island. Here the terrestrial world meets the marine and the concealing forest gives way to the open sea. The vast Pacific is not visible from Salt Spring, but it is ever present and felt in the currents that curl around the promontories and in the winter winds that storm in from the south. This nexus isn't just global, but cosmic, as the water's edge retreats and advances in eternal rhythm with the moon and the sun.

Ruckle Provincial Park has perhaps the finest section of coastline on Salt Spring, accessible via many kilometres of trails. Numerous coves alternating with rocky points give views of other islands across Captain Passage, Shingle Bay and down Swanson Channel. A lucky visitor may see porpoises or even a pod of orcas swim close past Yeo Point. The coast too is where geological history is well exposed, and some of the lustrous, variegated rock here prompts contemplation. The story locked in the stone is a very long one and anyone who looks at the multi-coloured complexity of a geological map of Salt Spring is quickly disabused of any thought of trying to summarize it. Most of British Columbia, its entire coast and far inland, not just the islands, consists of "exotic terranes," all accreted from distant islands arcs and fragments of seafloor crust. I have found reason for amazement in the mere knowledge that all of the island on which I live and the very bedrock under my house once came from somewhere in the far distant South Pacific.

When the tide retracts along the shoreline, the gaze is drawn downwards to investigate the beauty in the uncovered, fertile flats. I learned how to do this properly from our beloved dog, Shanti. That is, by taking time. Whenever we went to walk on one of the local beaches she, a Labrador retriever, was in her element, swimming and wading, looking at minnows, crabs and whatever else moved in the shallows under her. Her enthusiastic tail never ceased wagging, and no amount of cajoling and entreating could entice her to come home. Then one day to keep occupied I brought my cameras and started to explore the endless variety of colour, texture and fortuitous arrangements to be found in stones, driftwood, sea shells and drying seaweed exposed by the tide.

The resulting images became a catalyst for this book, when I realized that just the landscape and the details in nature alone on this relatively small island could sustain an entire volume of photography. In our complete absorption with the small wonders at our wet feet, Shanti and I became in sync. I sometimes wondered if she, and by extension other animals, had a sense of the beautiful, the sublime.

The sorts of animals living in and around Salt Spring have changed considerably over the last couple centuries. Gone are the wolves in the woods and the whales in the water. We now have an excess of deer, harmful to the regrowth of cedar stands through their appetite for the seedlings and saplings. The occasional black bear that arrives after a strenuous swim across Sansum Narrows often ends up shot in defense of the numerous local sheep. Sightings confirm that the more secretive cougars can survive here. Northern river otters are often seen swimming along the shore, sometimes briefly mistaken for the harbour seals that pop up here and there. The raccoon is also native to Salt Spring, as is the beaver, the red squirrel, the Douglas squirrel and the cute but unloved deer mouse. Not so the rabbit and the rat, which make one wish for more eagles, owls and hawks that are among the many birds on Salt Spring, where more than 300 different species have been spotted including herons, cormorants, gulls, mergansers and other ducks.

The most dominant species on Salt Spring is of course our own, *sapiens*, most of whom have also been introduced. To keep a consistent nature theme, I include no photos of people or their artifacts. Their stories and images could fill dozens of books. Many are writers, photographers, filmmakers, artists and sculptors, including some of the most recognized in Canada. Others are gardeners, organic farmers, artisans crafting a variety of goods, environmentalists and custodians of the numerous parks, nature reserves and sensitive habitats on the island. One could say that beauty is their business.

In British Columbia it is customary and proper to acknowledge that one resides on the traditional, ancestral territory of First Nations. Beyond the extensive historical, political and social conversation which that recognition entails, to whom the land belongs is perhaps not the question as much as who belongs to the land. In the case of Salt Spring Island it is the SENĆOŦEN and Hul'q'umi'num' speaking peoples who have been here the longest and cared for it the most. I owe particular gratitude to the STÁUTW – Tsawout, who welcome all to their reserve land on which many of the photos herein were taken. It is to them that this book is dedicated.

J. A. Kraulis
Fulford Harbour
December 2025

High tide at the Tsawout Reserve, looking southeast towards Russell Island.

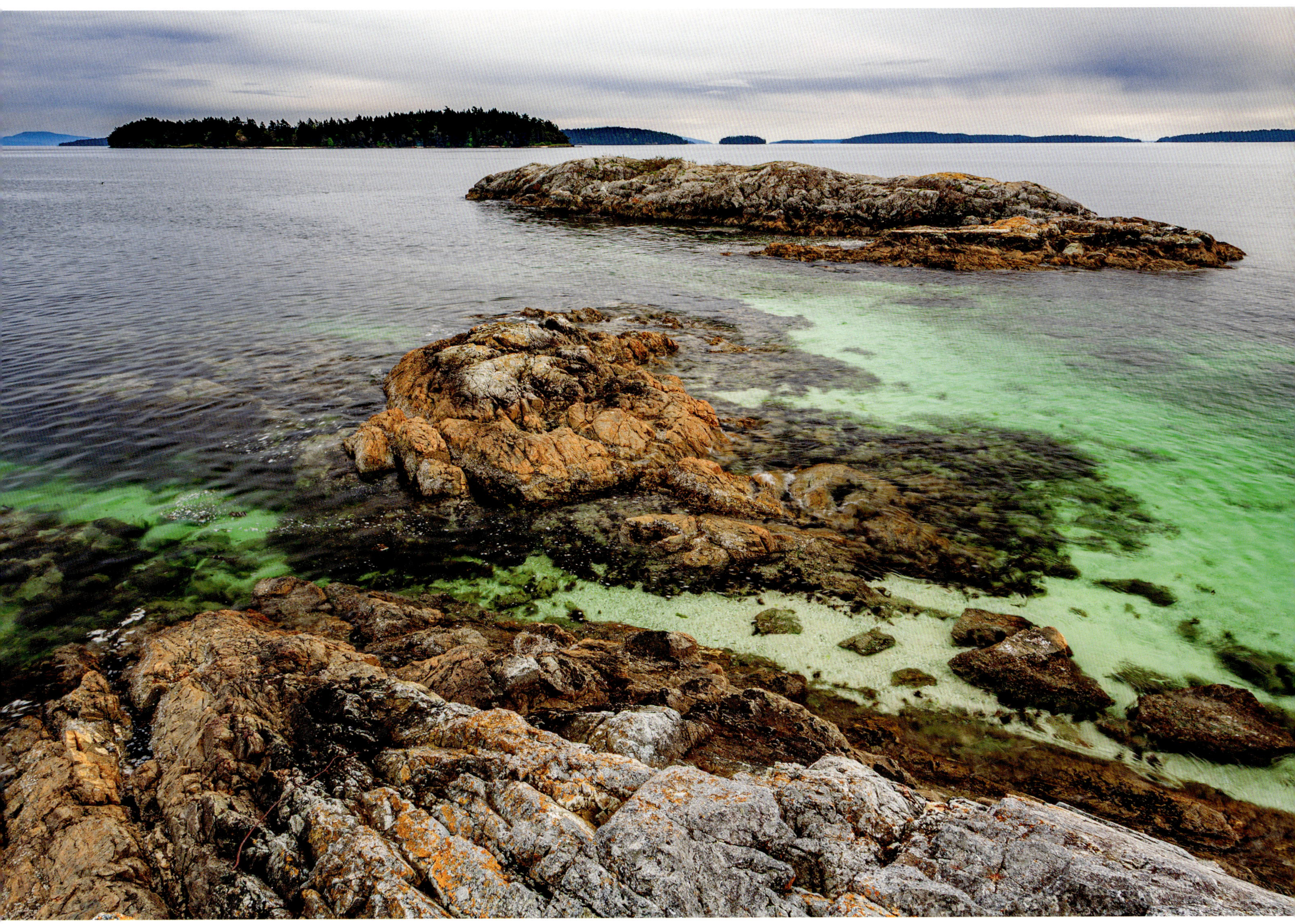

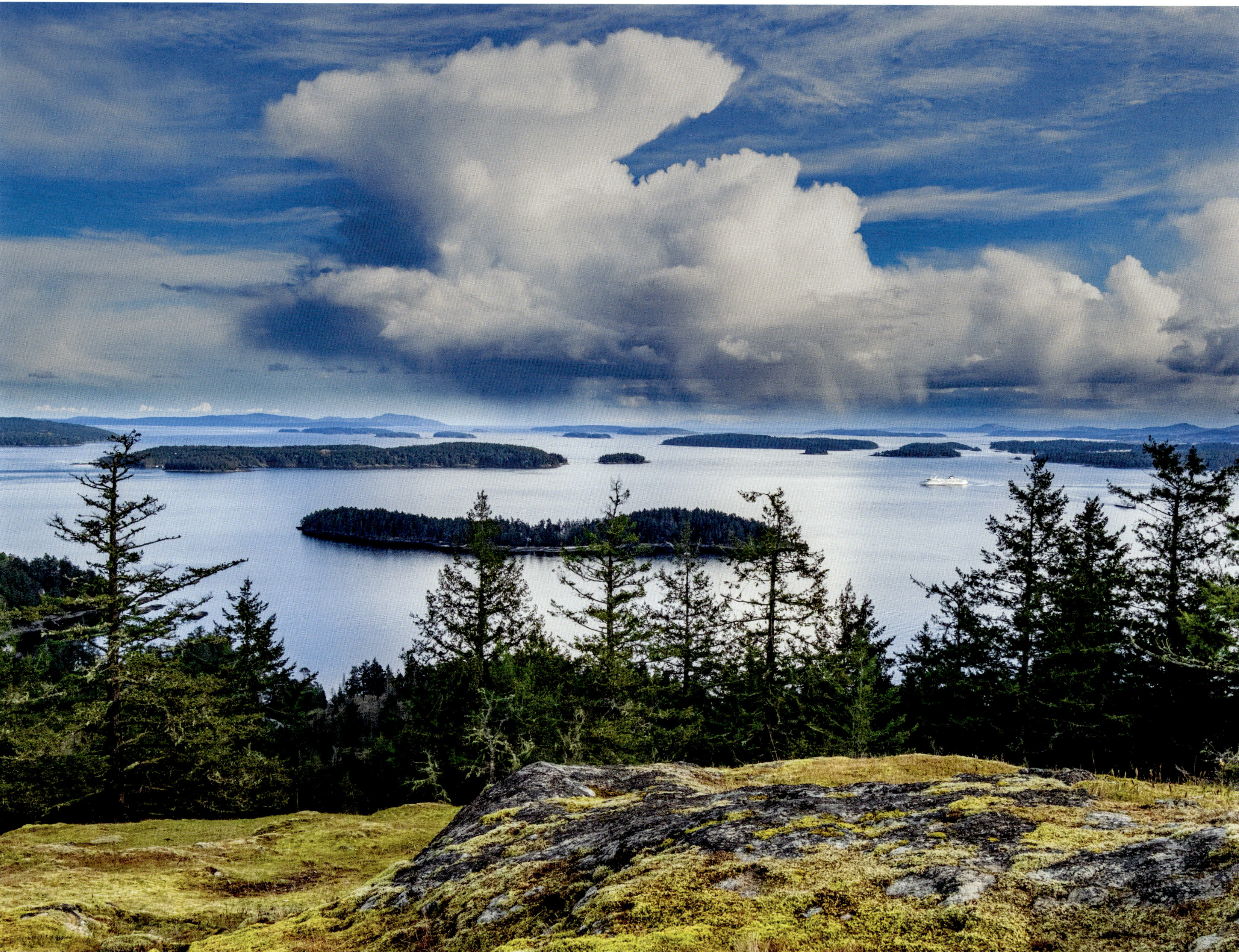

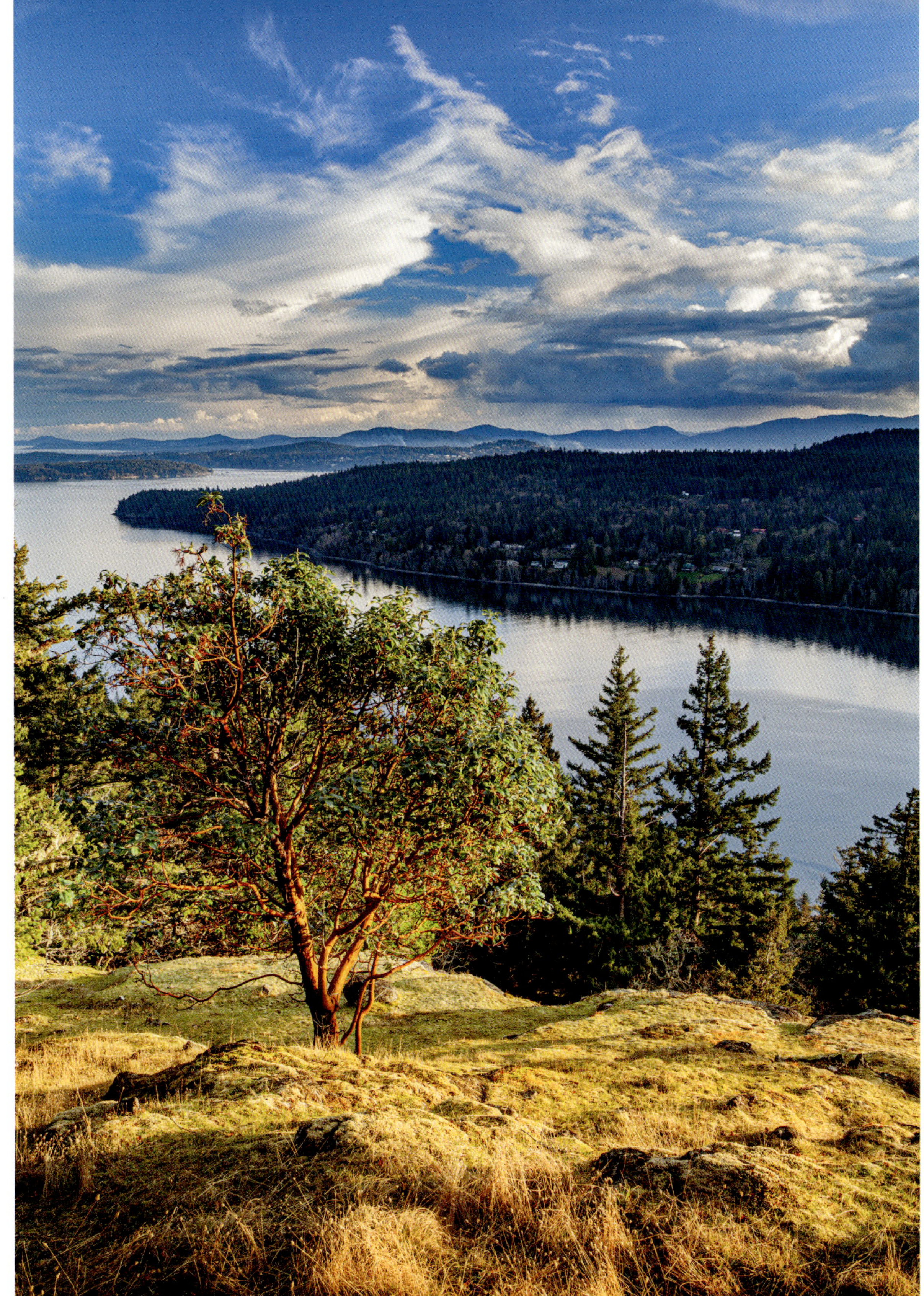

From different locations on Reginald Hill: a view of Russell, Portland, Brackman, Coal and other Gulf Islands with Washington in the distance (left), and across Fulford Harbour to Isabella Point (right).

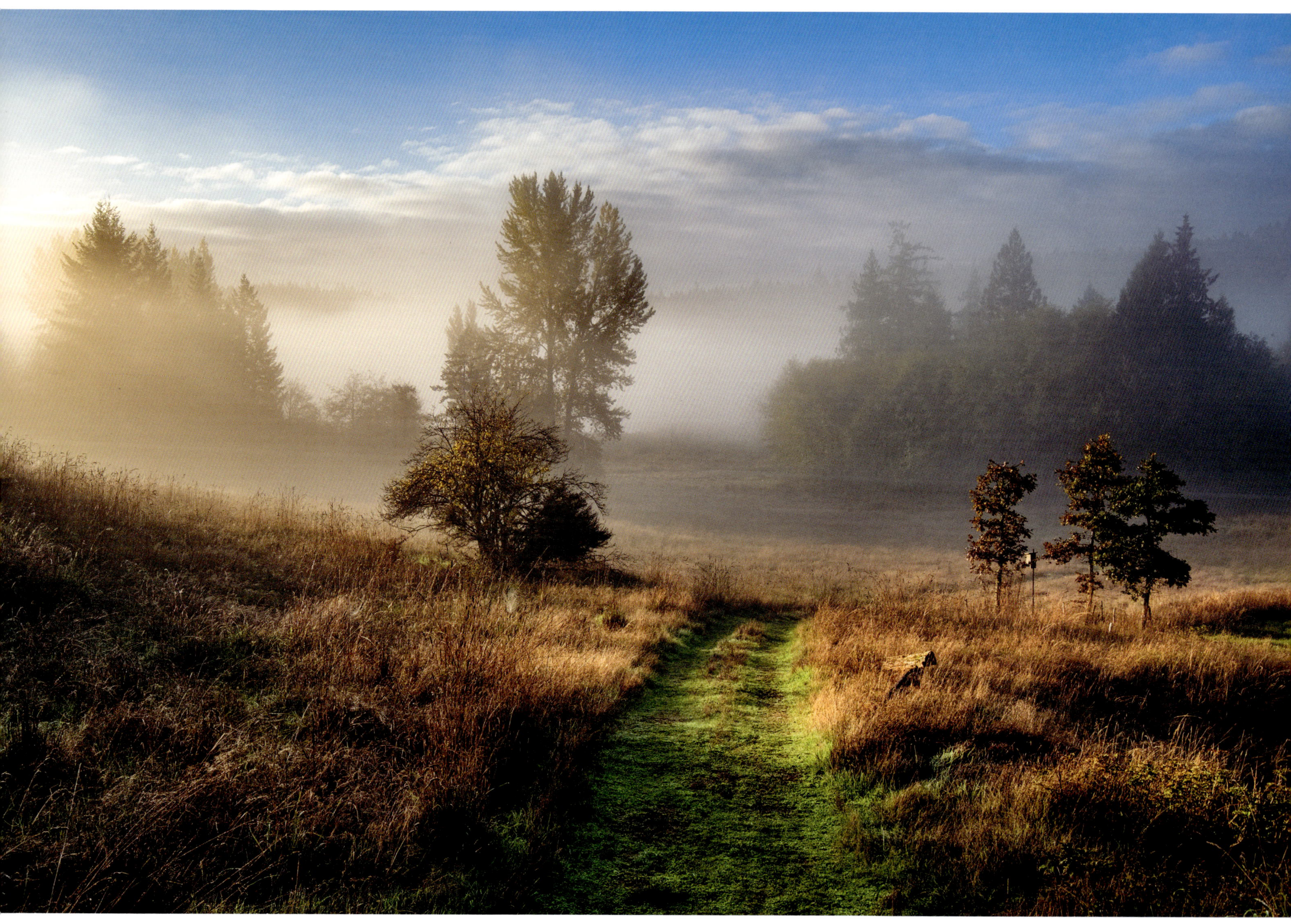

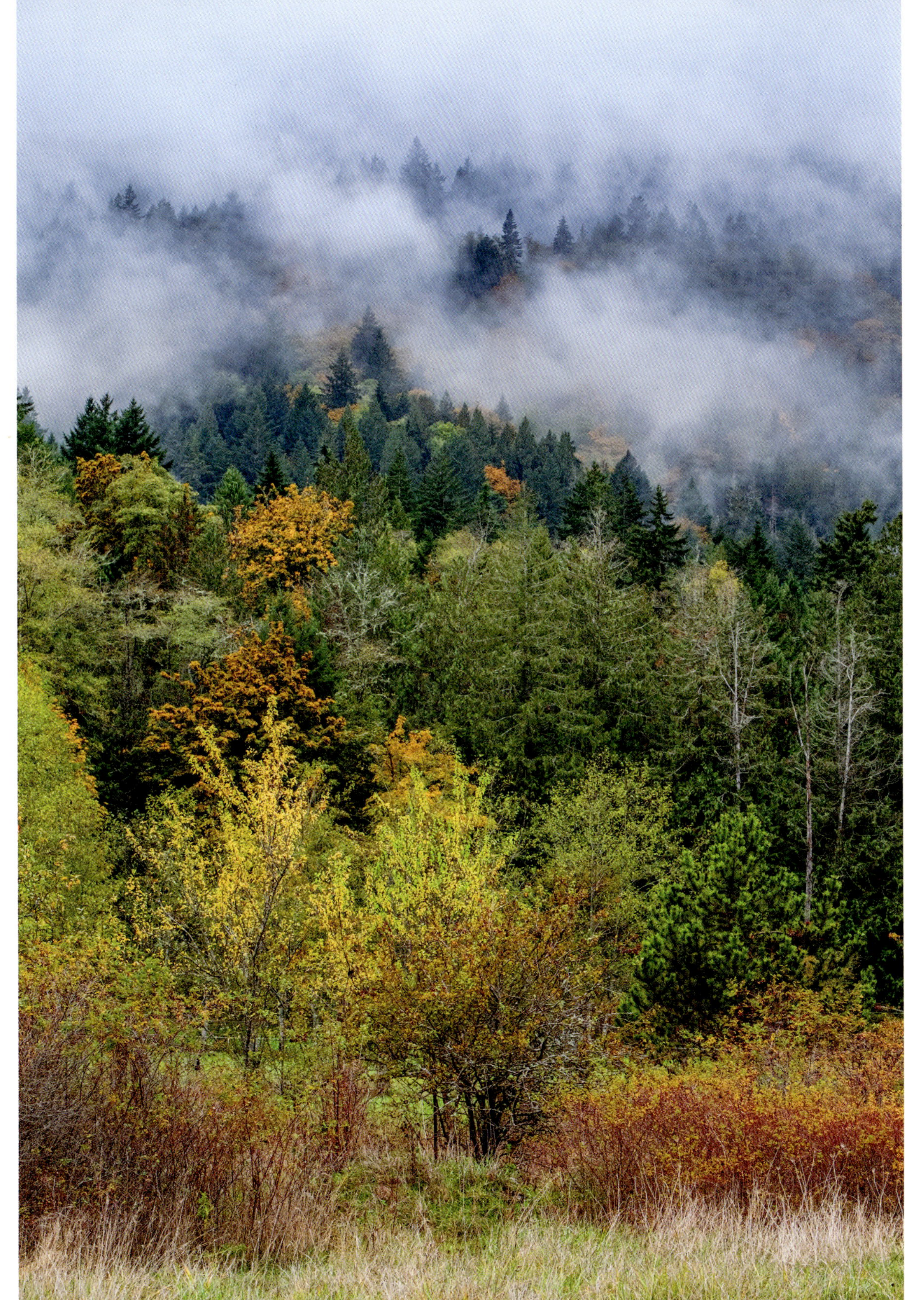

Mid-October weather: morning mist at Blackburn Lake Nature Reserve (left) and shifting low cloud on the slopes of Mount Bruce from Fulford Valley (right).

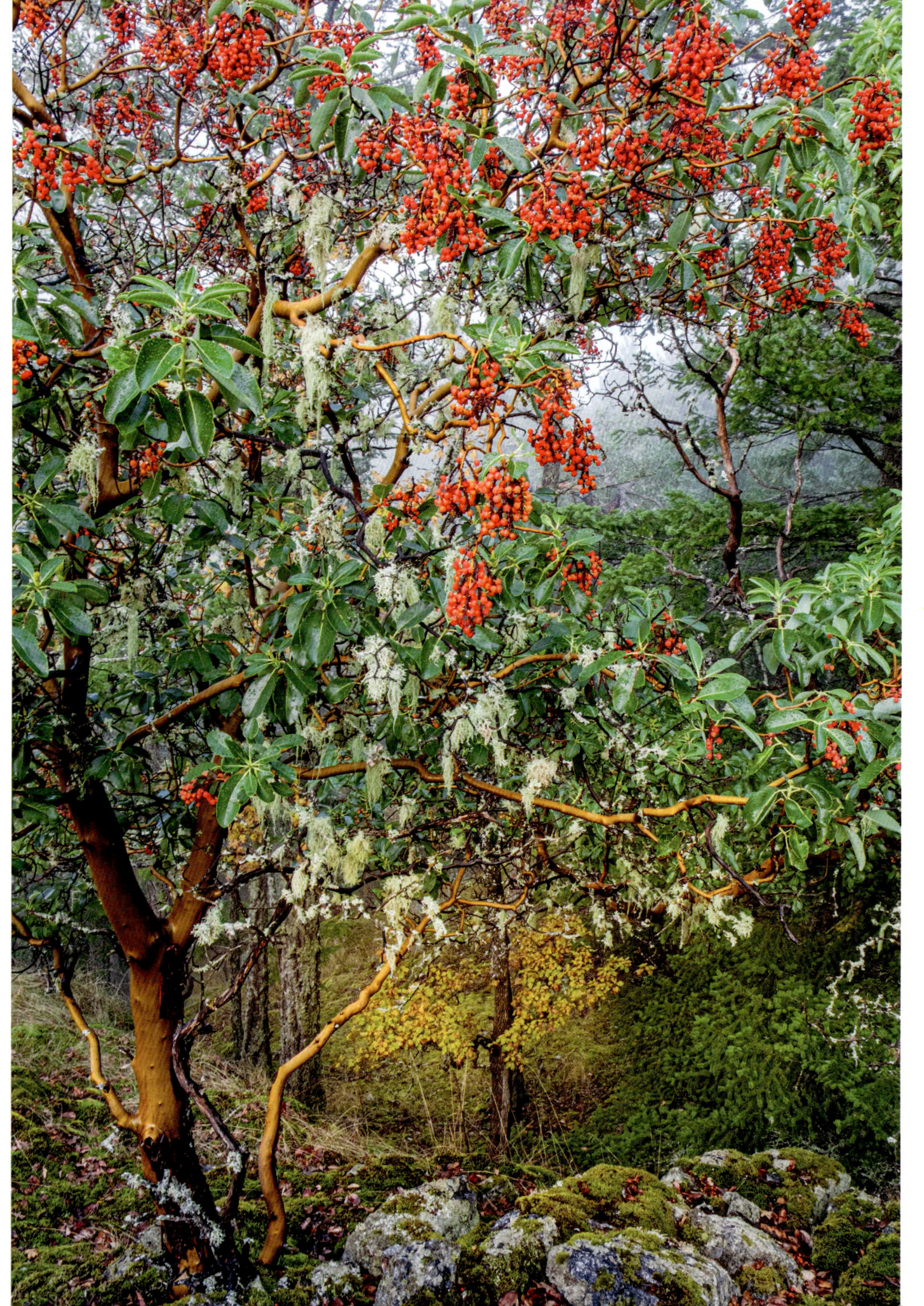

Early November colour in arbutus berries (left), and on a bigleaf maple, framed by the trunks of conifers (right).

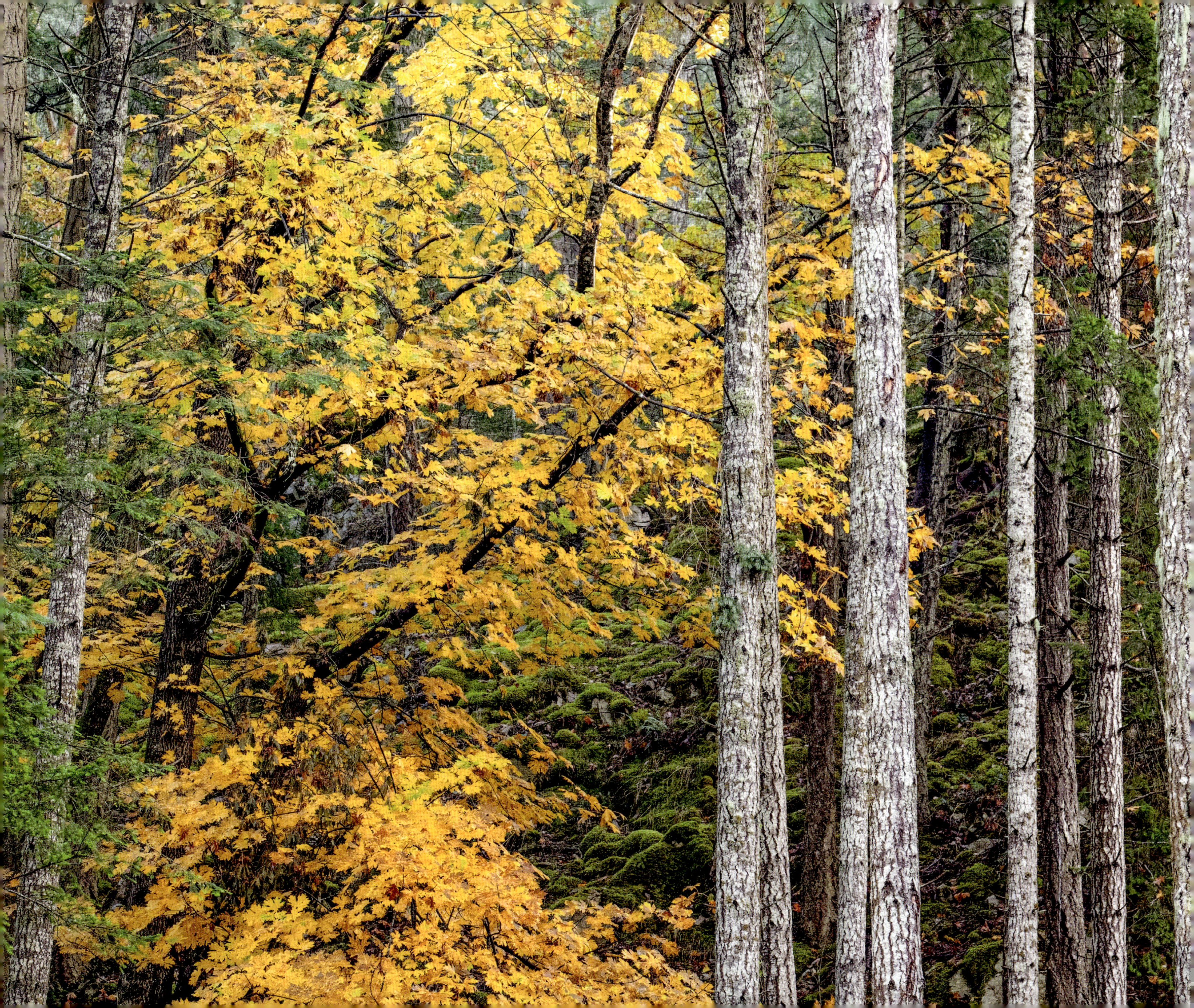

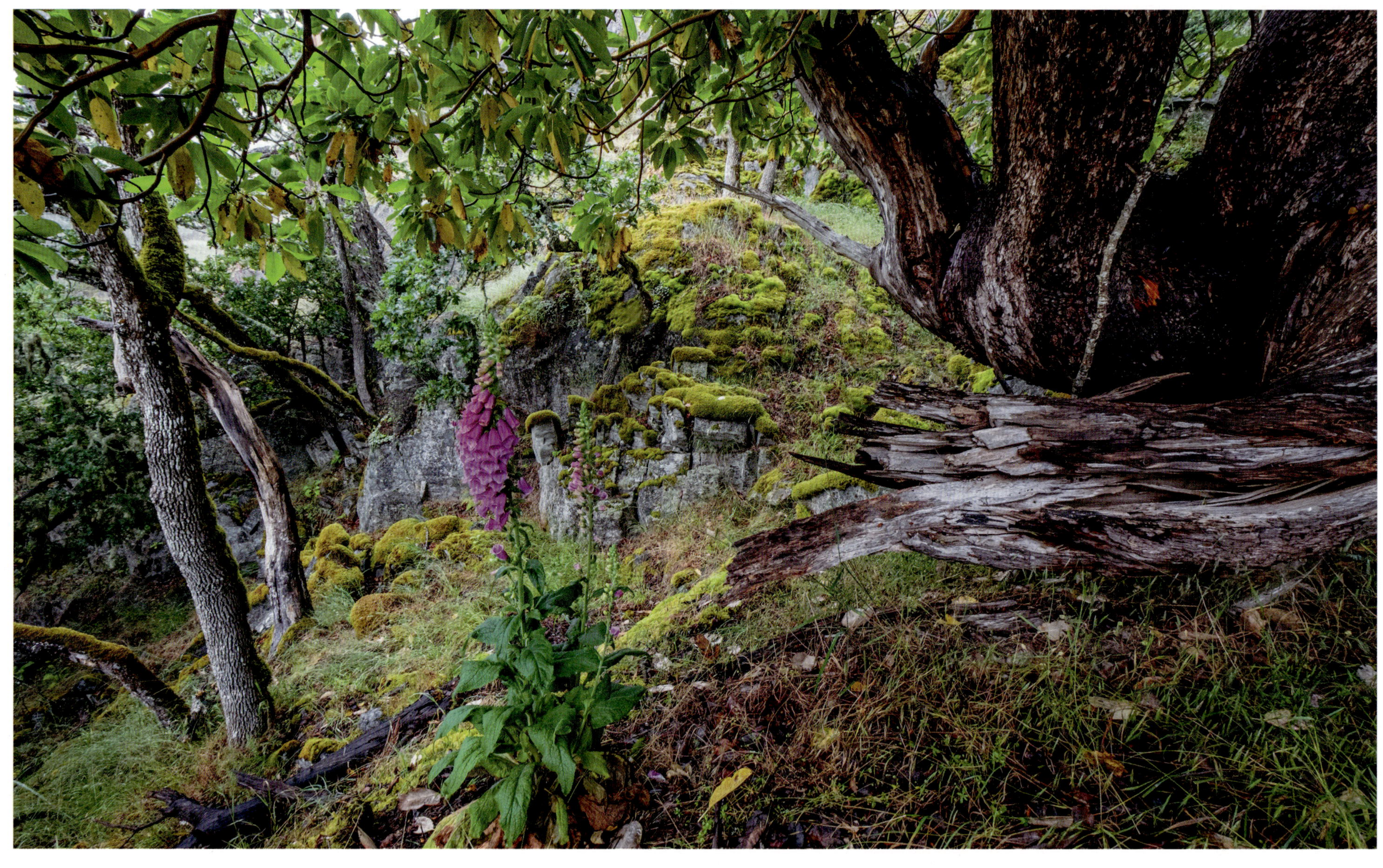

Foxglove amidst Garry oak and a robust, mature arbutus (above), and cornflowers, poppies, daisies and foxglove on a berm along Furness Road (right), both in June.

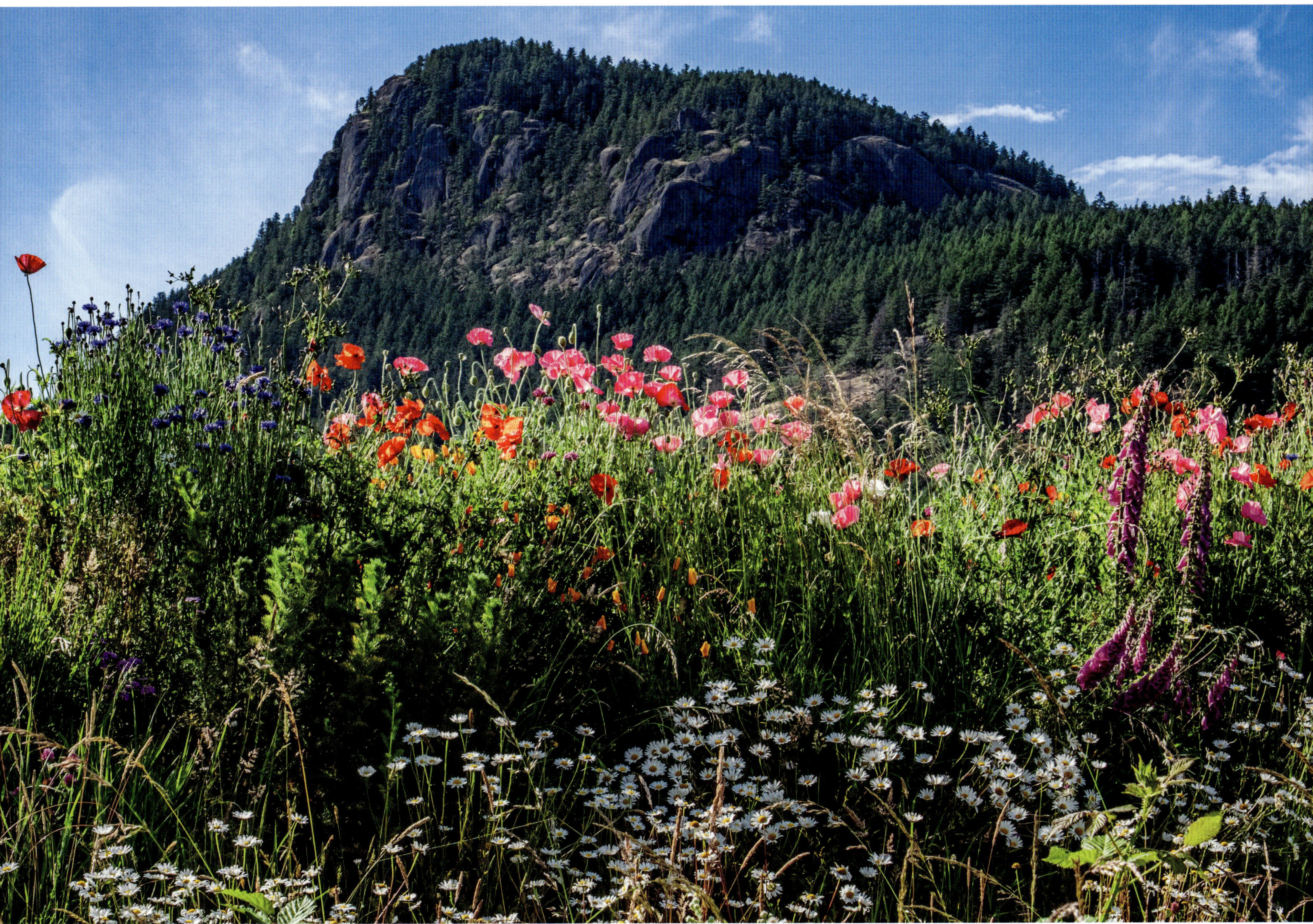

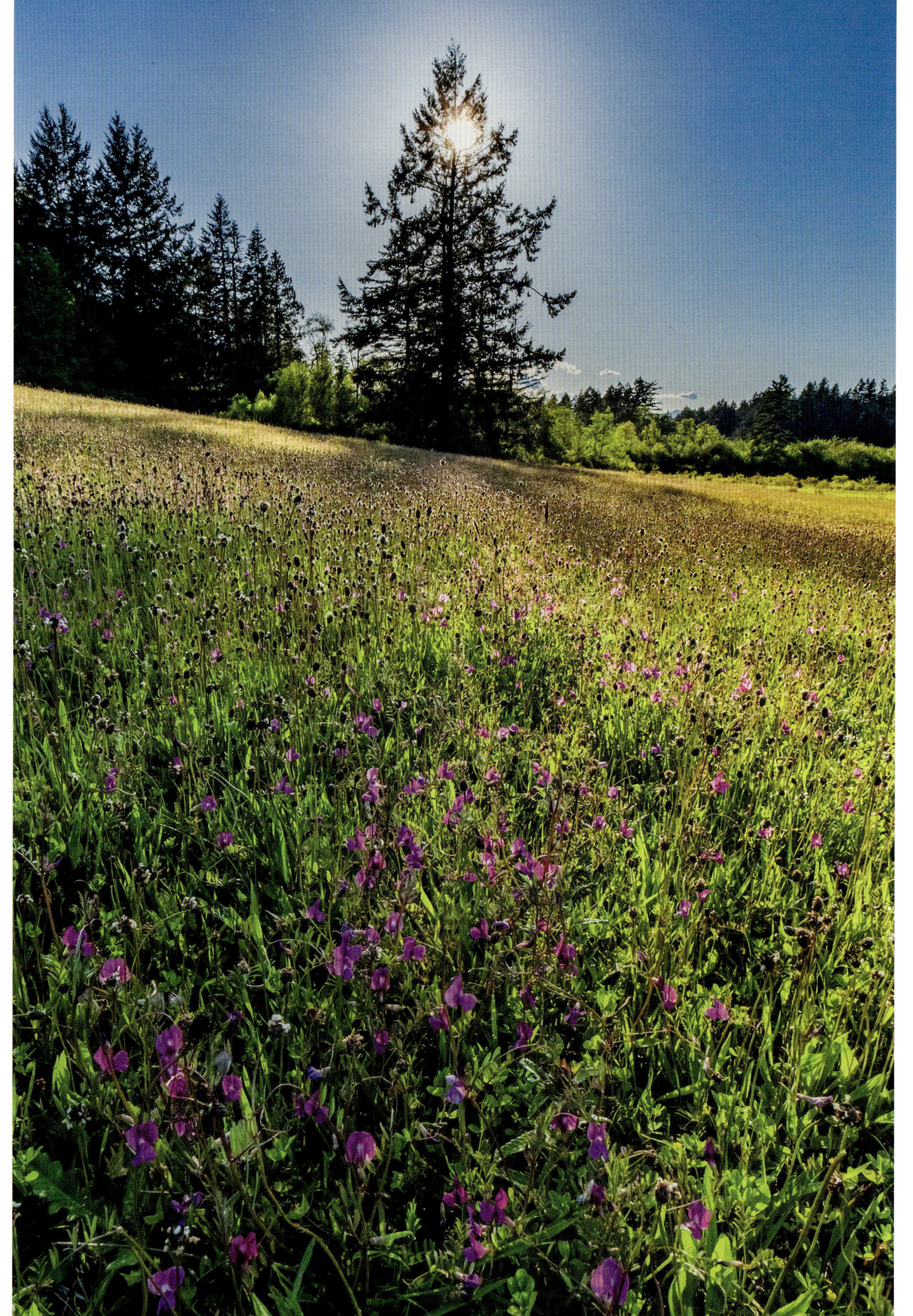

Pea flowers (left) and daisies (right), in the meadows of Burgoyne Bay Provincial Park in May.

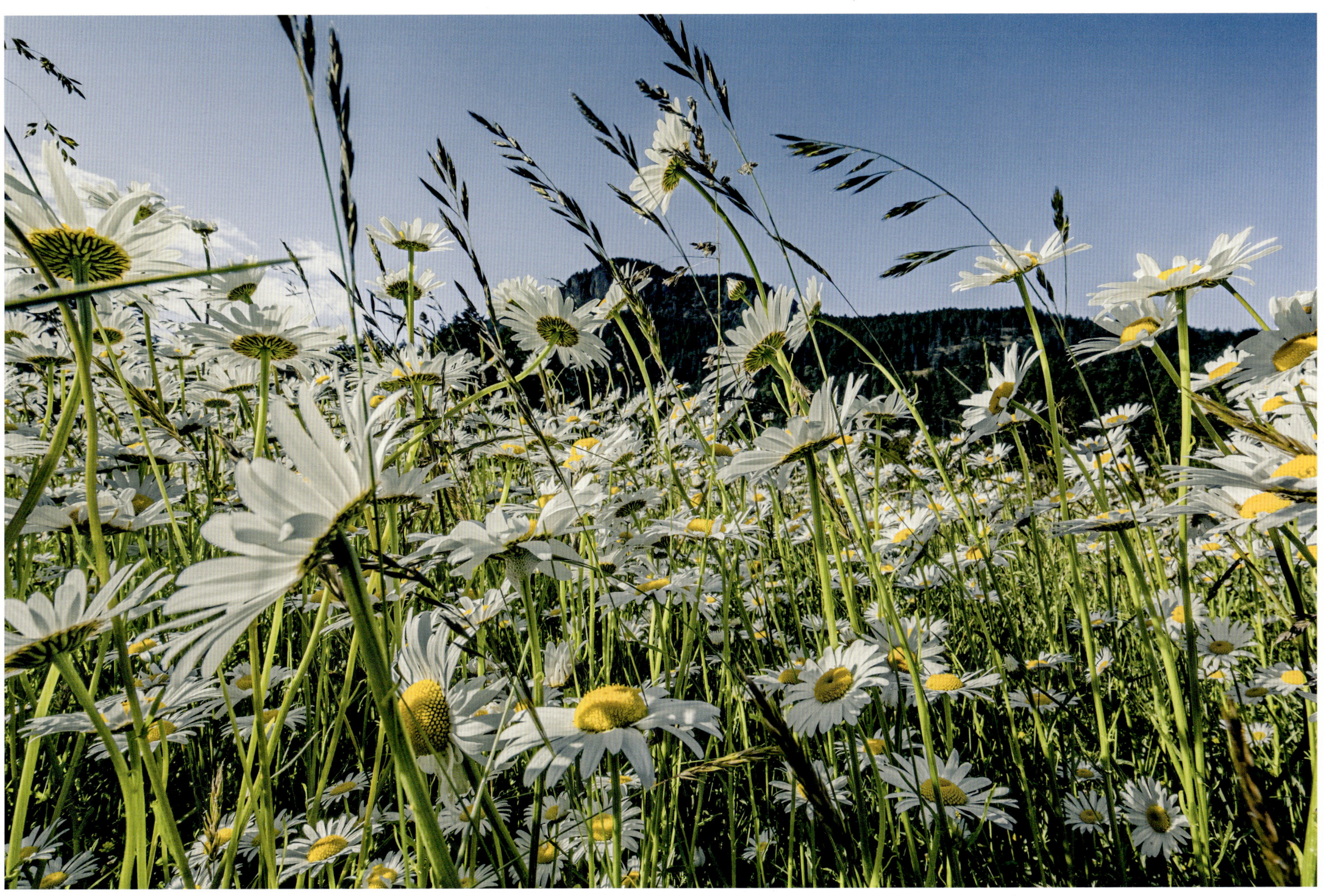

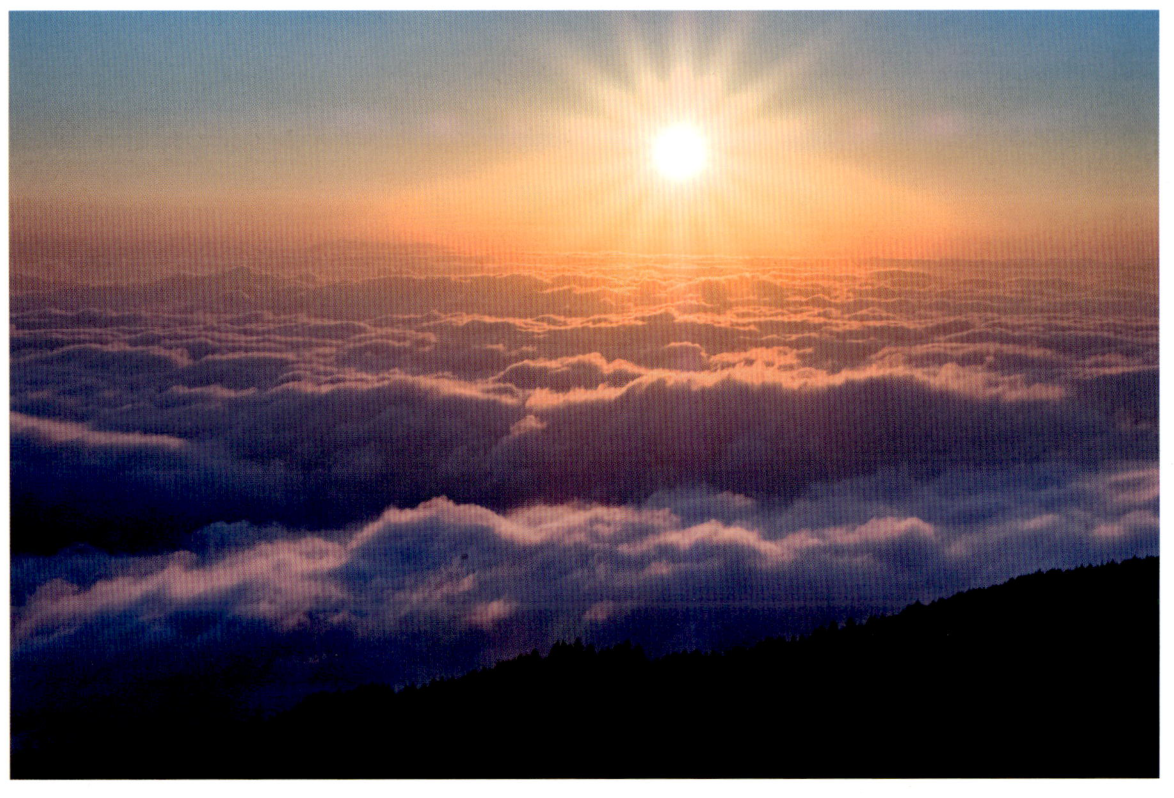

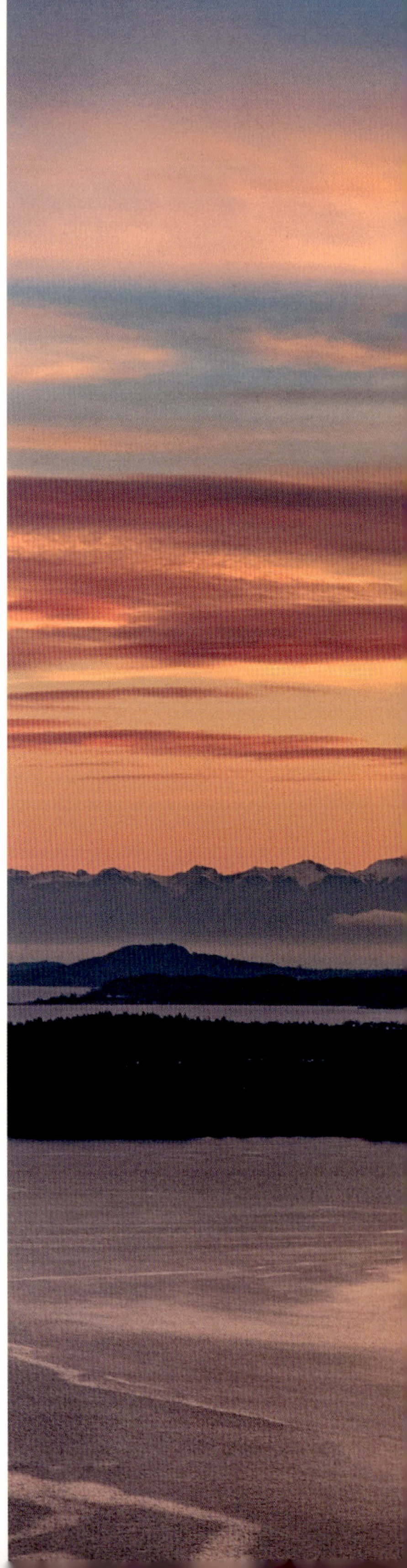

Sunrise over a fogbound sea from the summit of Mount Bruce in late October (above).

A January sunset from Reginald Hill, looking beyond Isabella Point to the Olympic Mountains in Washington on the horizon (right).

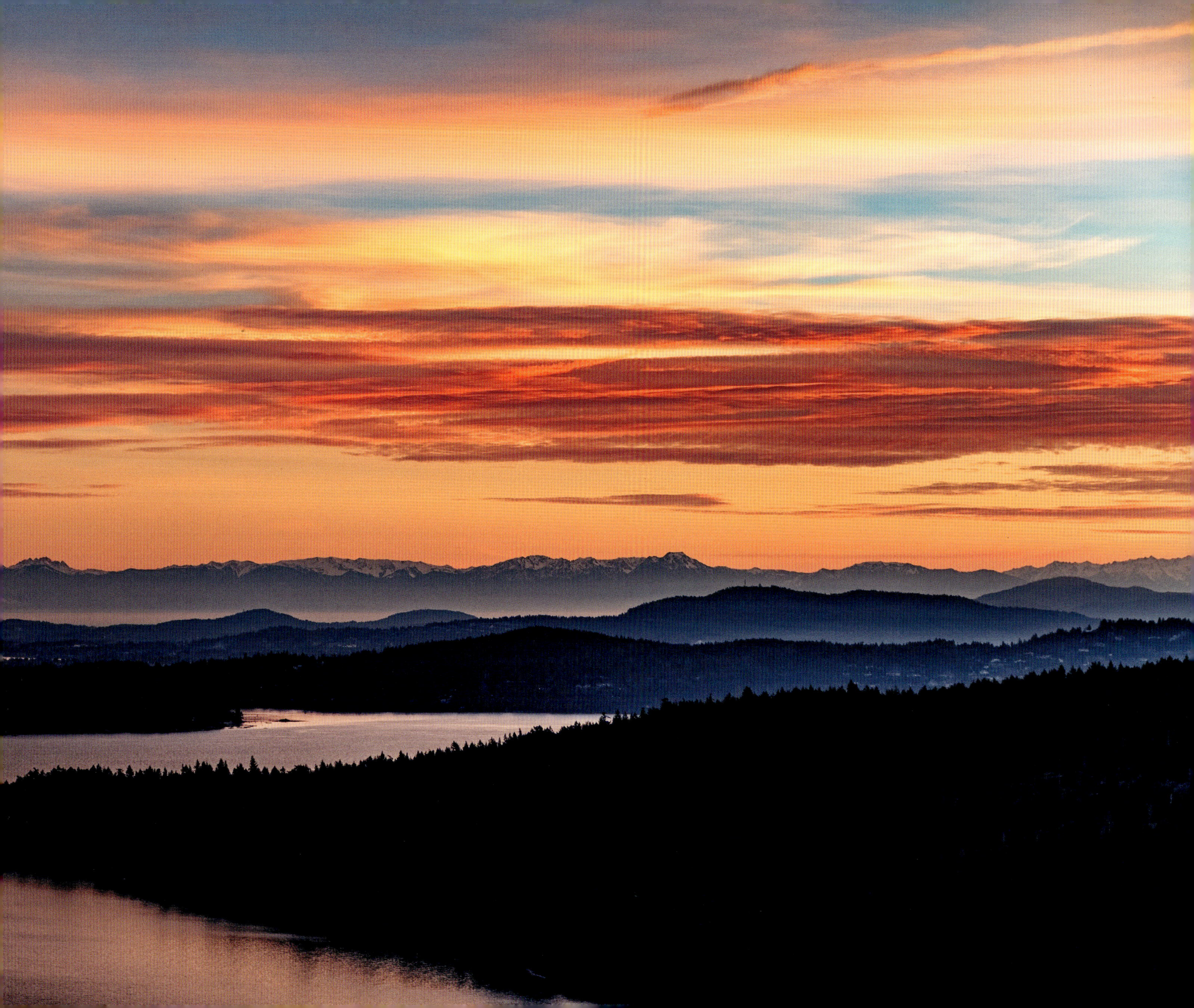

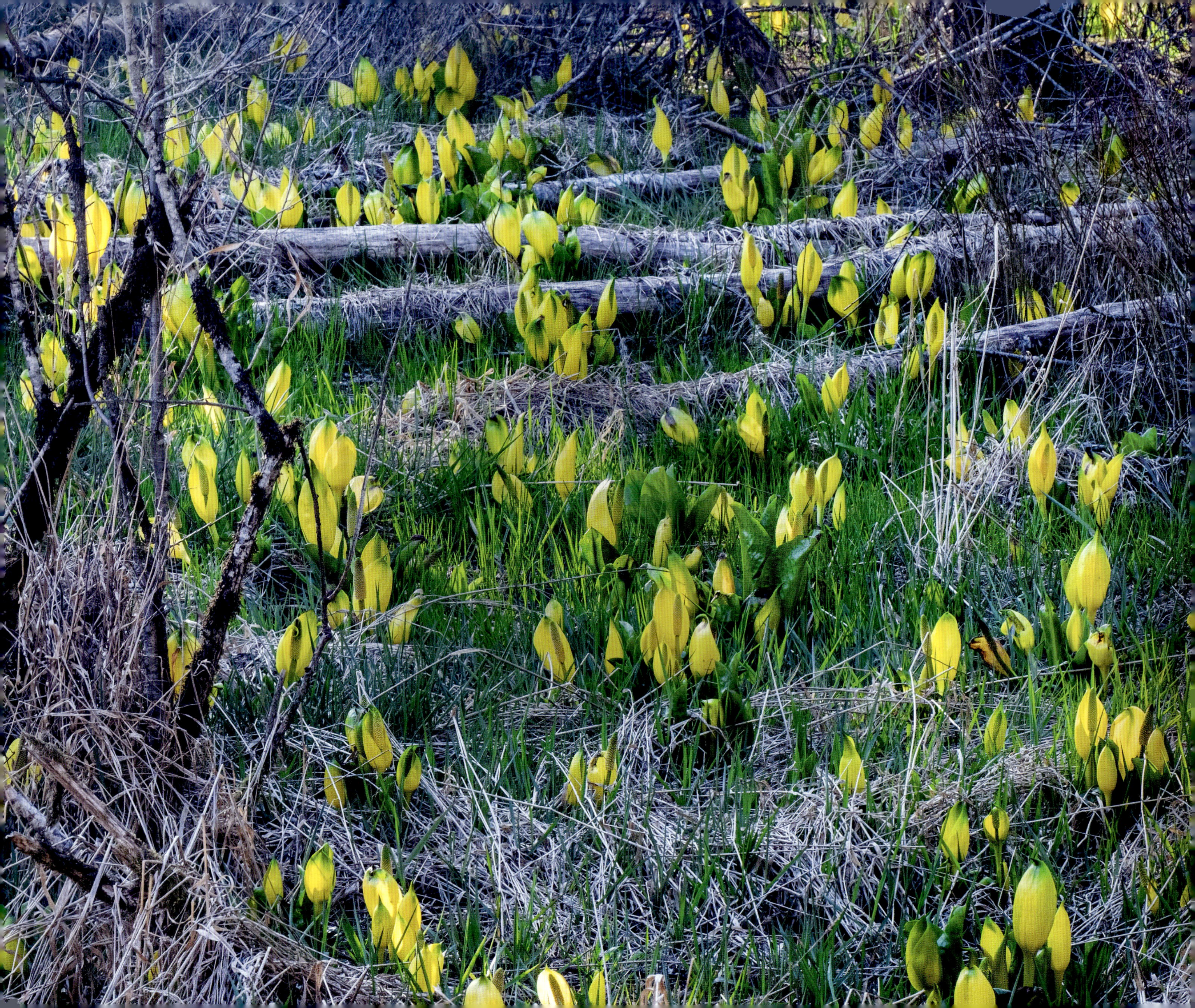

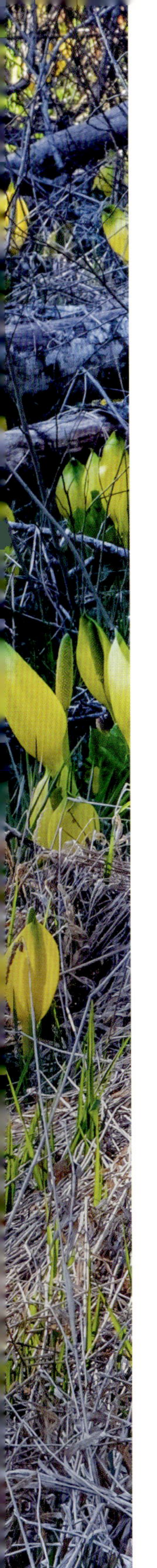

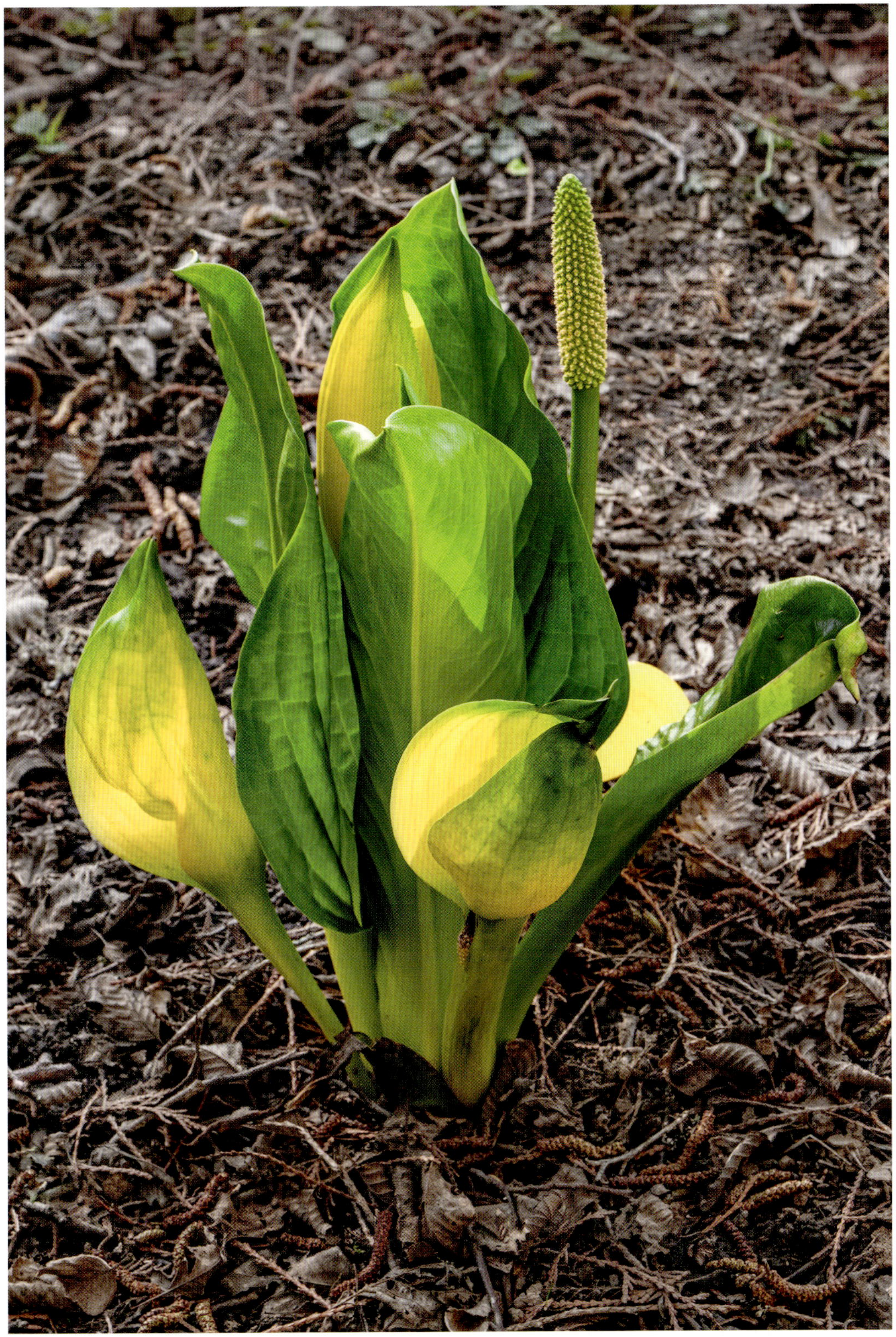

Skunk cabbage is at its most colourful in late March and early April.

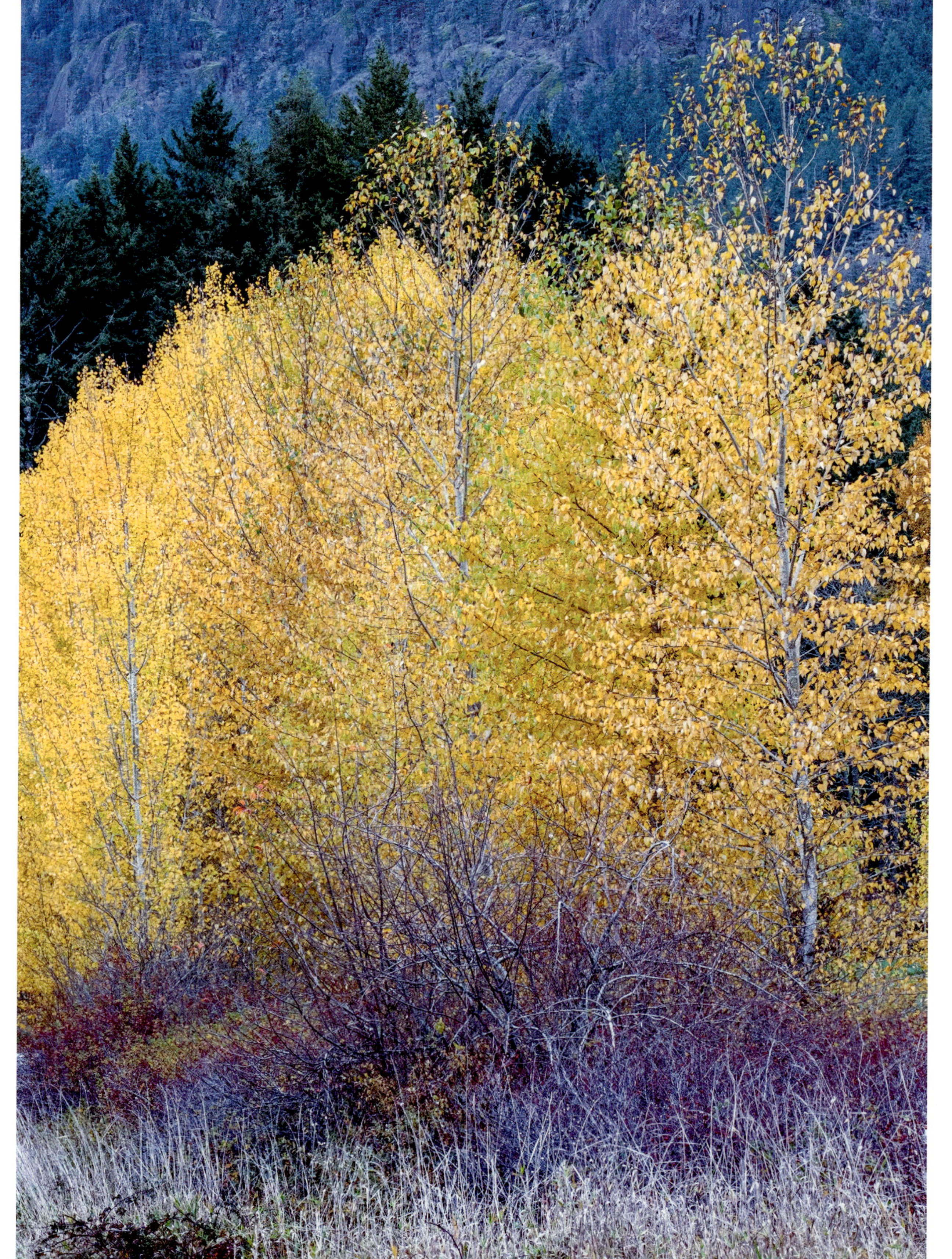

Aspen in autumn at the junction of Fulford-Ganges and Burgoyne Bay Roads (left), and orchard blossoms at the end of King Road (right).

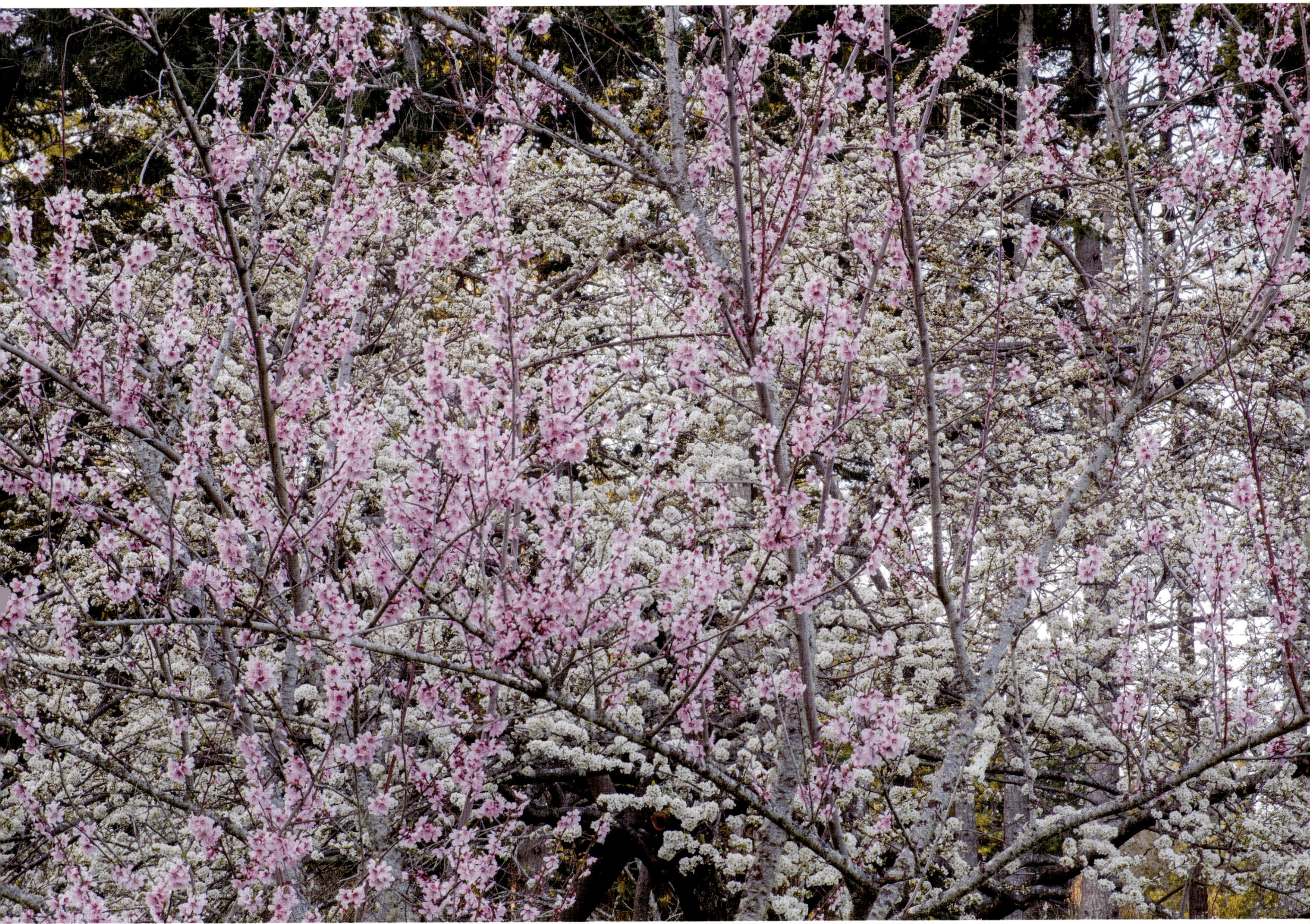

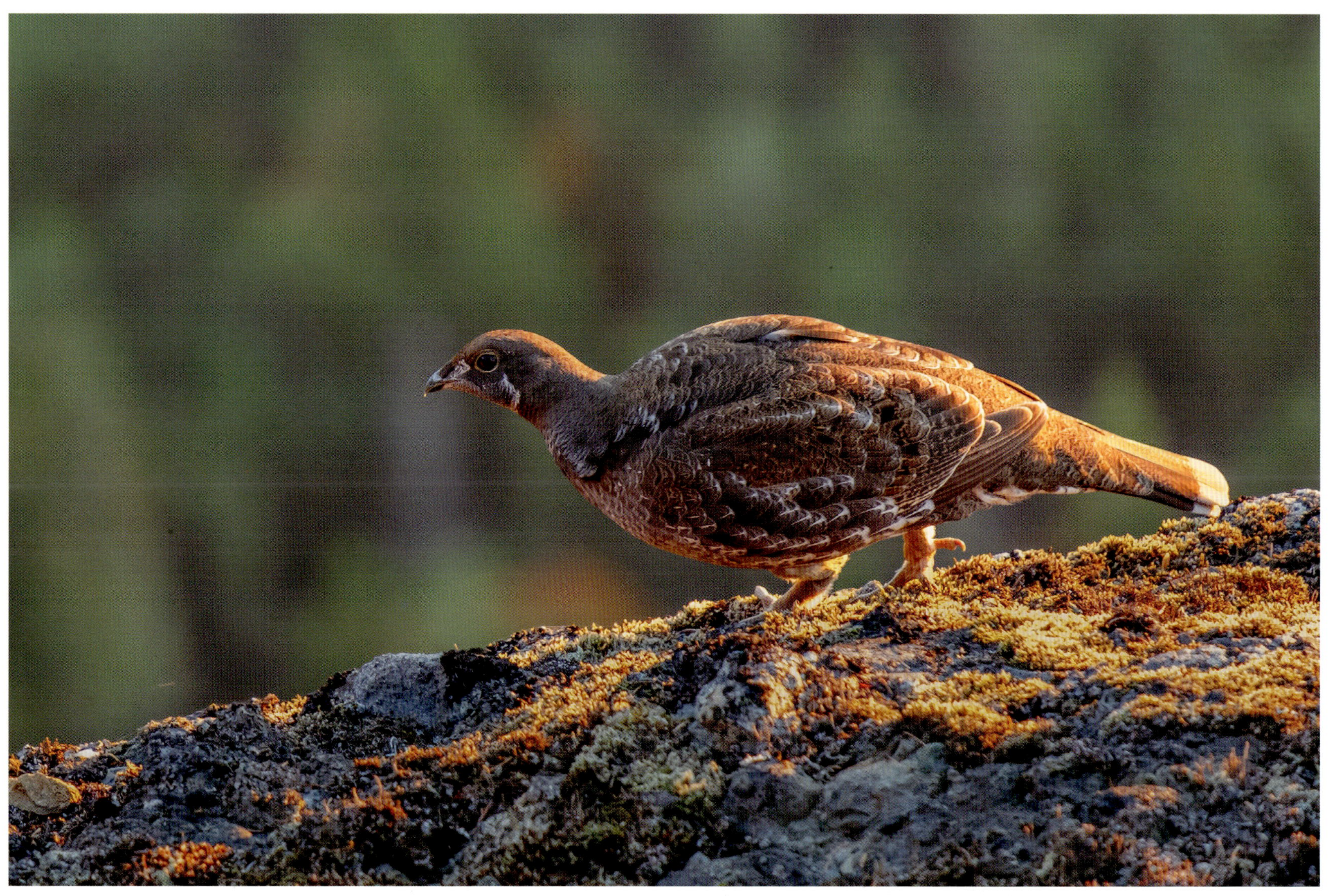

A sooty grouse walks the cliff edge at the summit of Baynes Peak (above), and a bald eagle surveys Fulford Harbour (right).

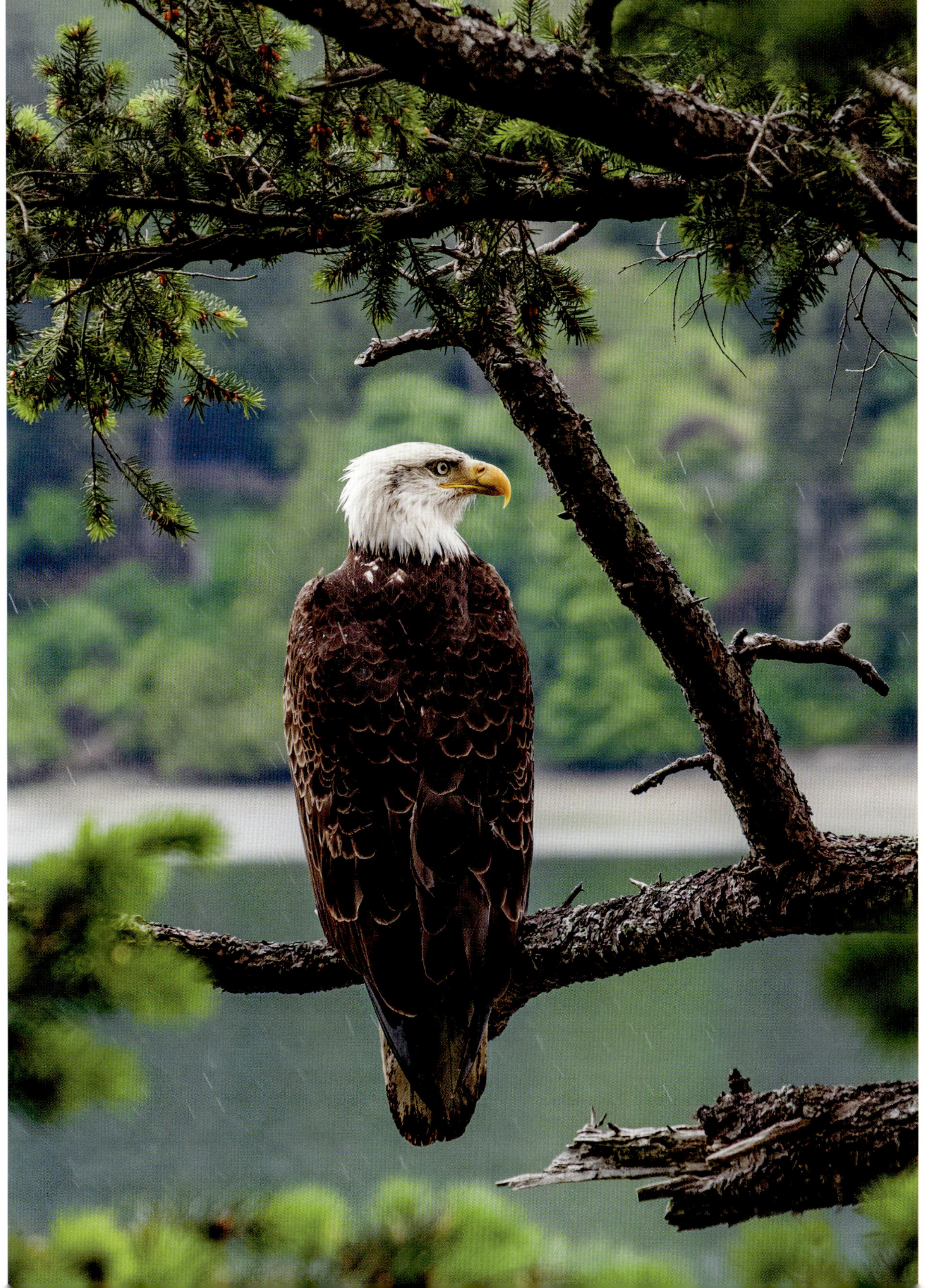

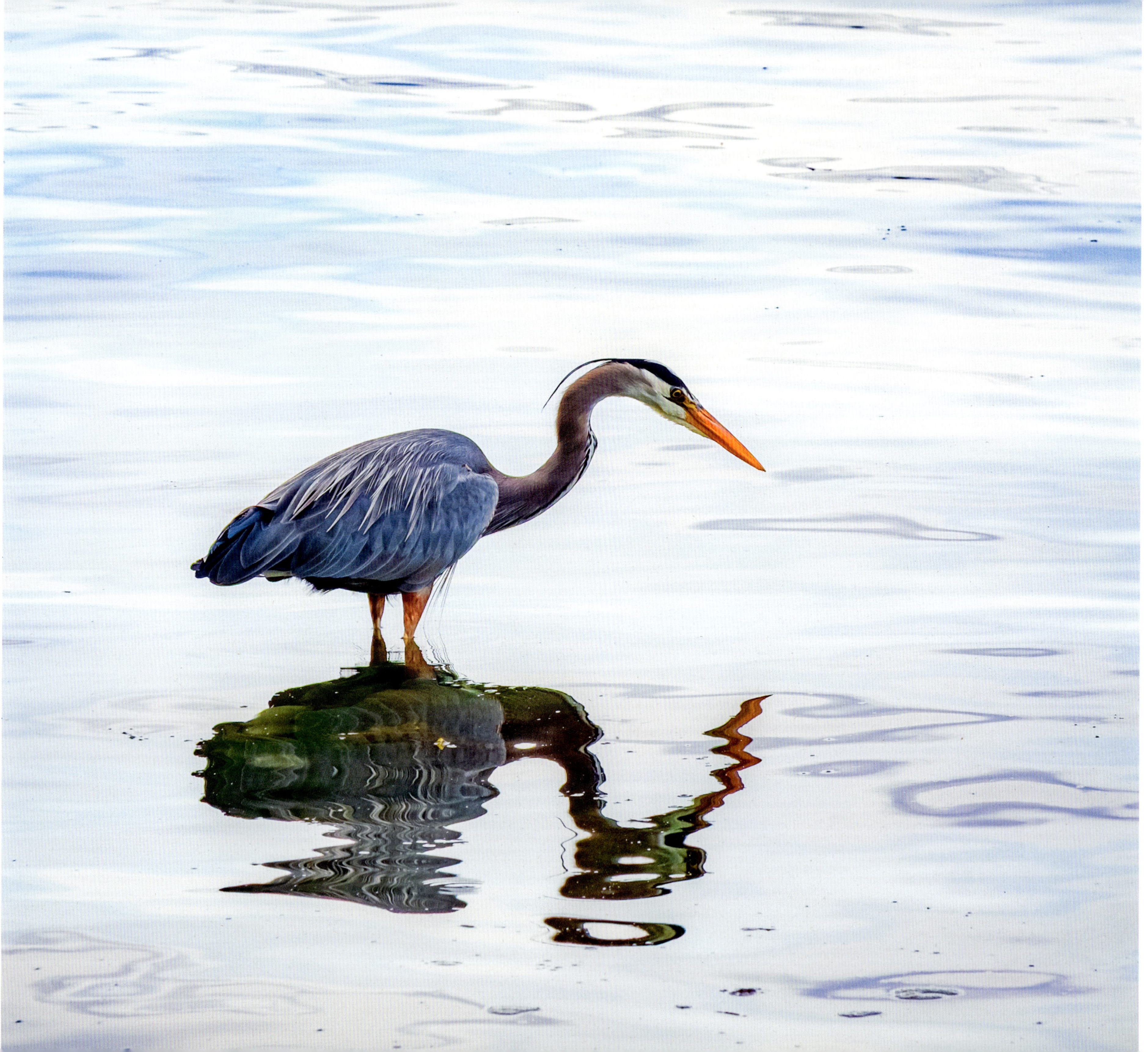

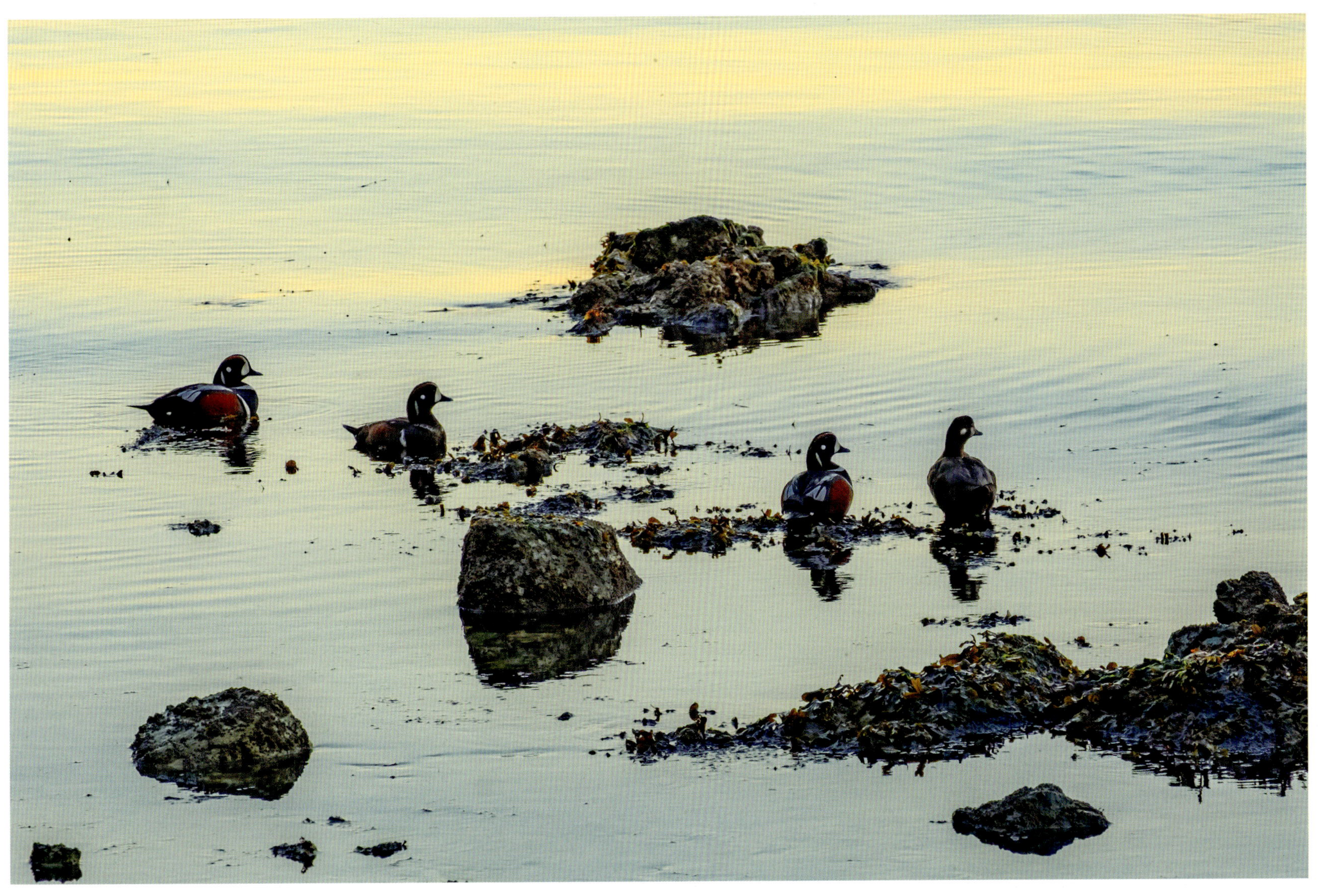

Great blue herons and harlequin ducks are regularly seen year-round in the waters around the island.

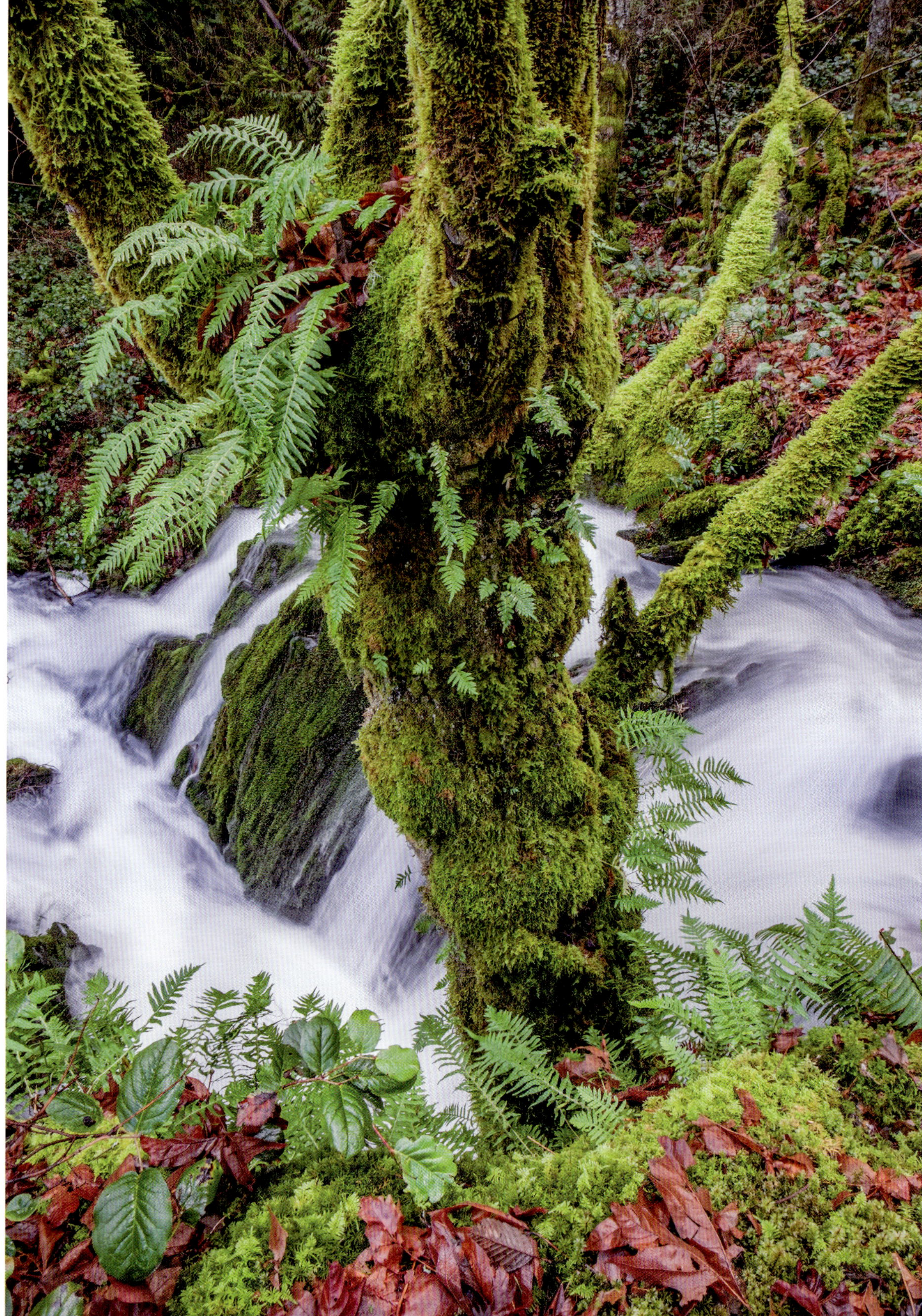

Licorice fern on a mossy bigleaf maple over a waterfall in Mount Tuam Ecological Reserve in January (right).

Foxglove and arbutus on a rainy day in early July (far right).

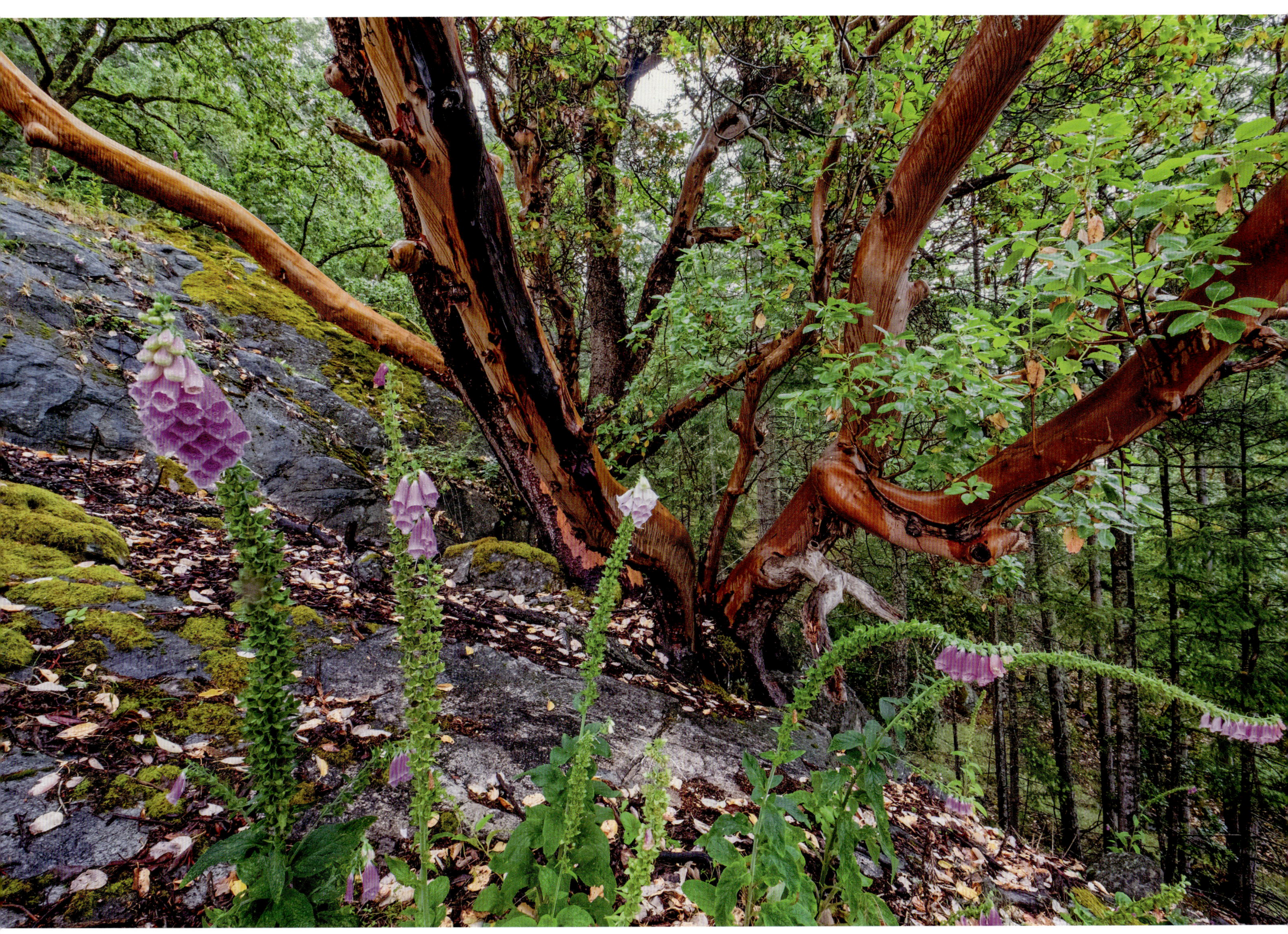

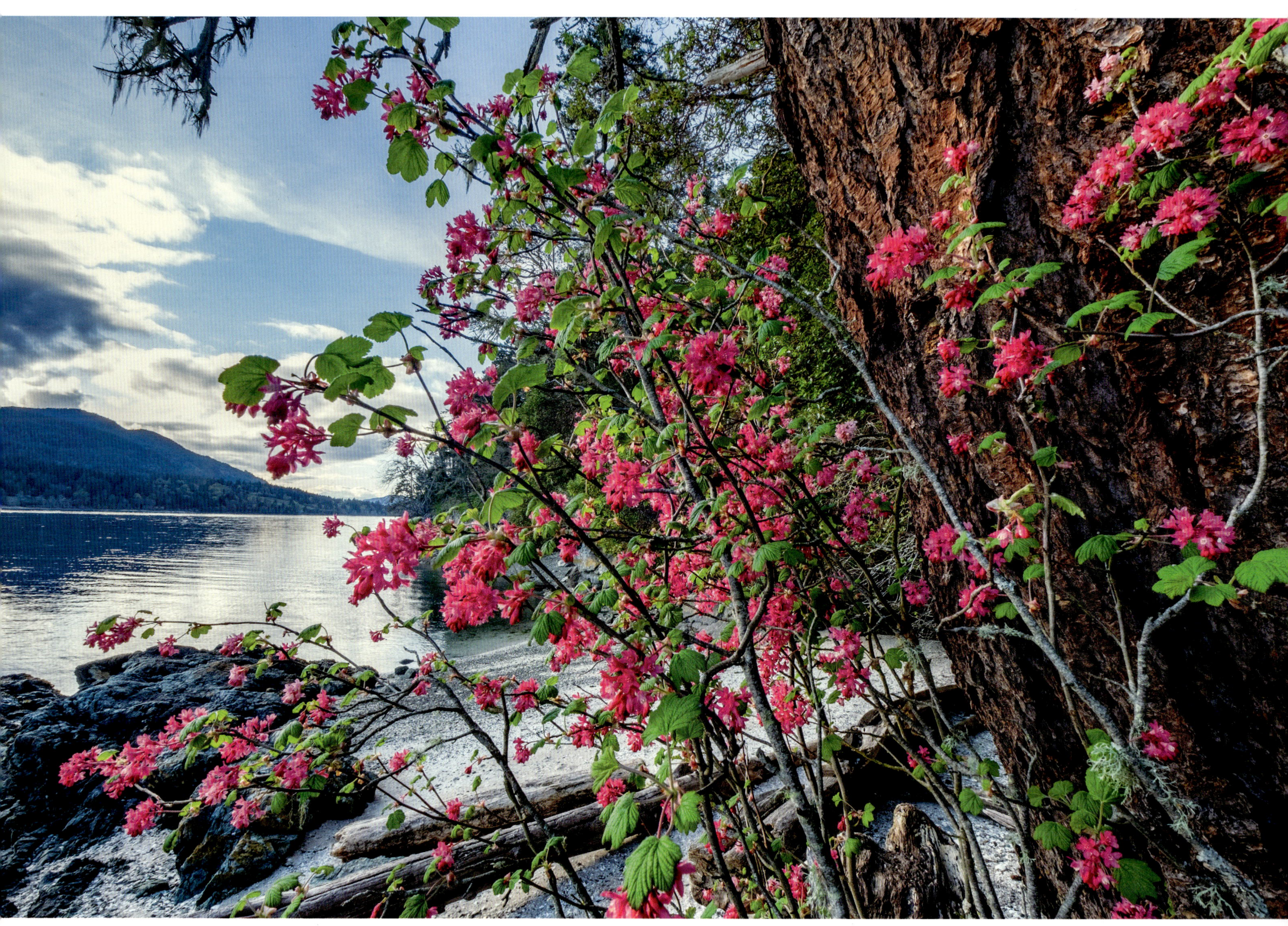

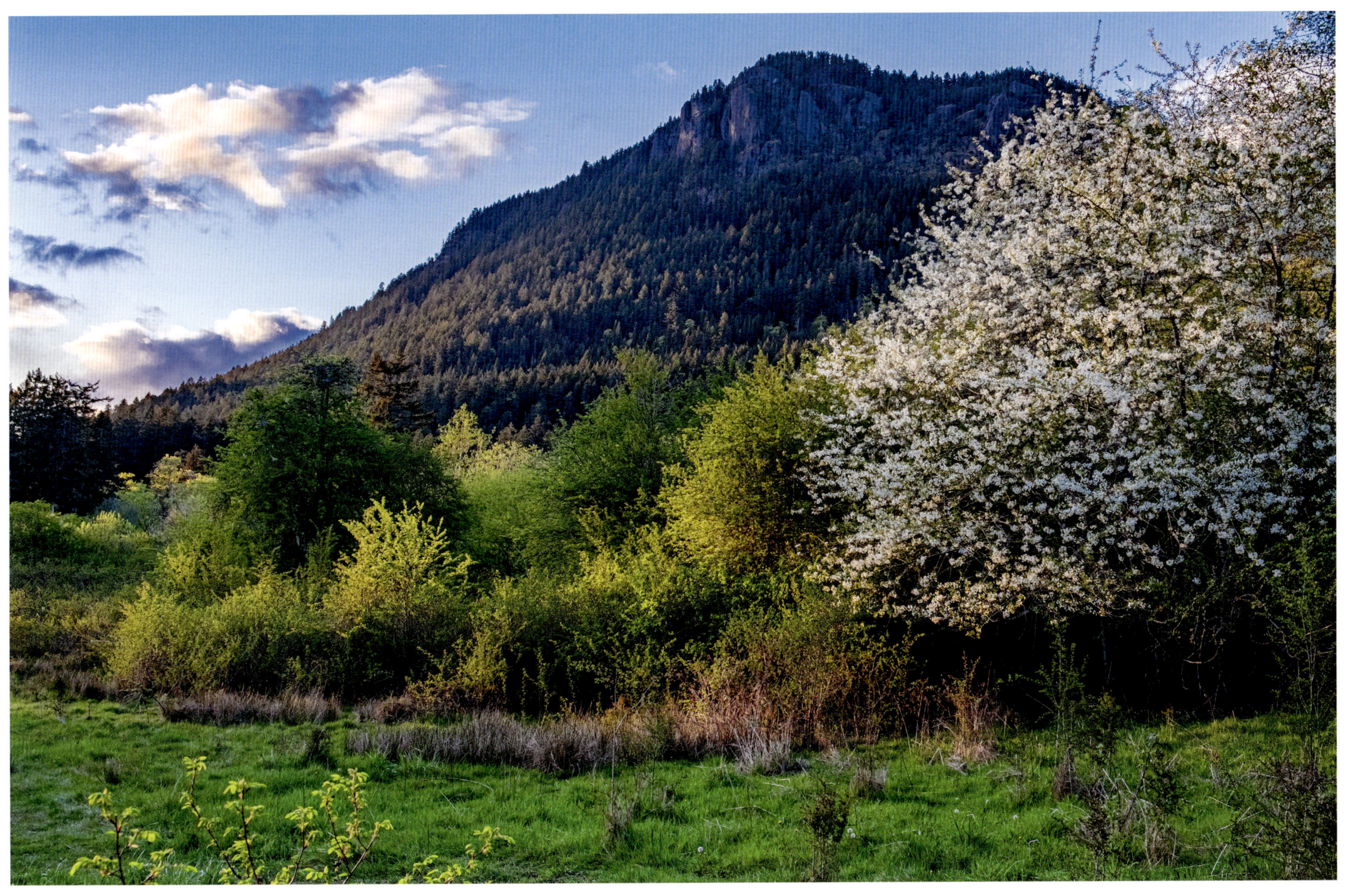

Red-flowering currant along the shoreline in the Tsawout Reserve in late March (left).

April in the meadows below Baynes Peak (Mount Maxwell) in Burgoyne Bay Provincial Park (above).

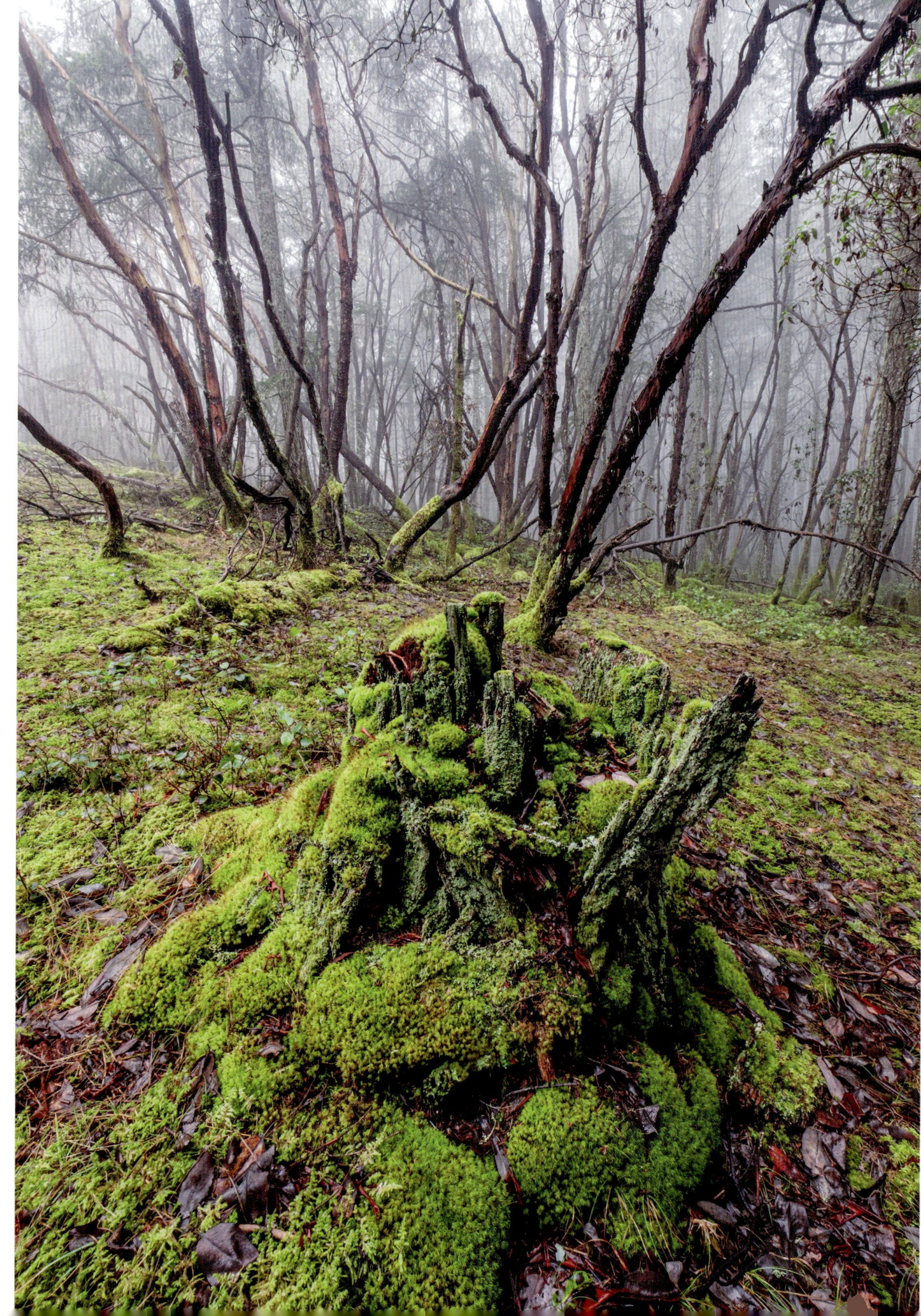

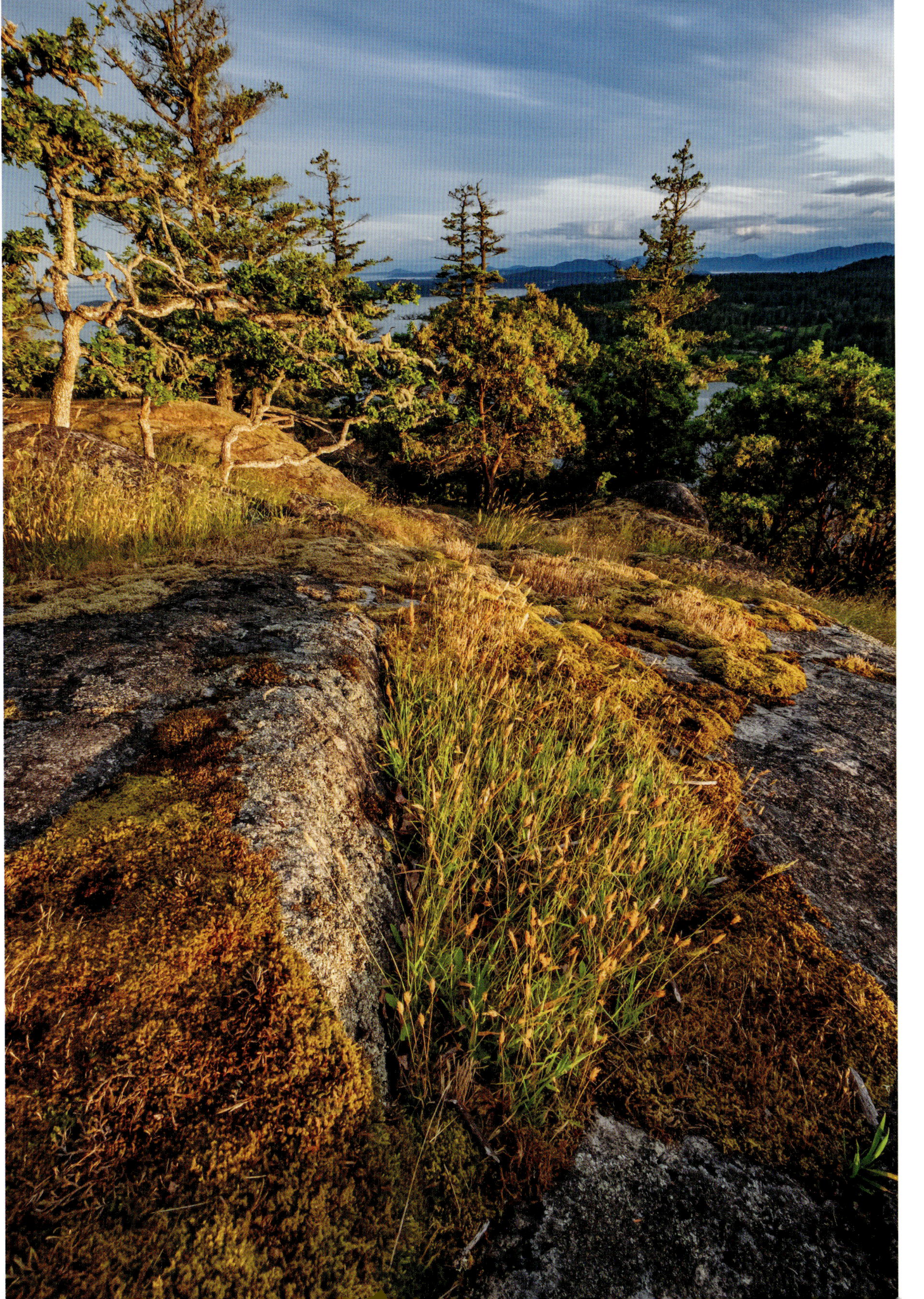

A foggy January day along the trail up Reginald Hill (far left), and a late evening view from the top in mid-June (left).

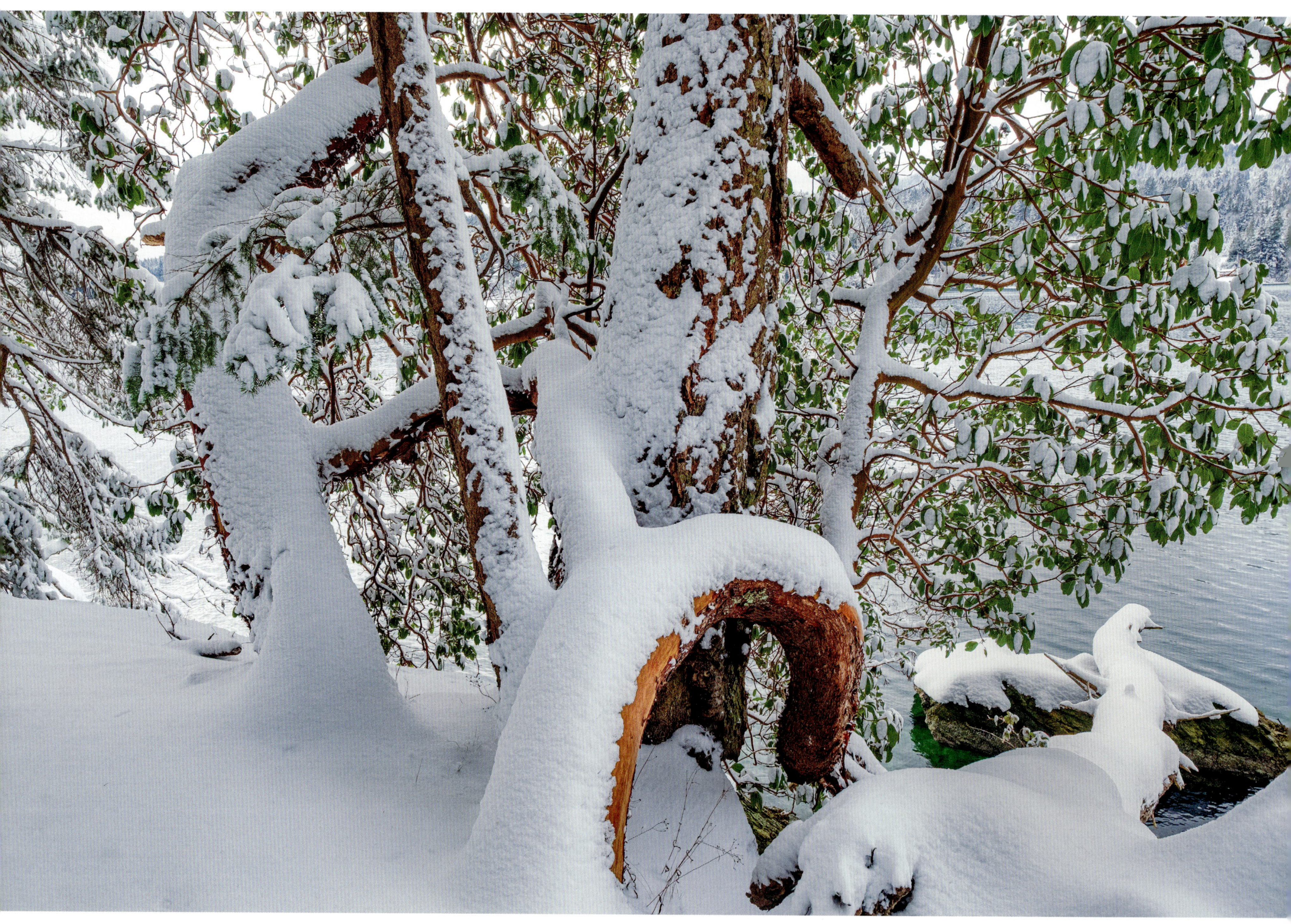

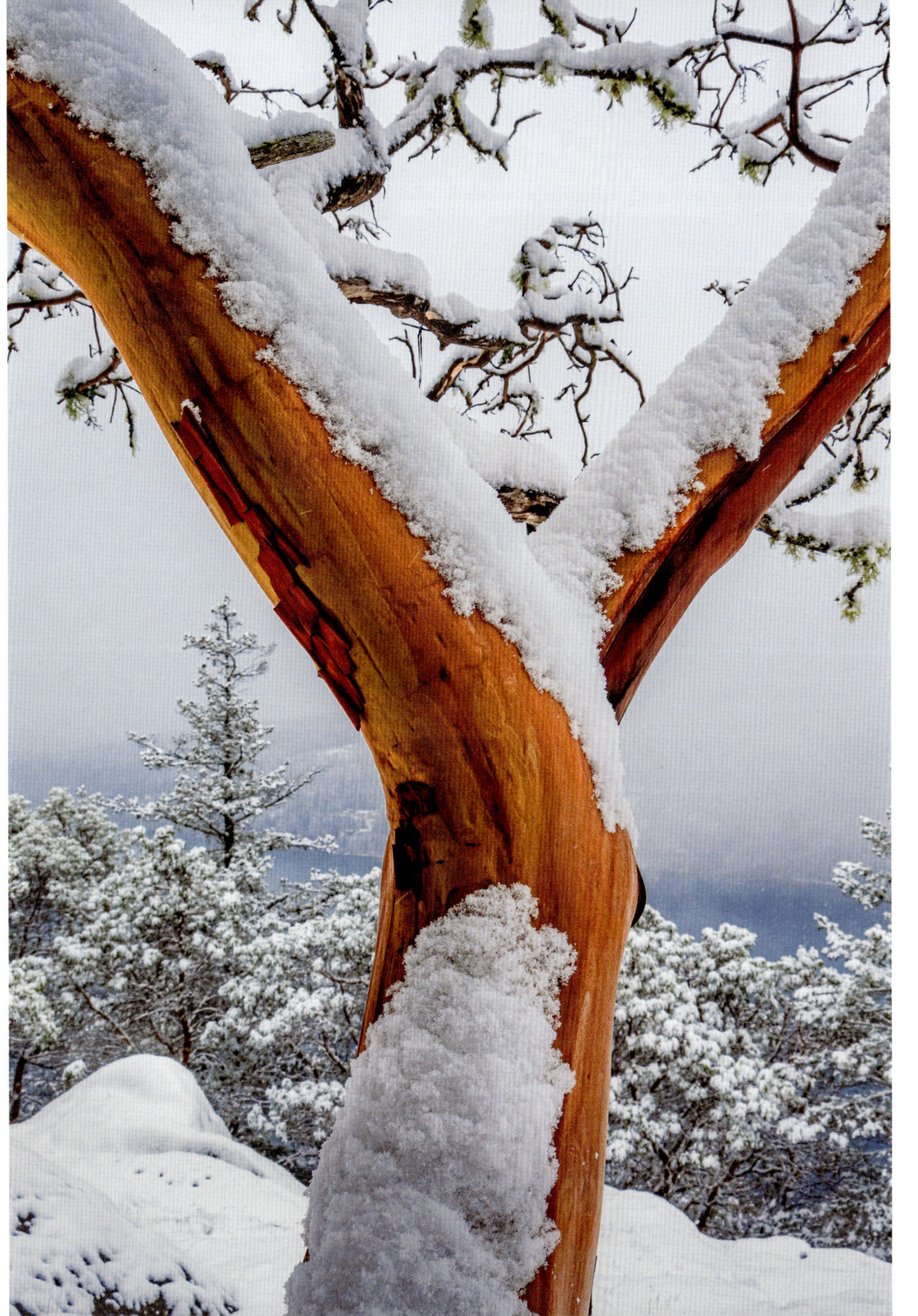

Arbutus, Canada's only native broadleaf evergreen tree, is especially striking after a fresh February snowfall.

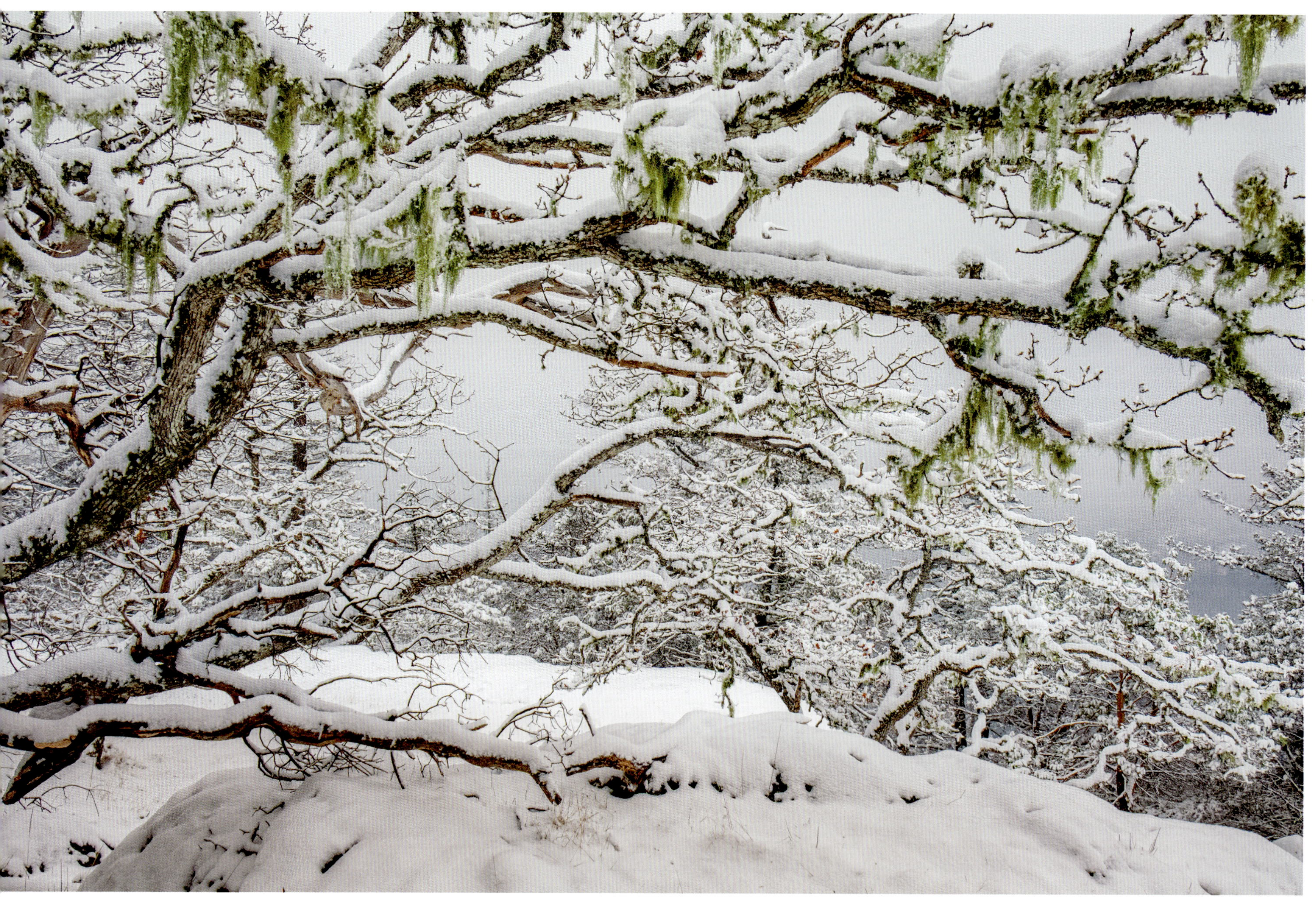

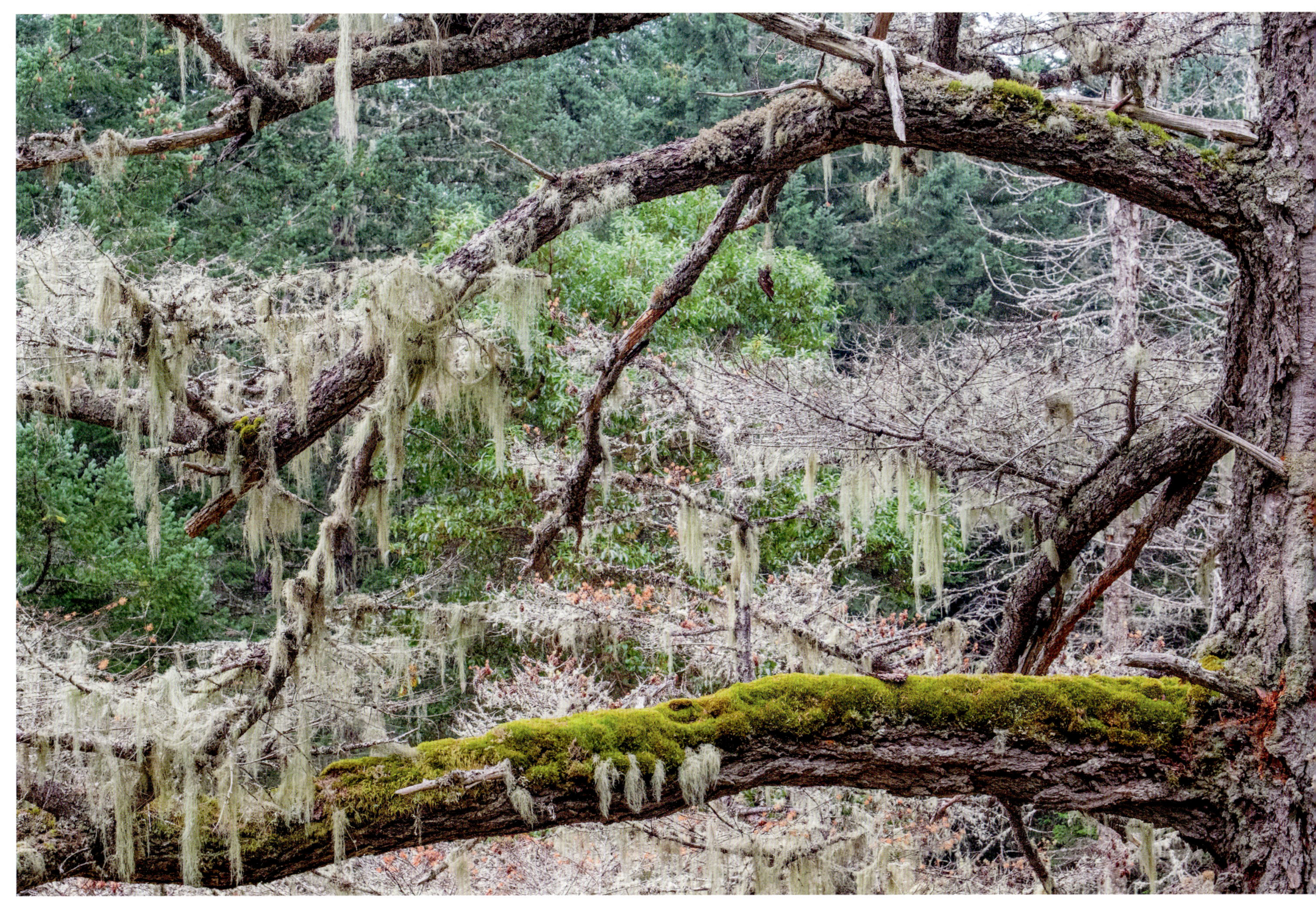

Beard lichen hangs from the branches of a Garry oak (left) and a Douglas fir (above).

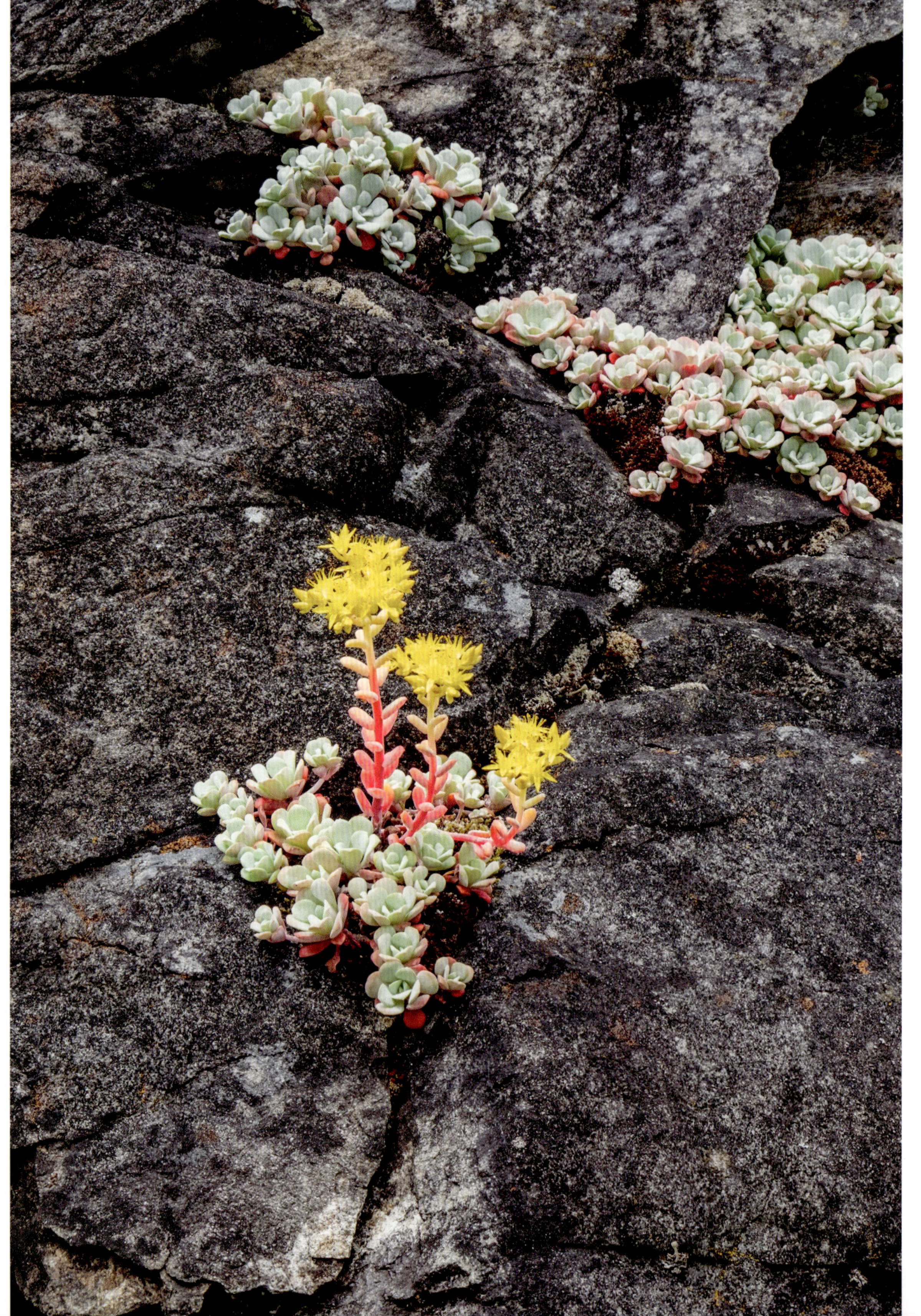

The drought- and heat-resistant broadleaf stonecrop finds a foothold in rocky outcrops at Churchill Beach in Ganges Harbour (left), and along the shoreline in Ruckle Provincial Park (right).

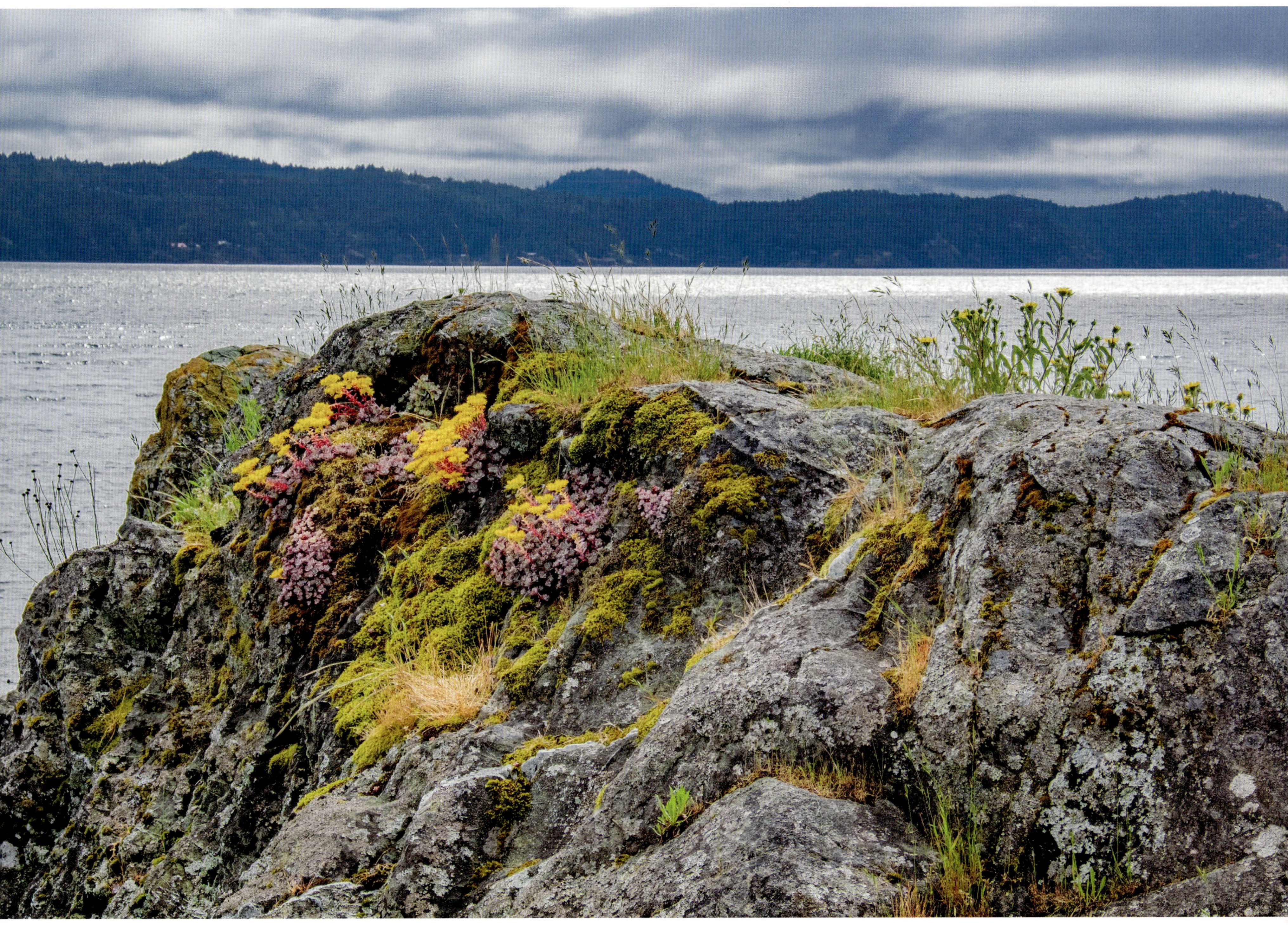

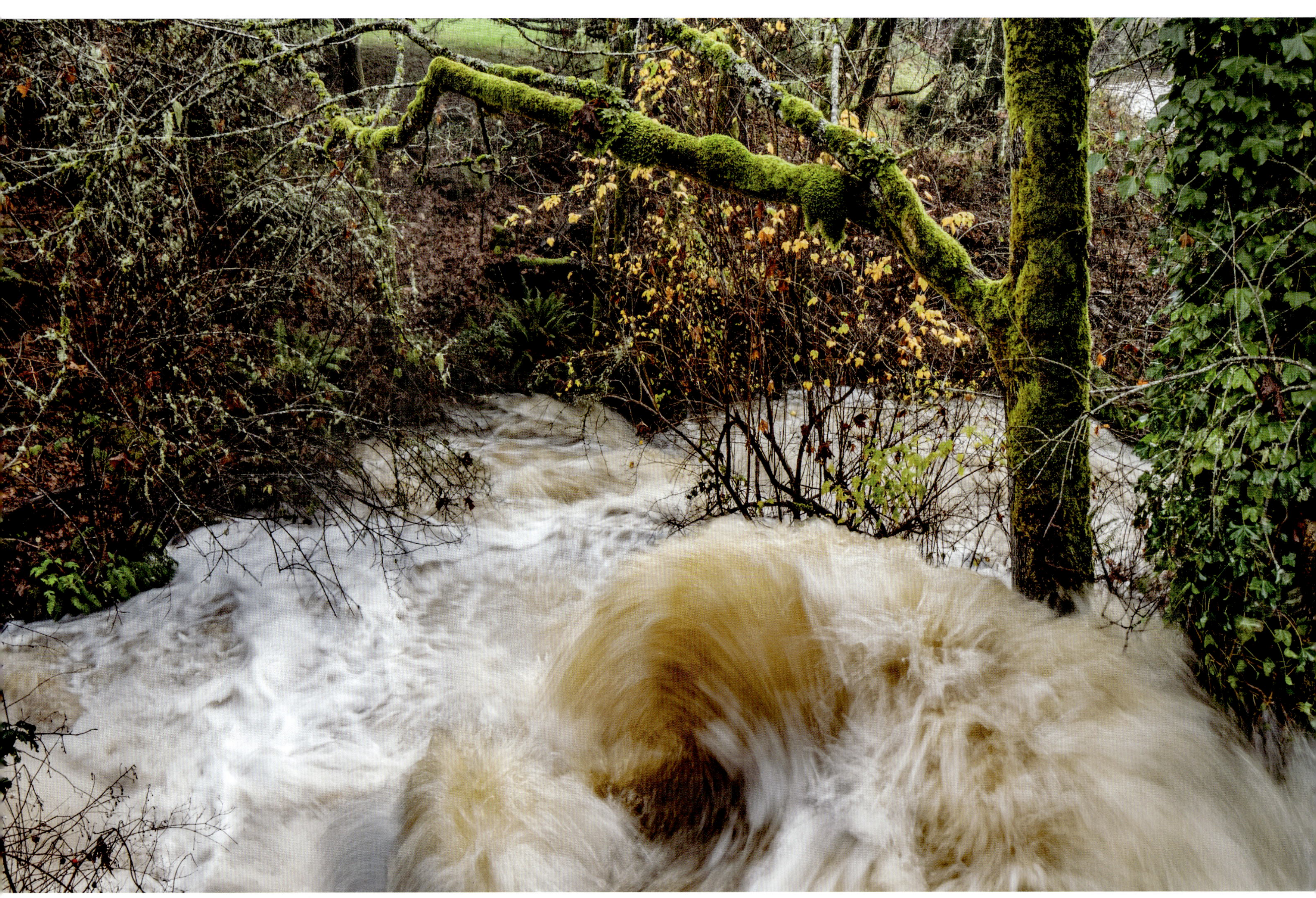

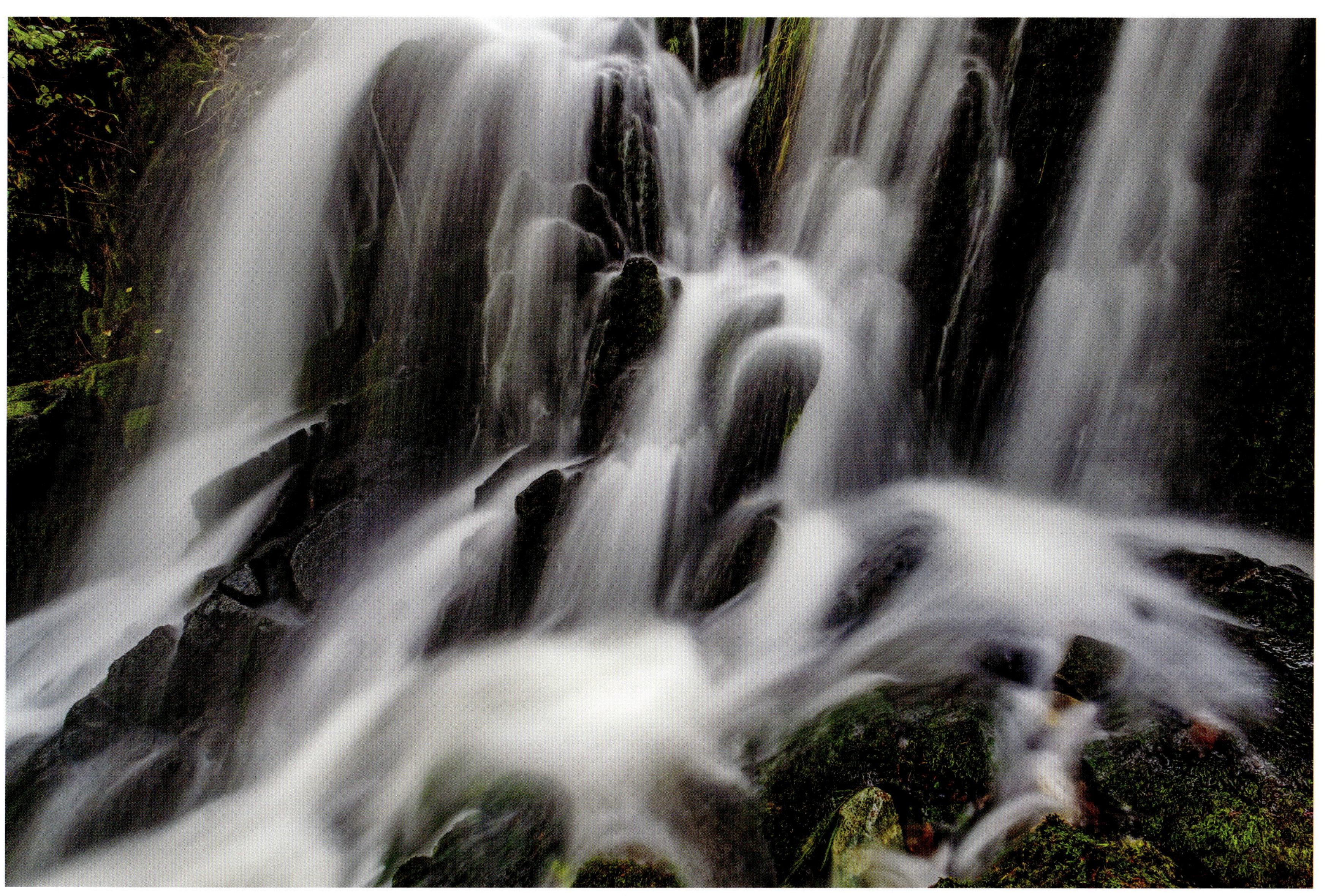

An exceptionally violent runoff on Stowell Creek in mid-November 2021, when an "atmospheric river" caused widespread flooding across British Columbia (left).

A waterfall off Mountain Road in Mount Tuam Ecological Reserve in November (above).

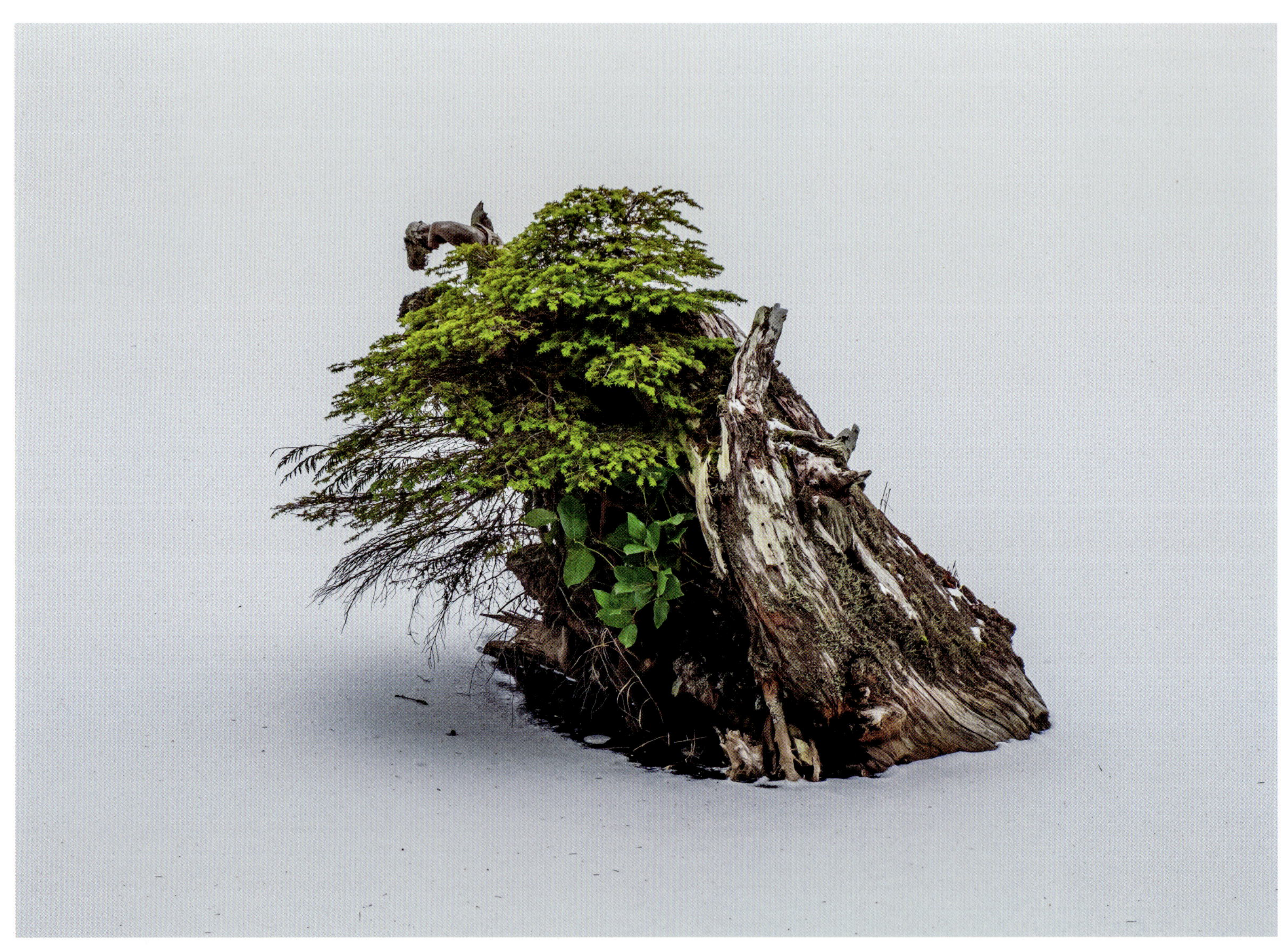

A submerged stump in frozen, snow-covered Rosemurgy Lake on Mount Bruce (above), and a meadow detail in Burgoyne Bay Provincial Park (right), both in mid-February.

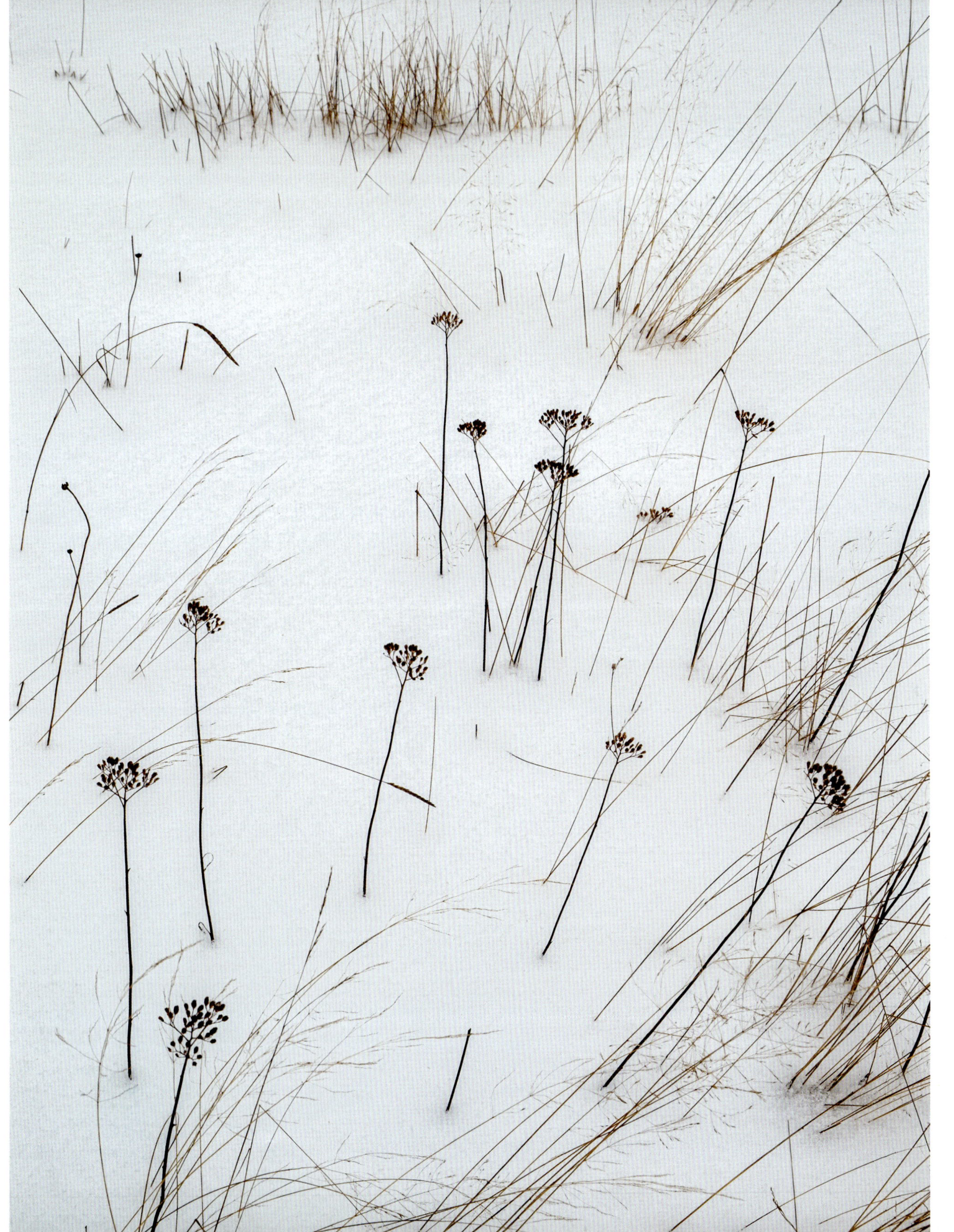

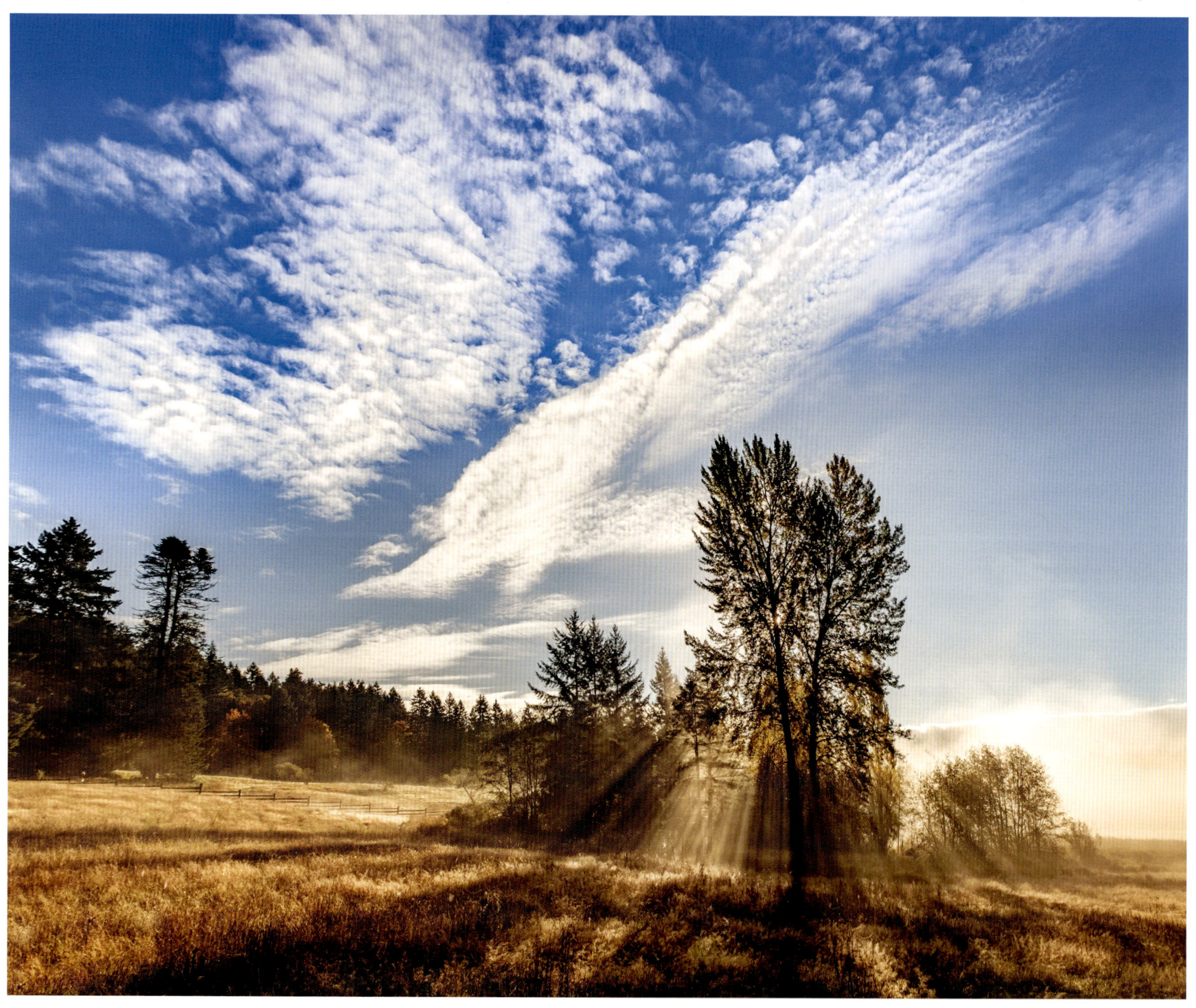

Clearing mist at Blackburn Lake Nature Reserve on an October morning (above).

A view from Reginald Hill of the islands and passages near Sidney (right).

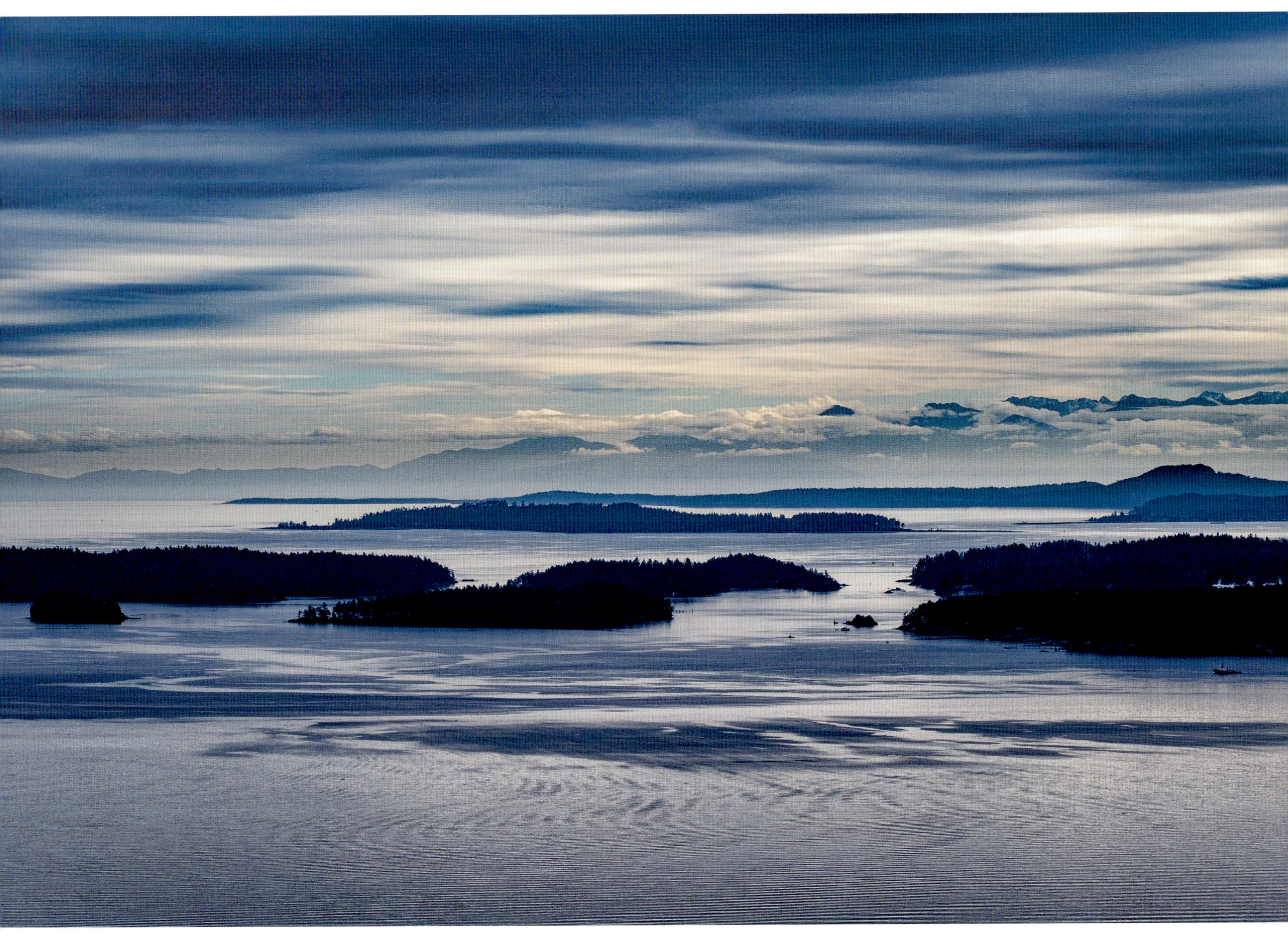

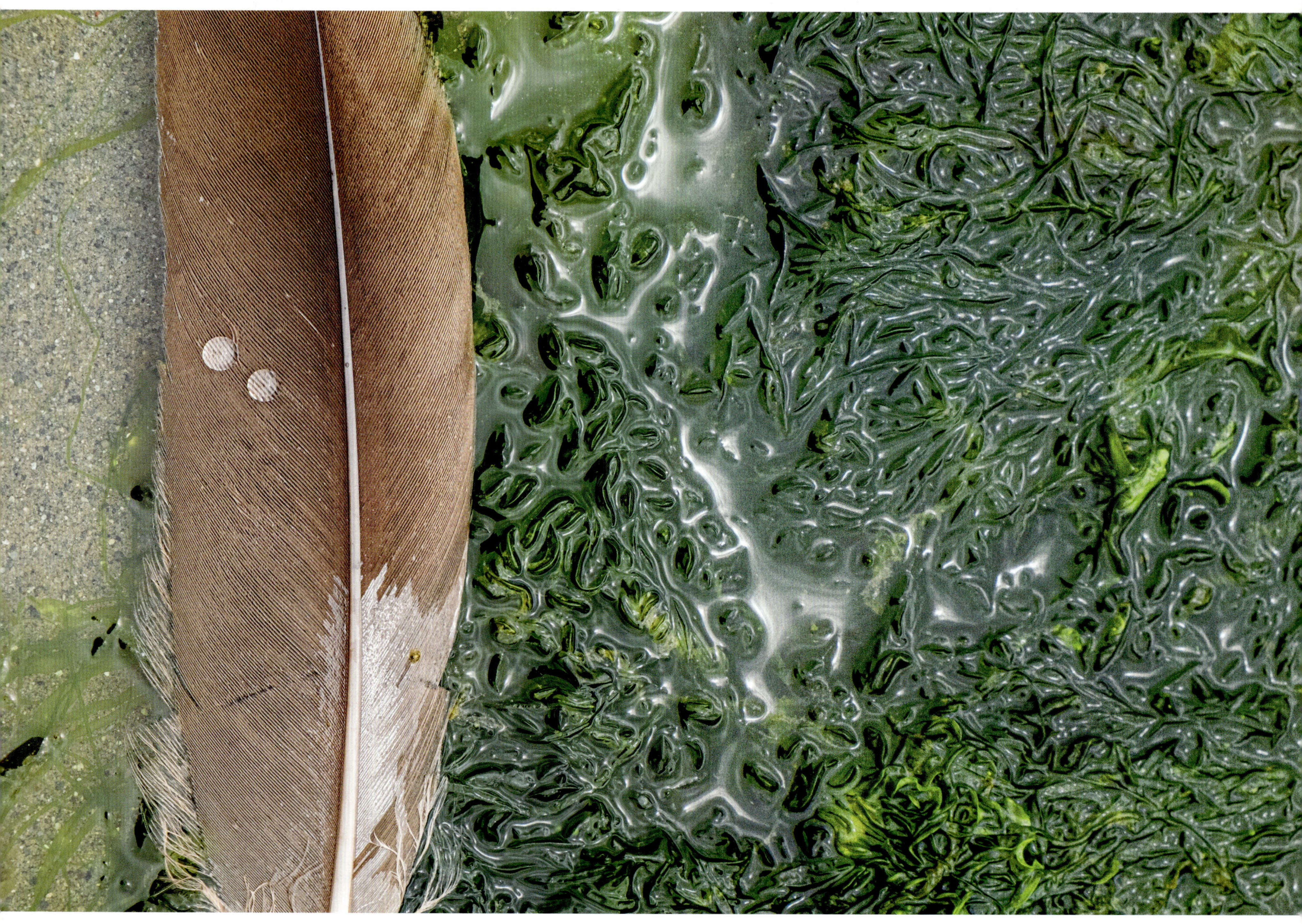

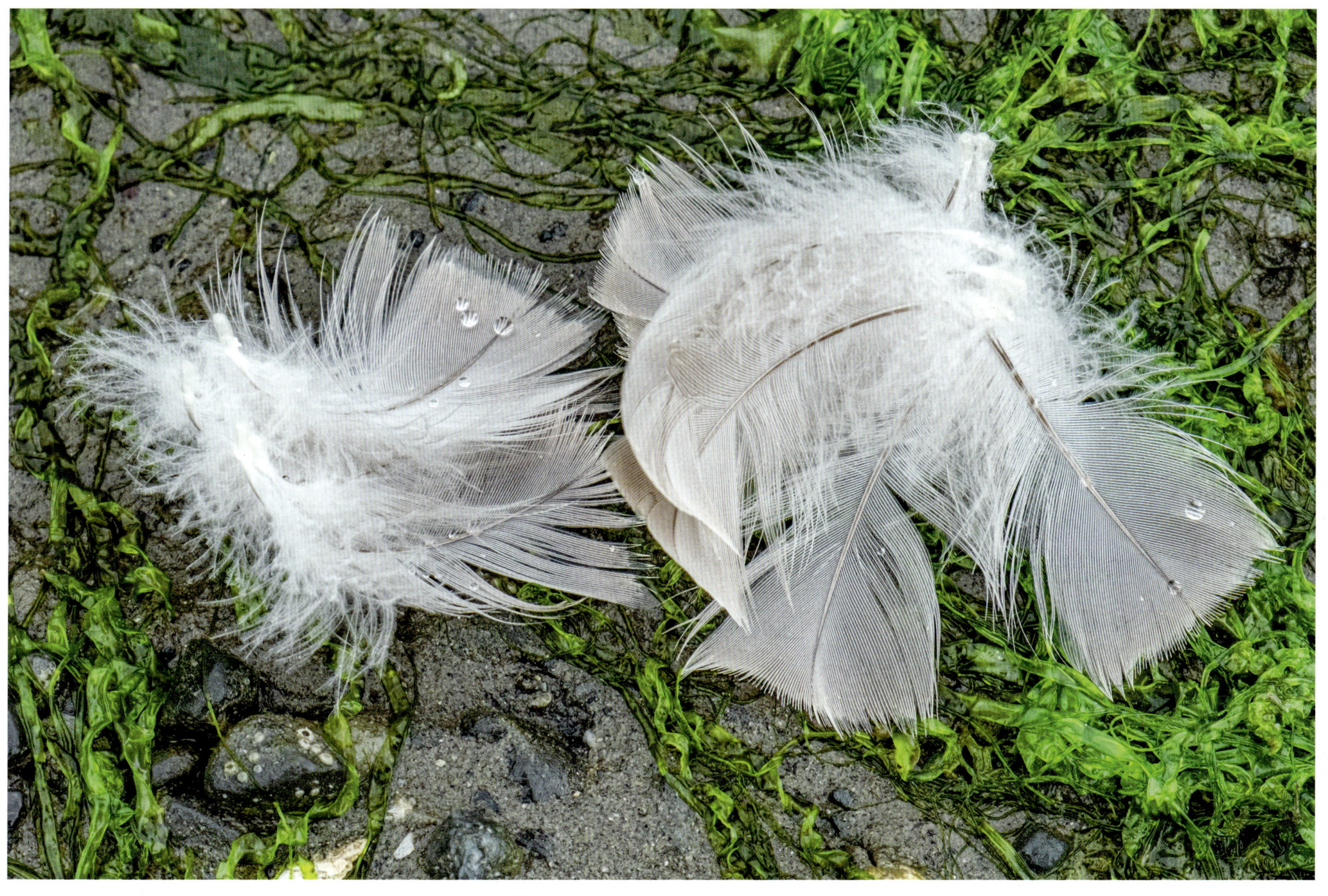

Bird feathers on tidal flats at low tide.

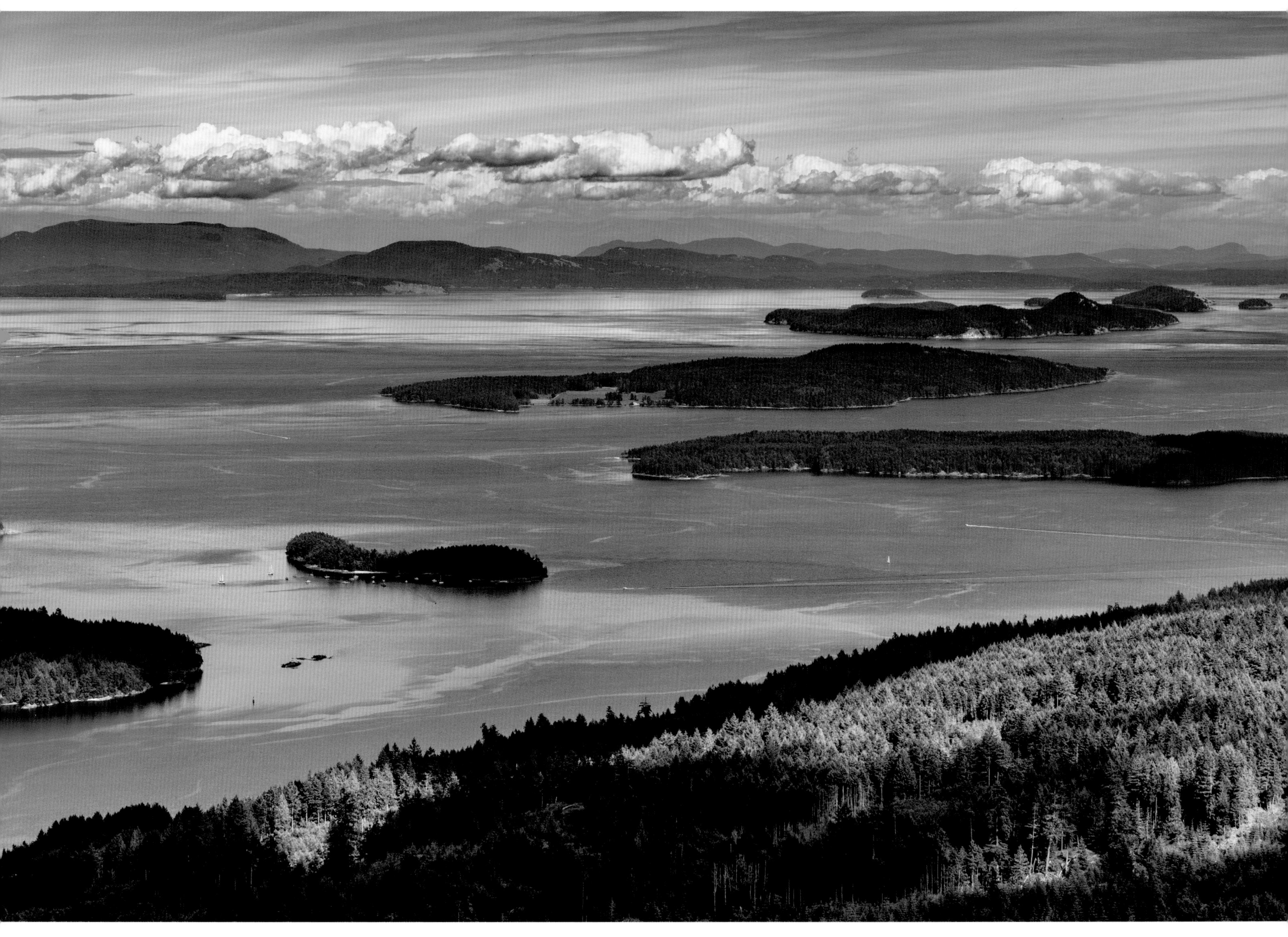

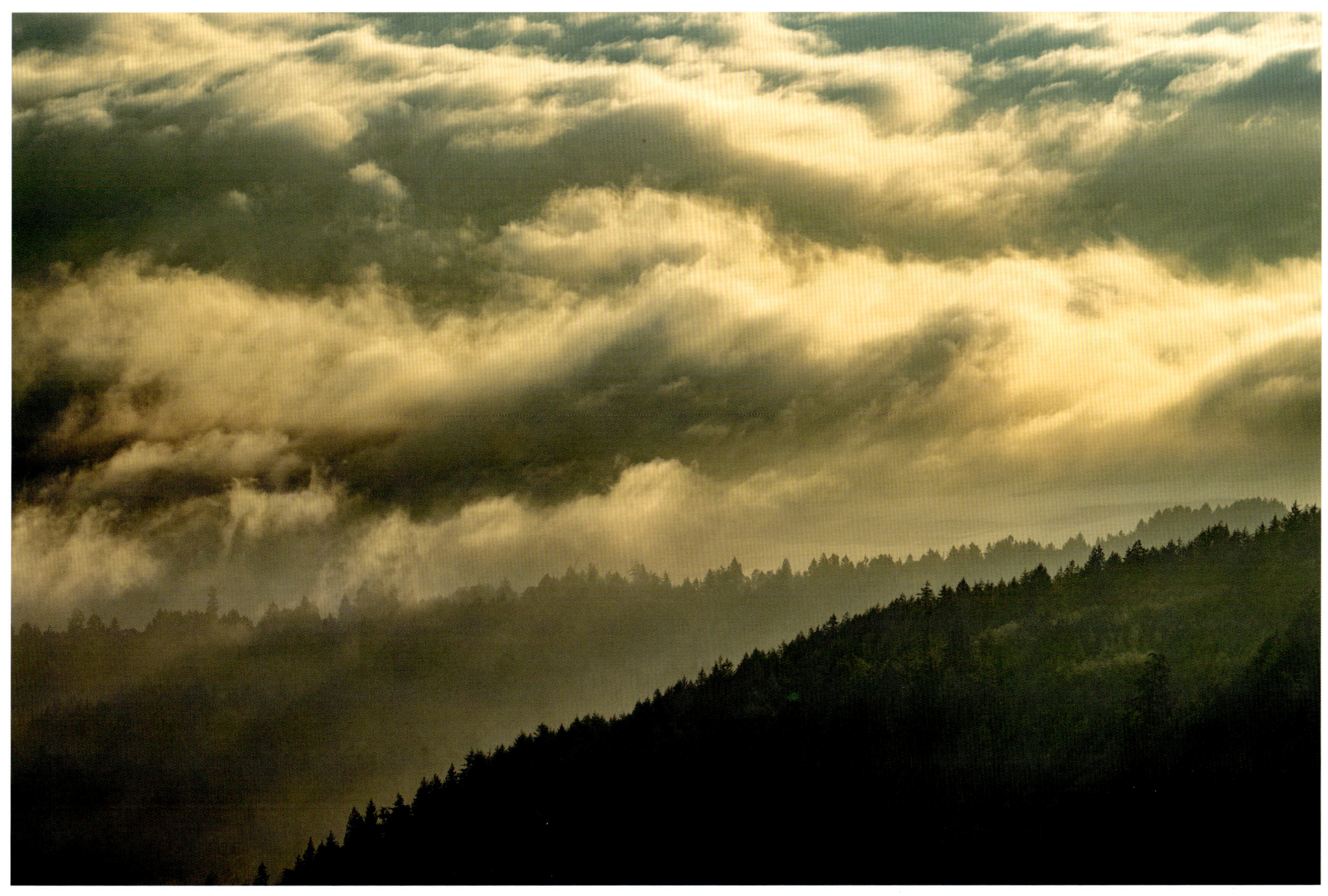

Russell Island, Portland Island, Moresby Island and the San Juan Islands beyond, viewed from the summit of Mount Bruce in June (left).

Looking down from Mount Bruce on a morning fog bank in October (above).

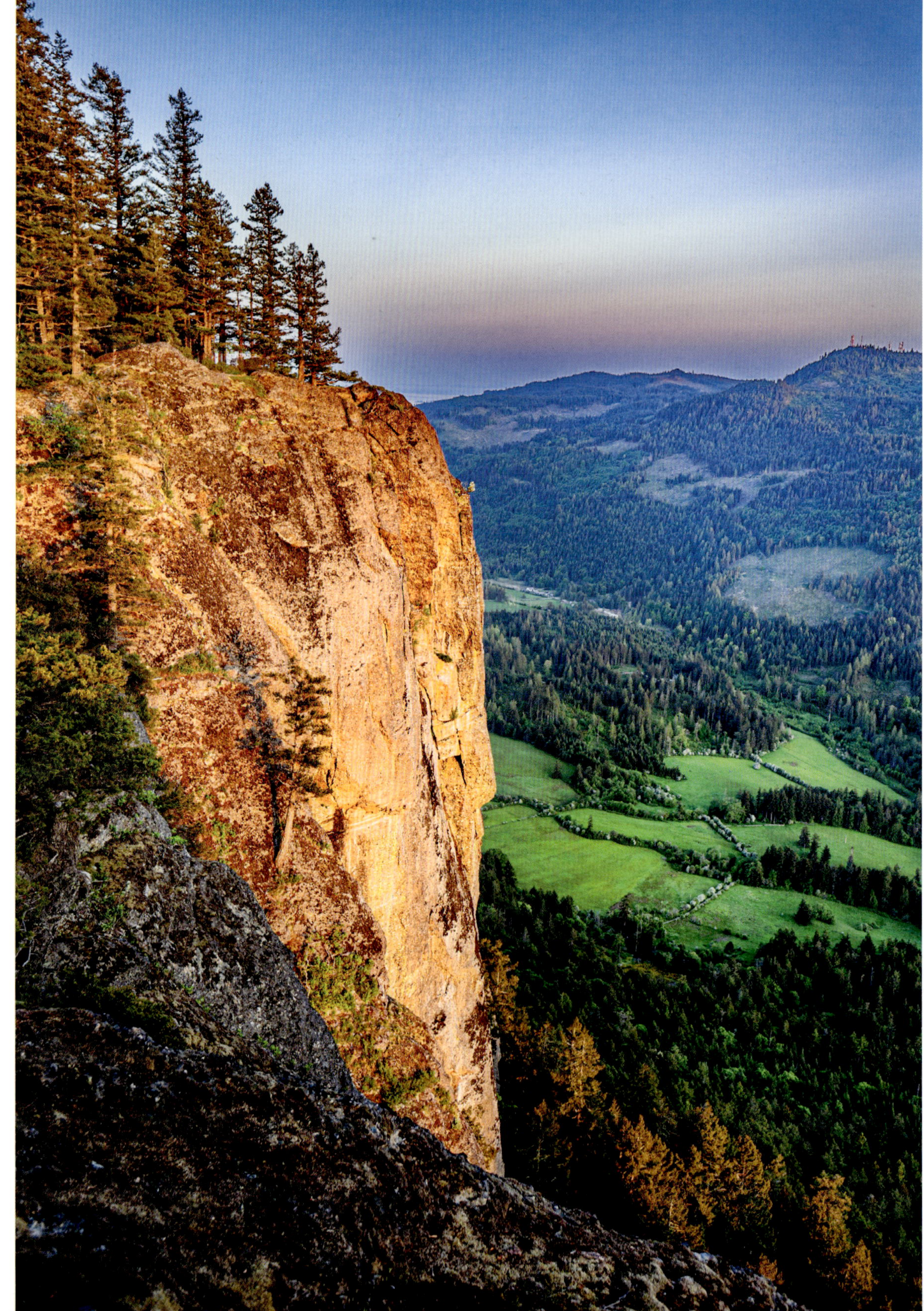

The views from Baynes Peak in Mount Maxwell Provincial Park, looking down on the meadows in Burgoyne Bay Provincial Park in May.

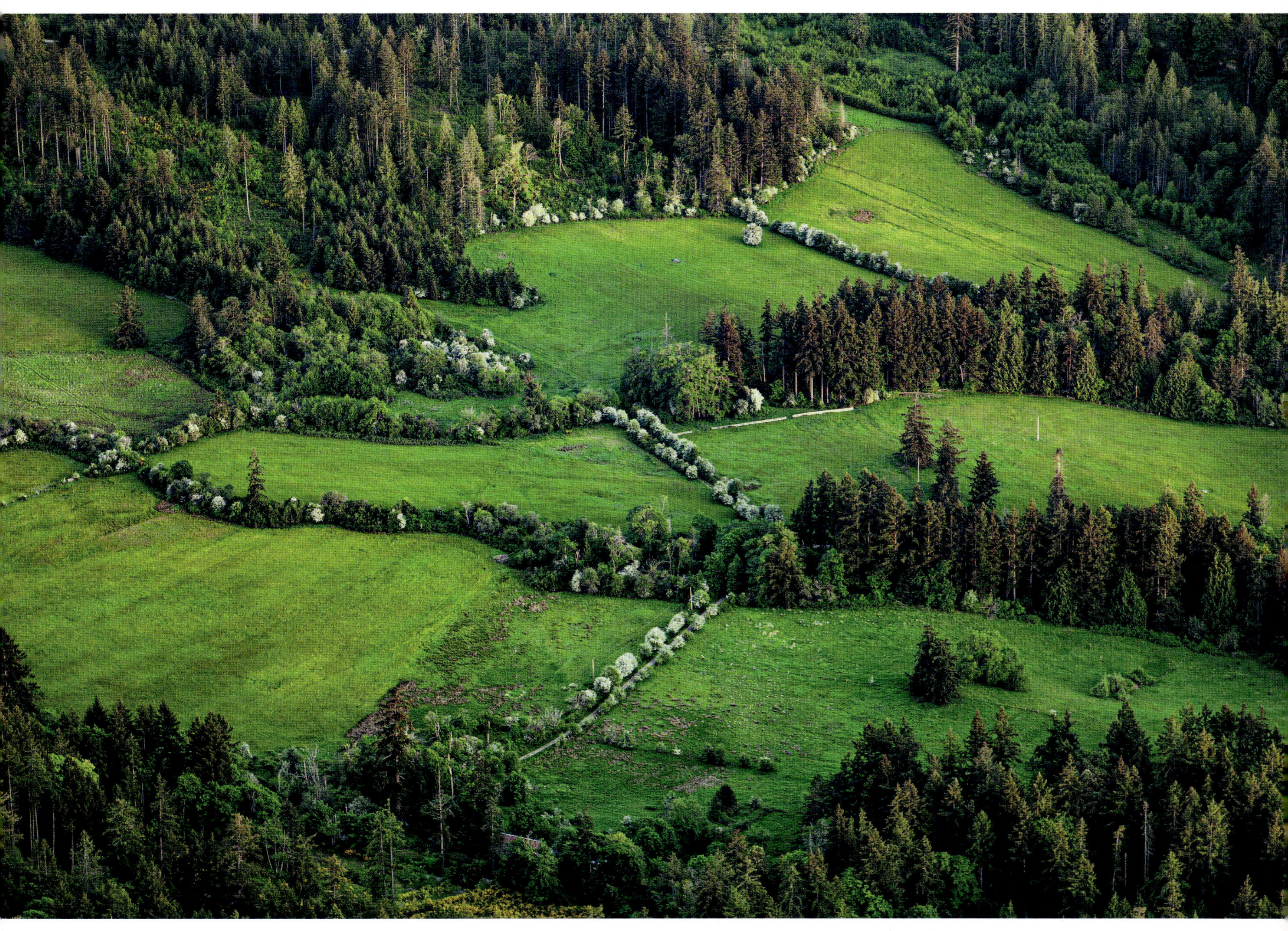

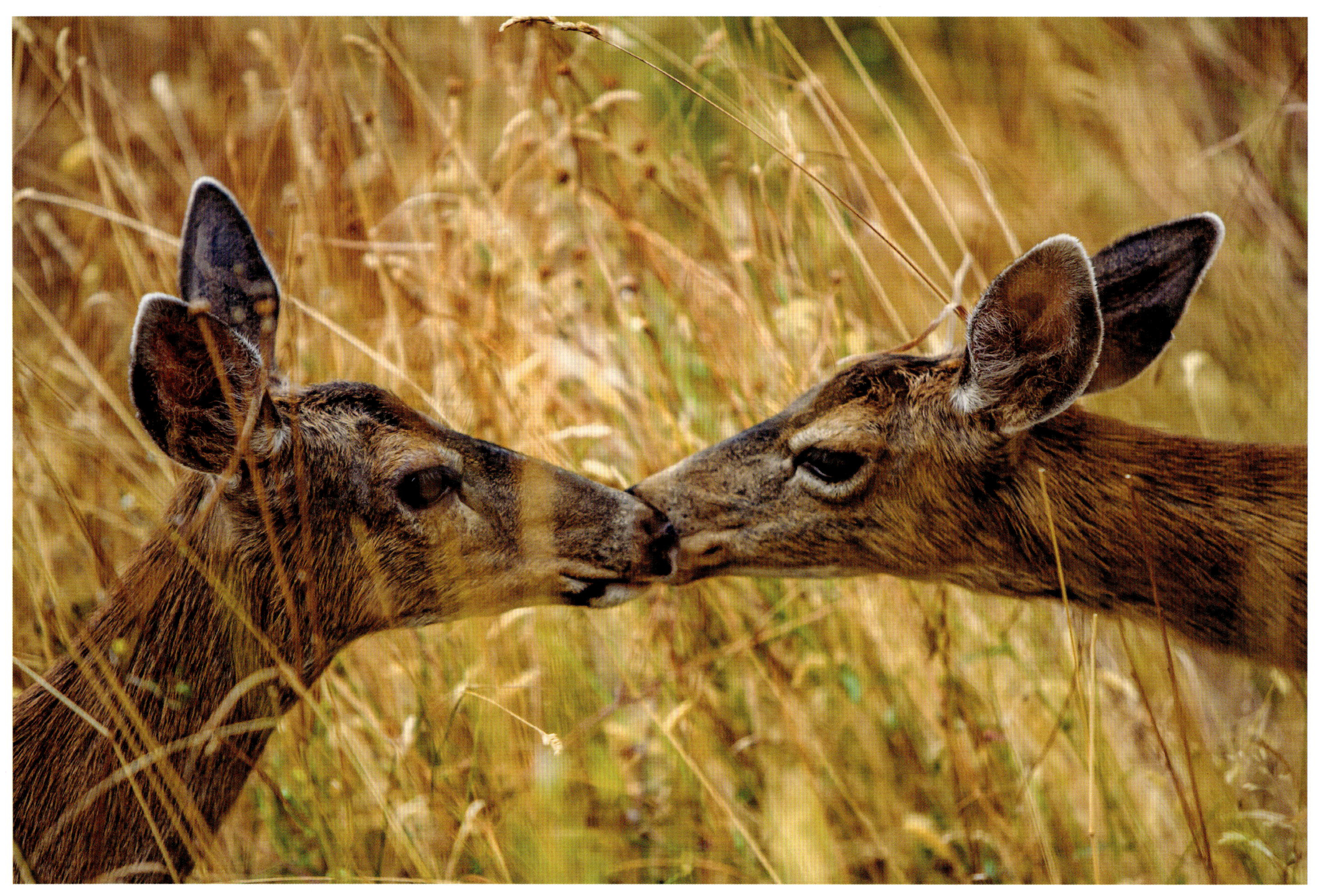

Black-tailed deer thrive in overabundance as a result of the elimination of wolves, bears and most cougars on the island.

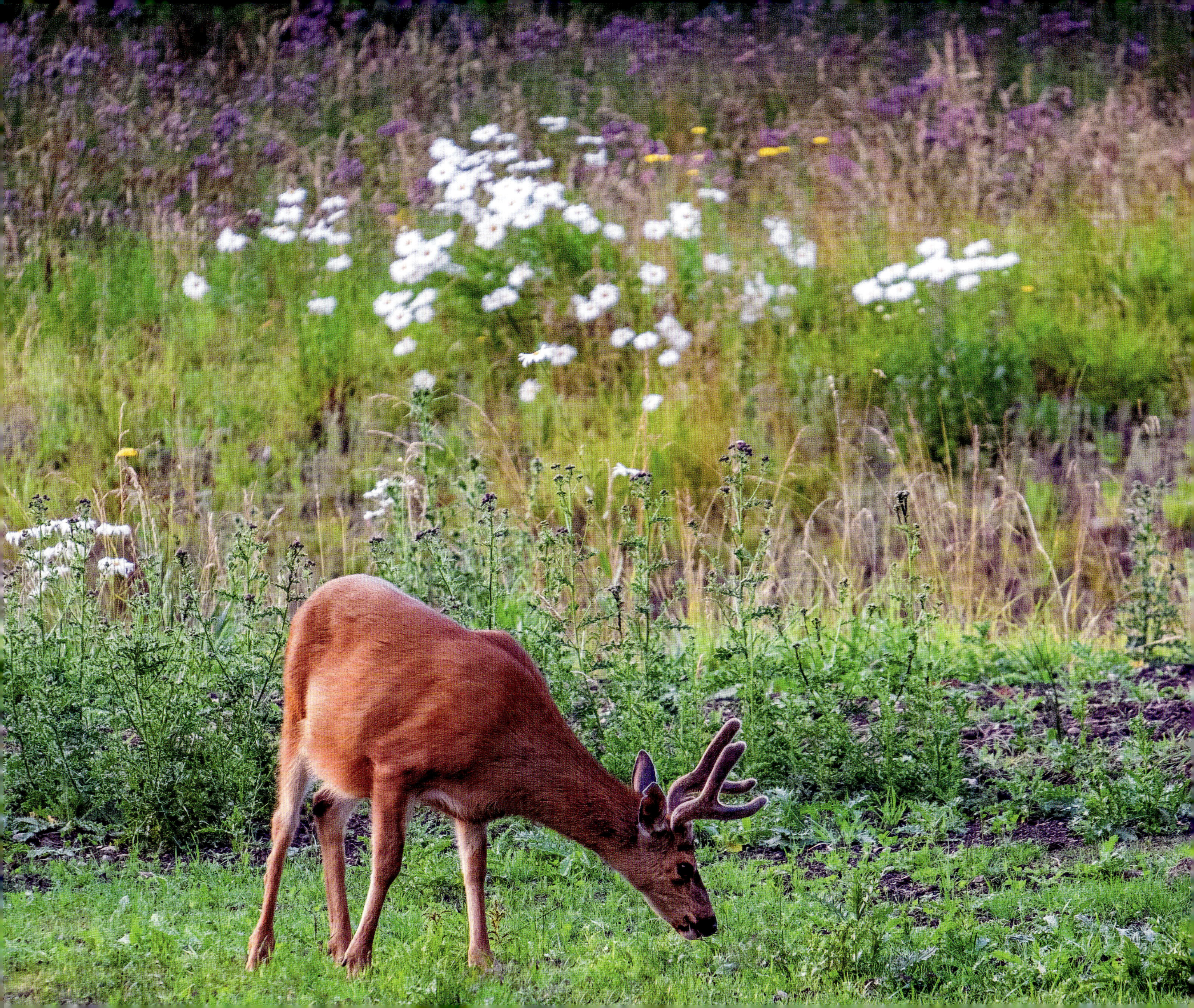

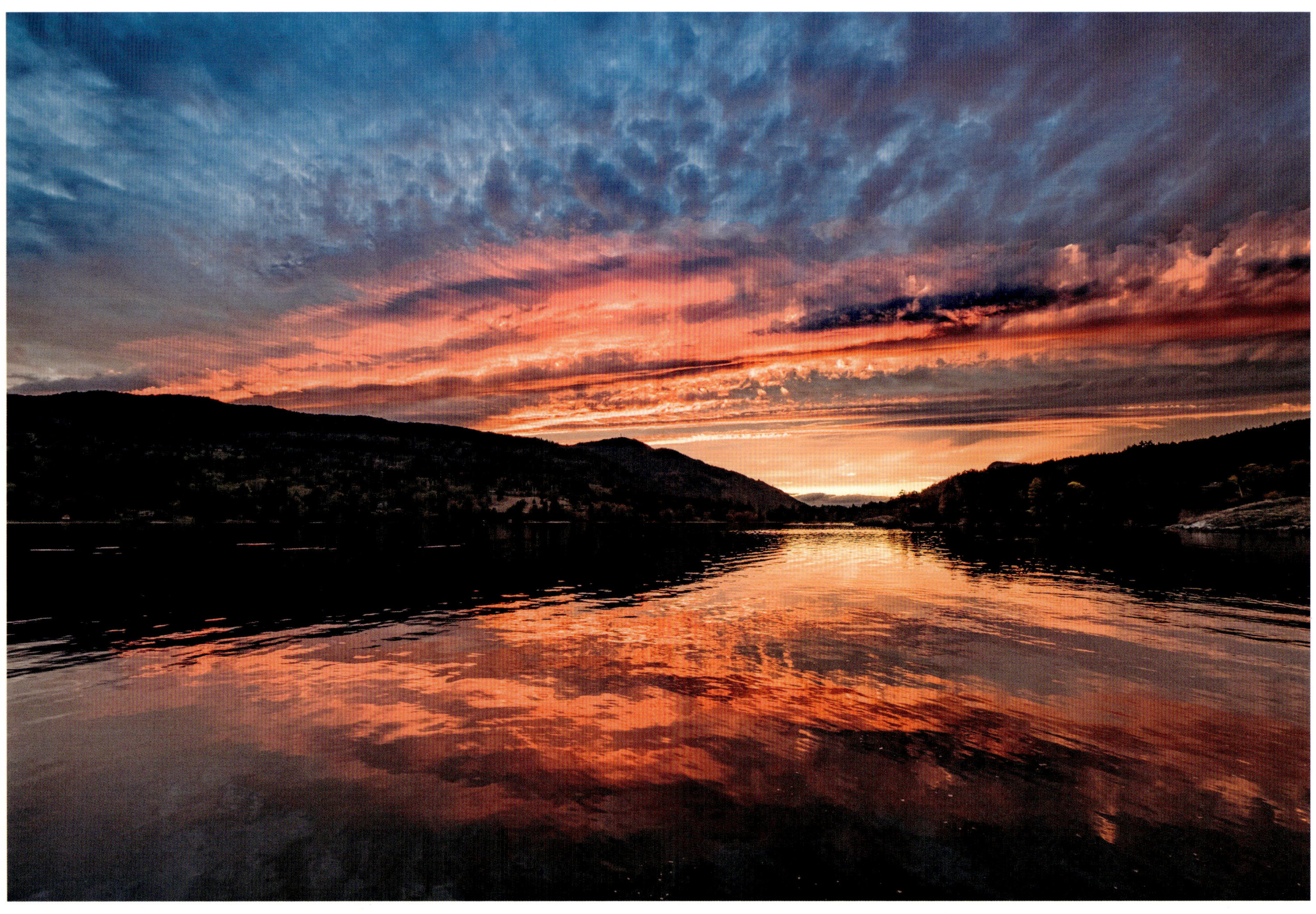

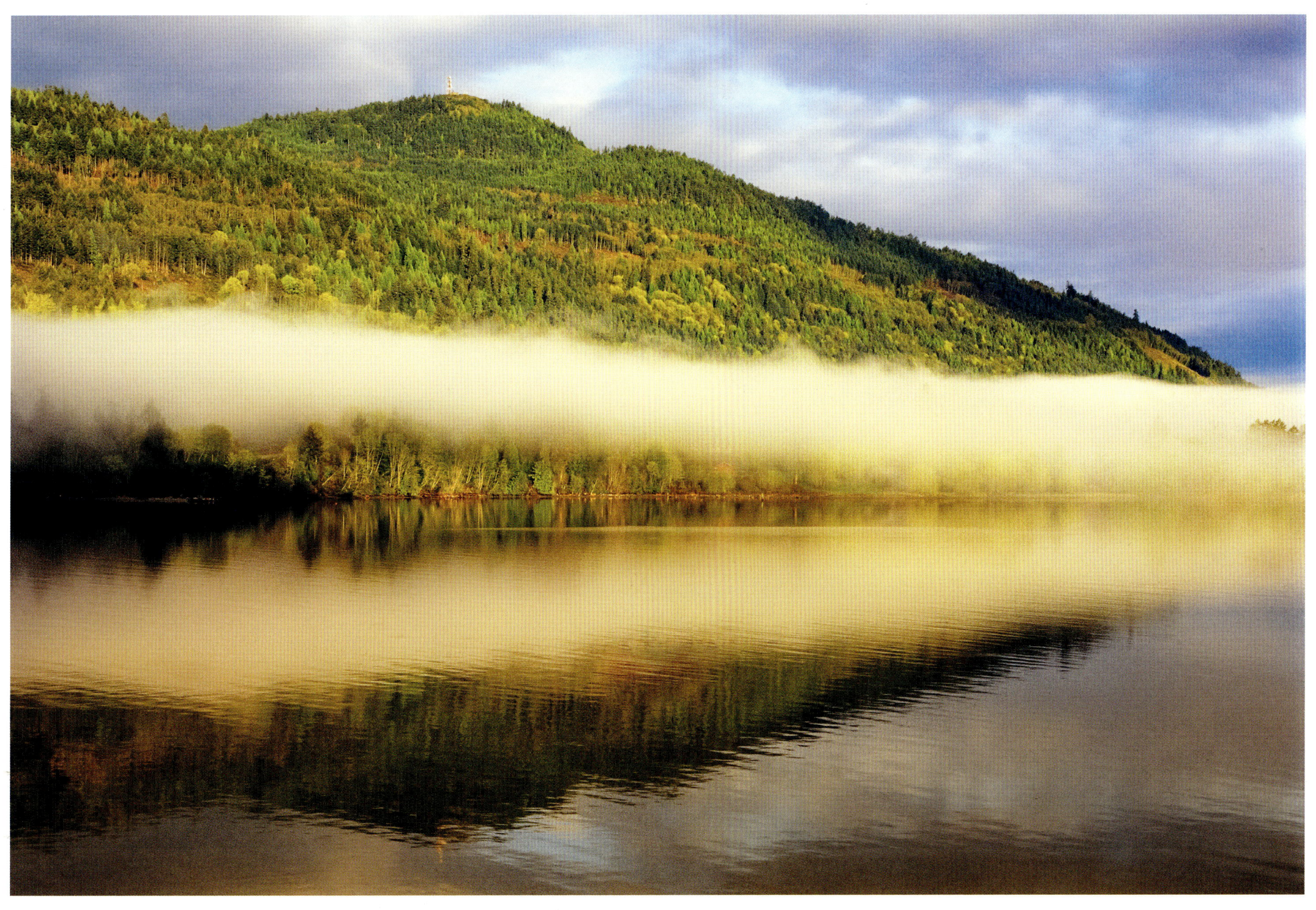

A sunset and morning fog at Fulford Harbour in September.

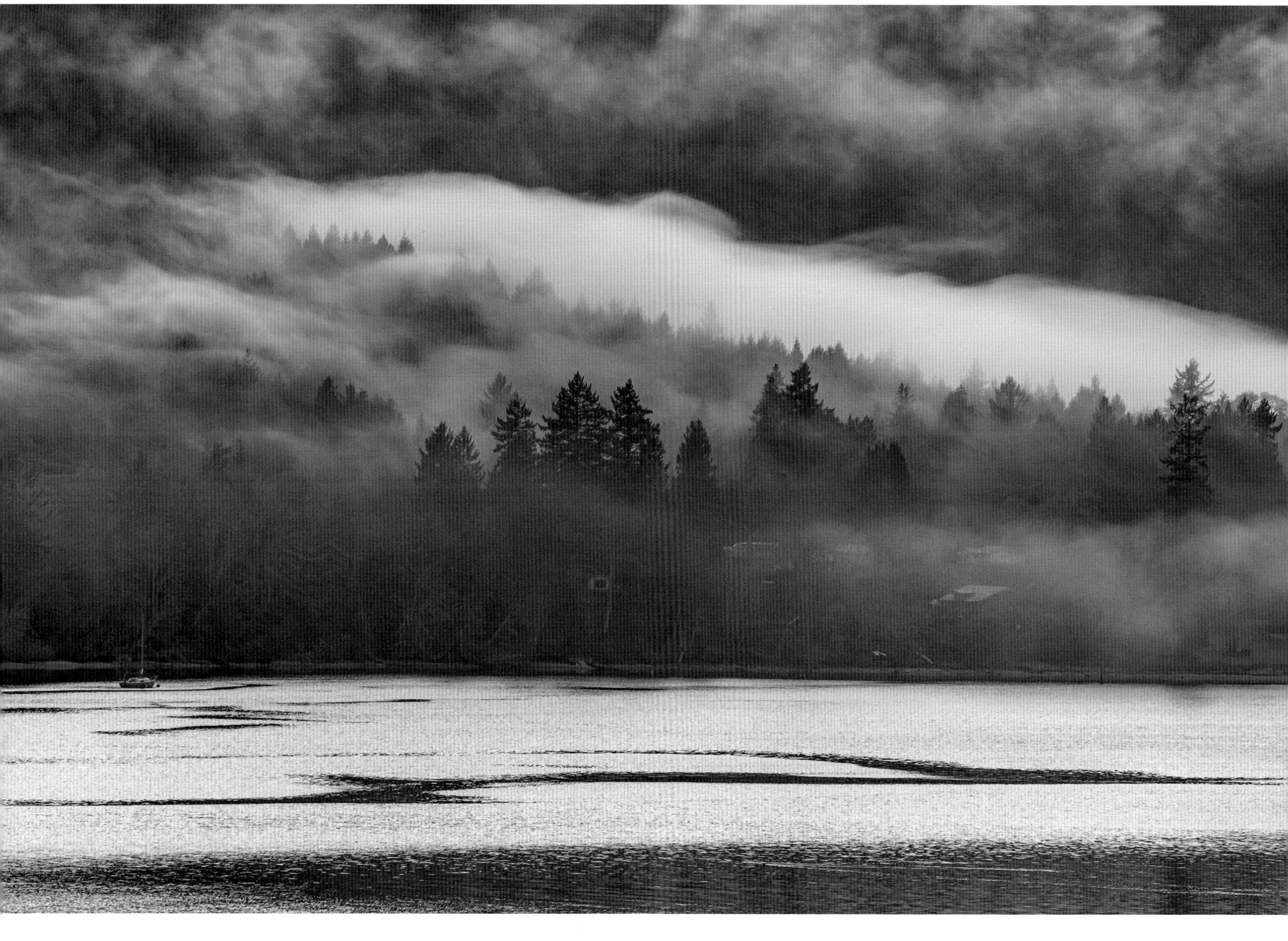

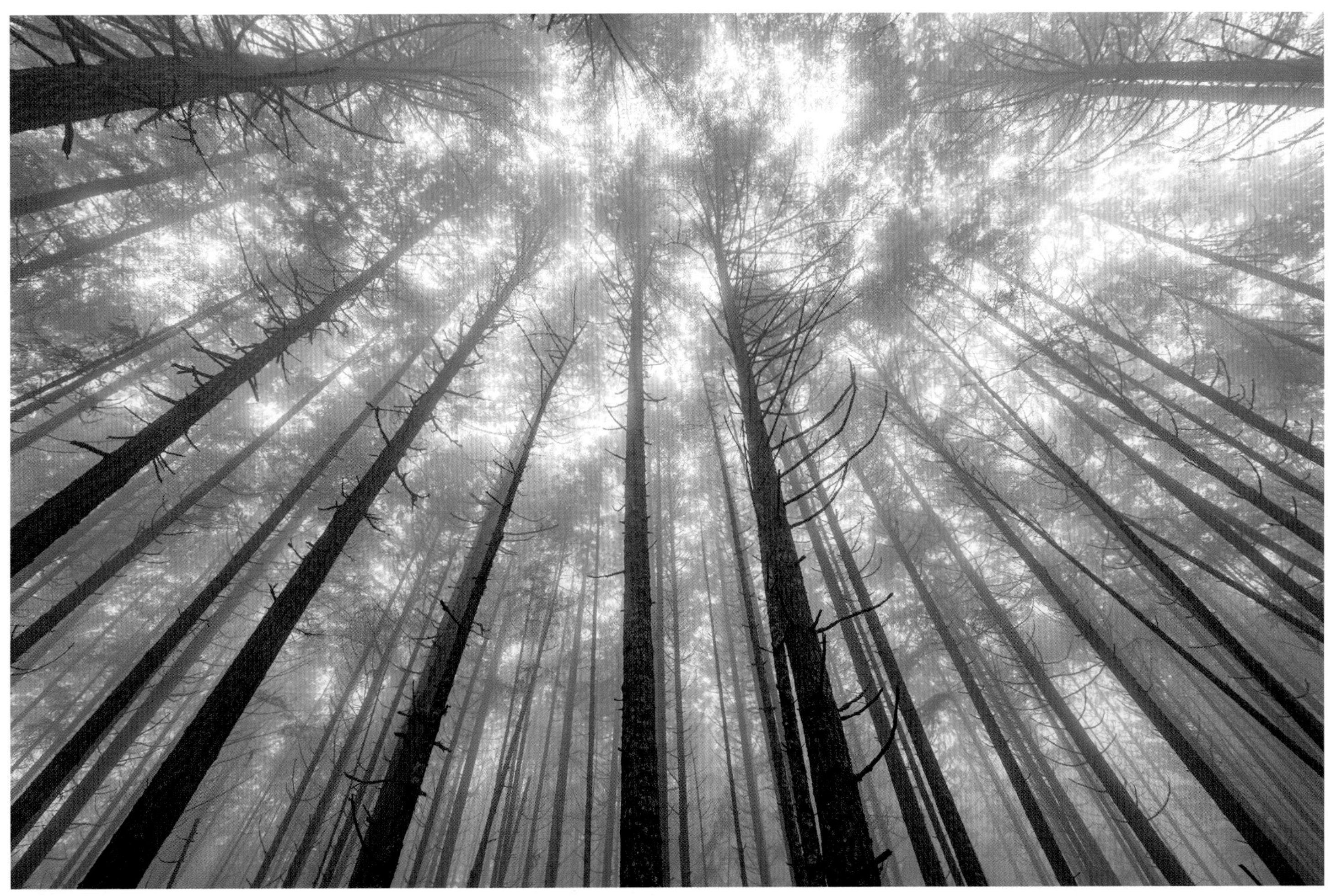

Cloud and mist drift across the slope of Mount Bruce above Fulford Harbour on Christmas Day (left).

Tall fir and hemlock trees soar into the mist on Channel Ridge (above).

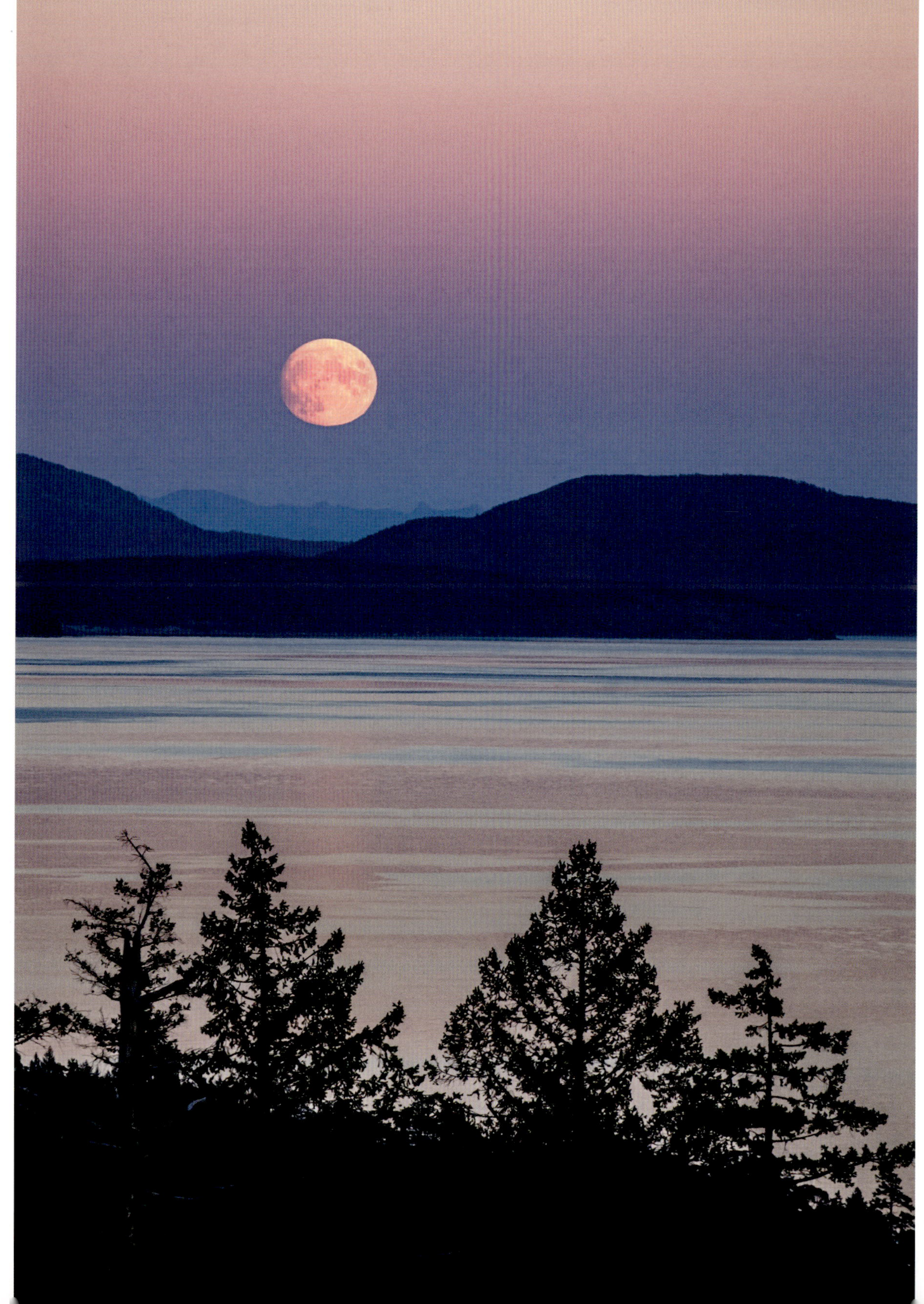

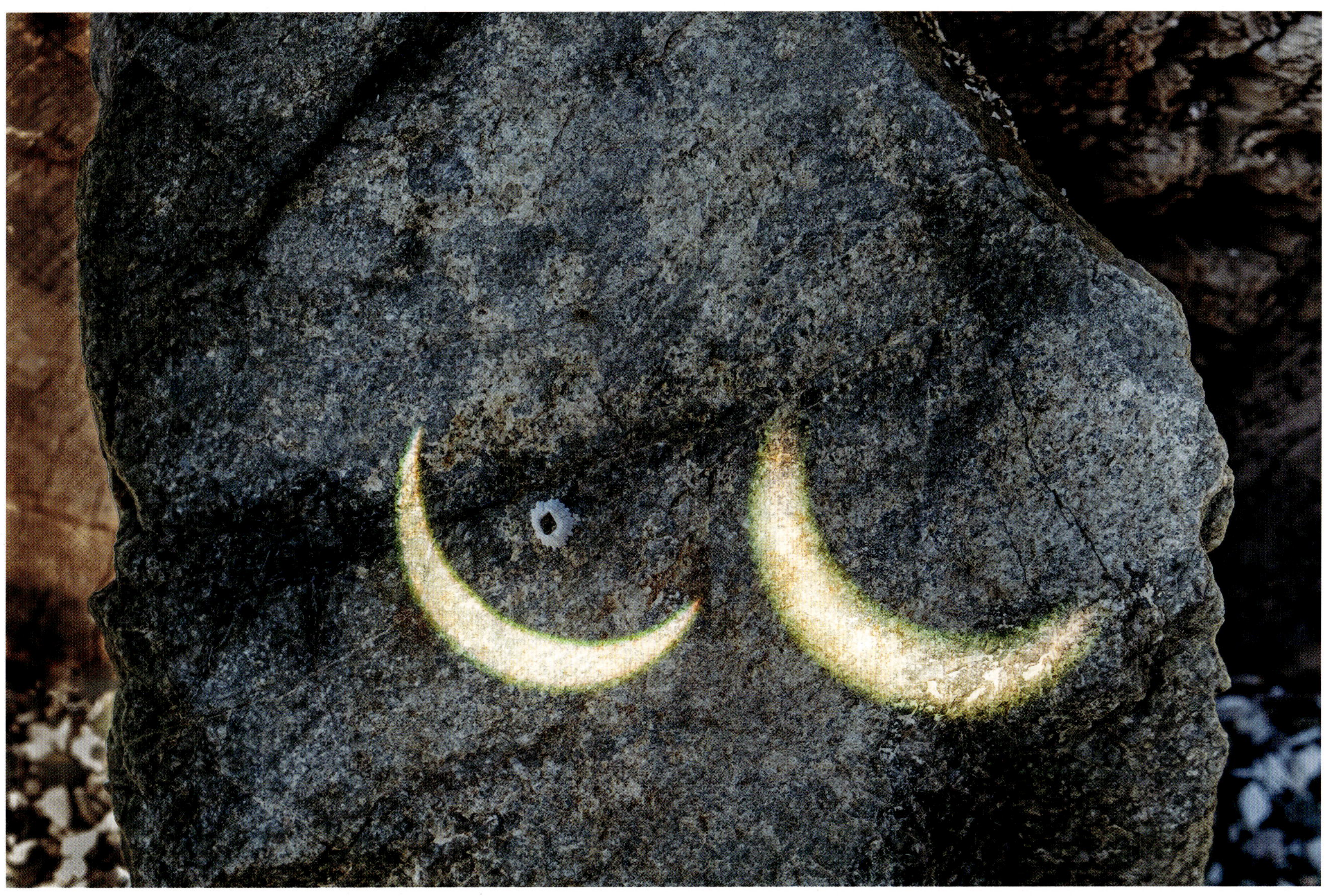

Moonrise in September over Swanson Channel (left).

The solar eclipse of August 21, 2017 at its local maximum projected through binoculars (one lens deliberately defocussed) onto a seaside boulder in the Tsawout Reserve (above).

(Following page) The view from Baynes Peak towards Fulford Harbour at dusk in July. The islands in the panorama include Stuart (USA), Moresby, Portland, Brackman, Brethour, Domville, Gooch, Forrest, Coal, Pym, Knapp, Goudge, Piers, Sidney and D'Arcy.

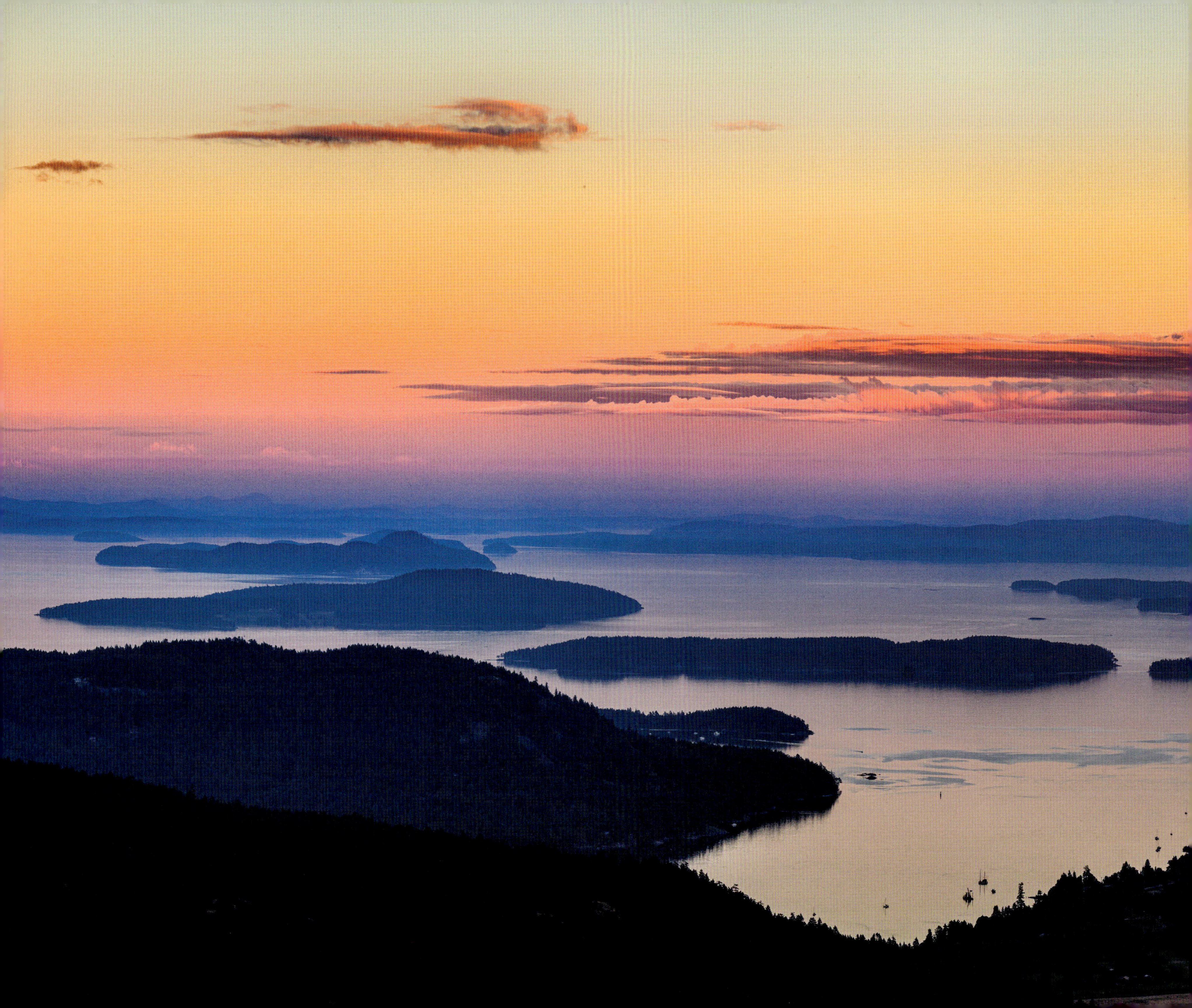

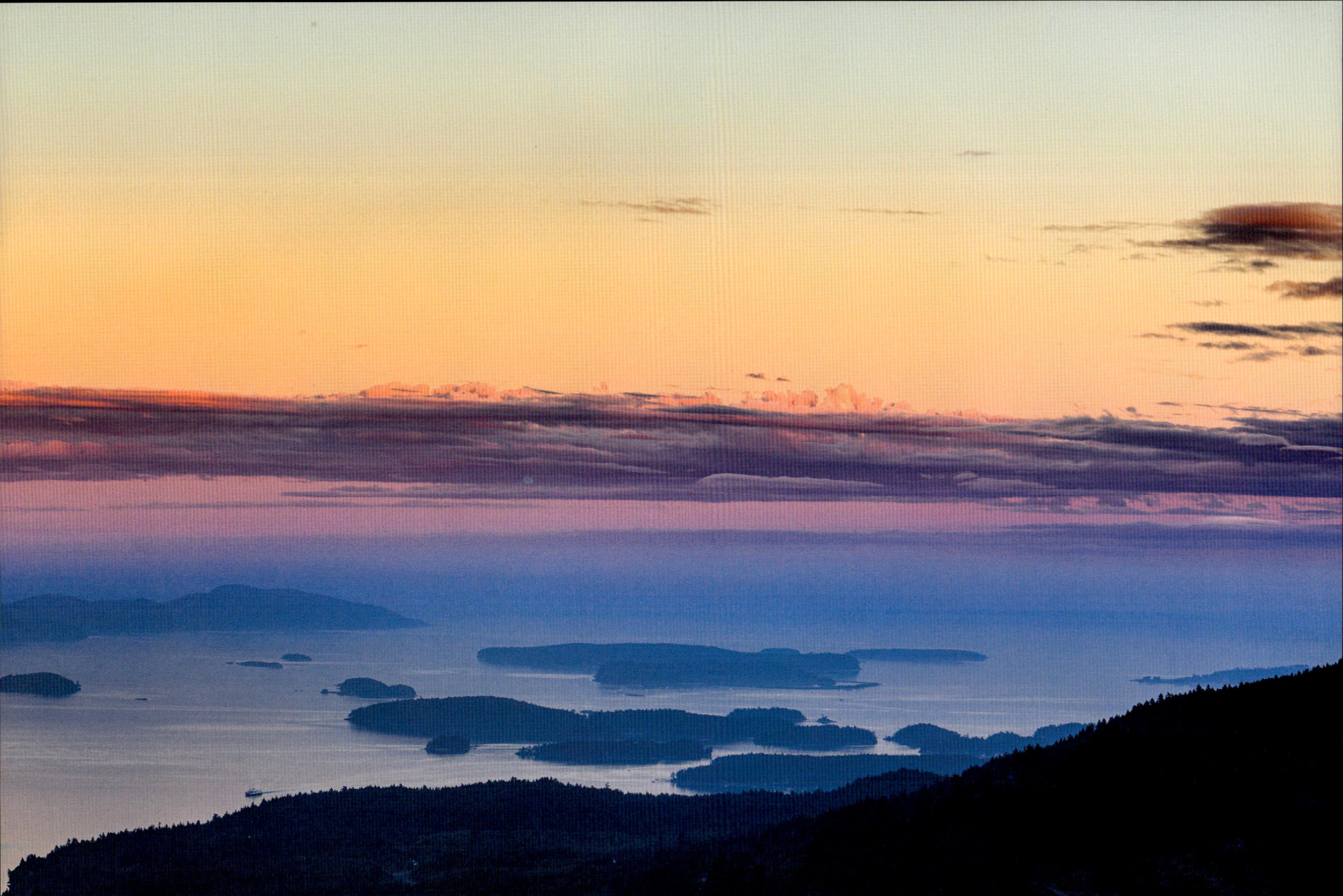

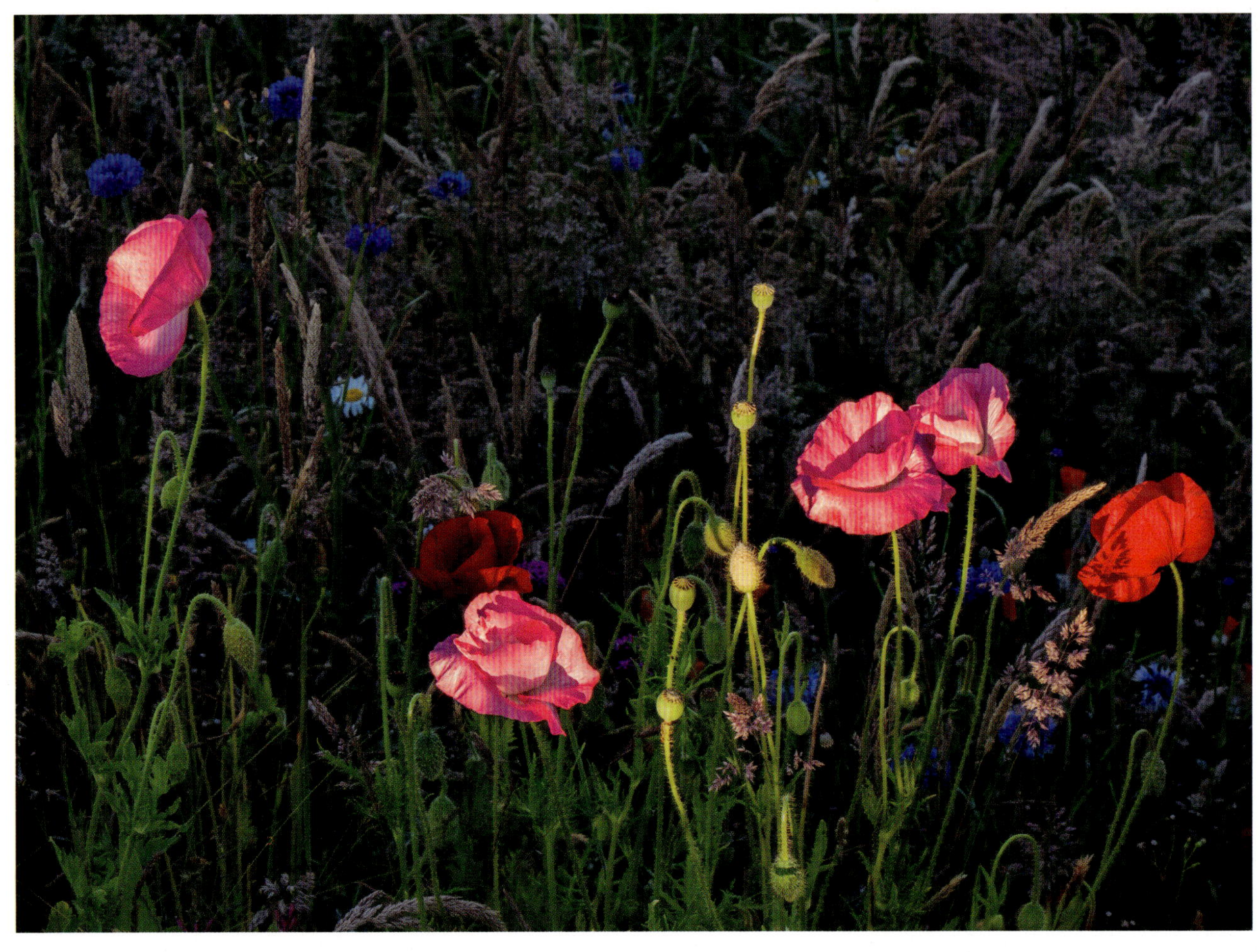

Poppies by the roadside in Fulford Valley and a black-tailed deer doe in Burgoyne Valley, both in June.

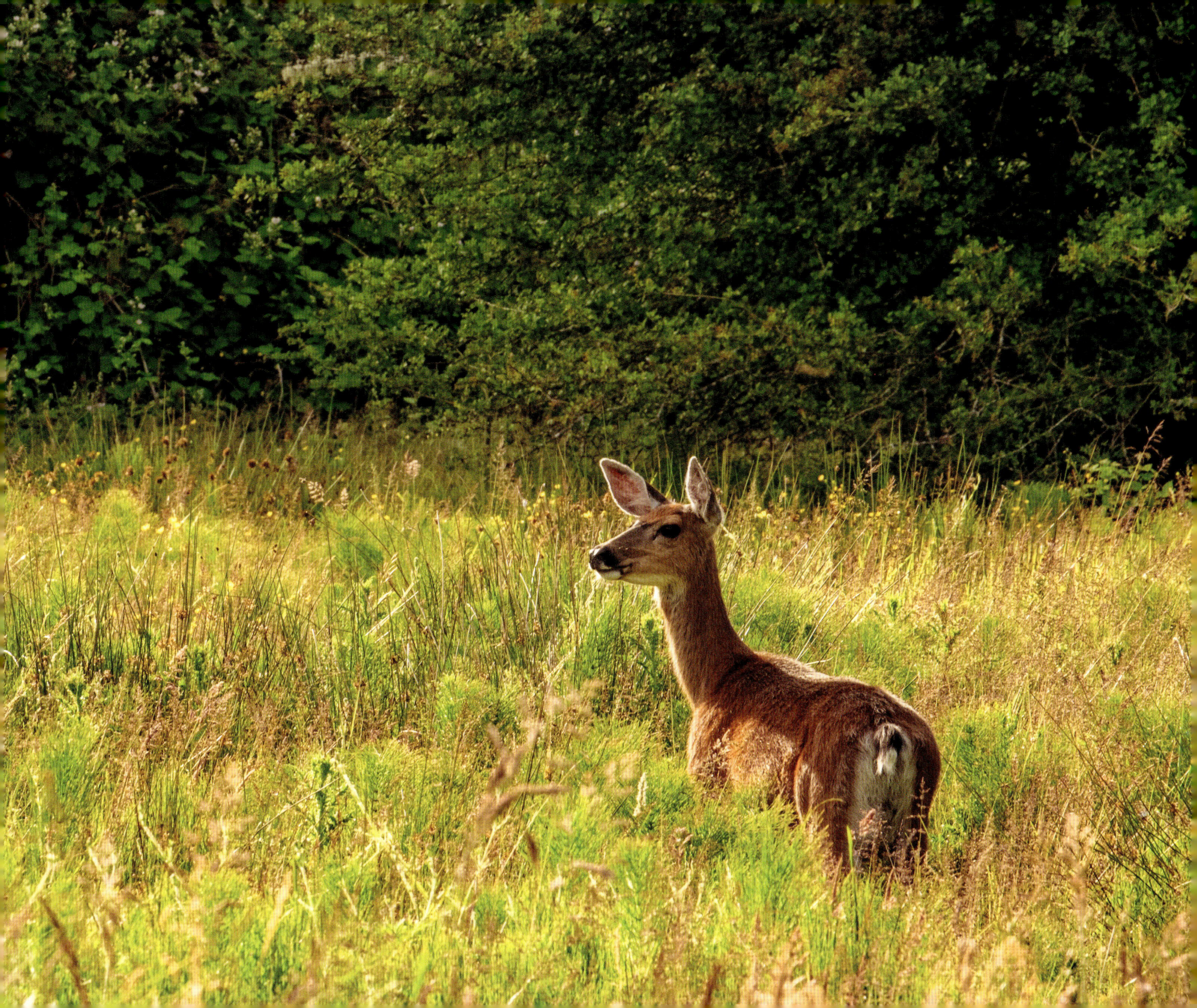

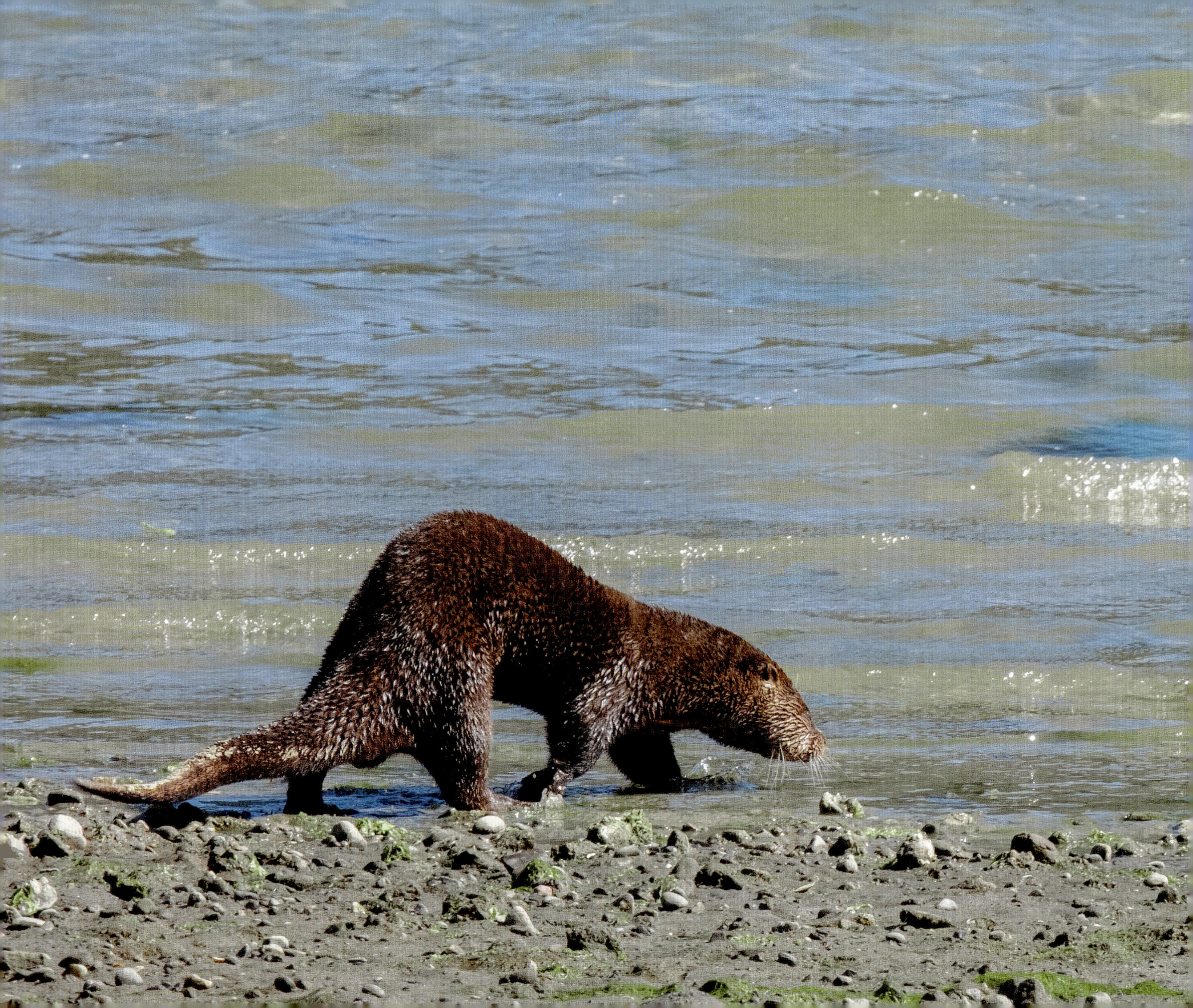

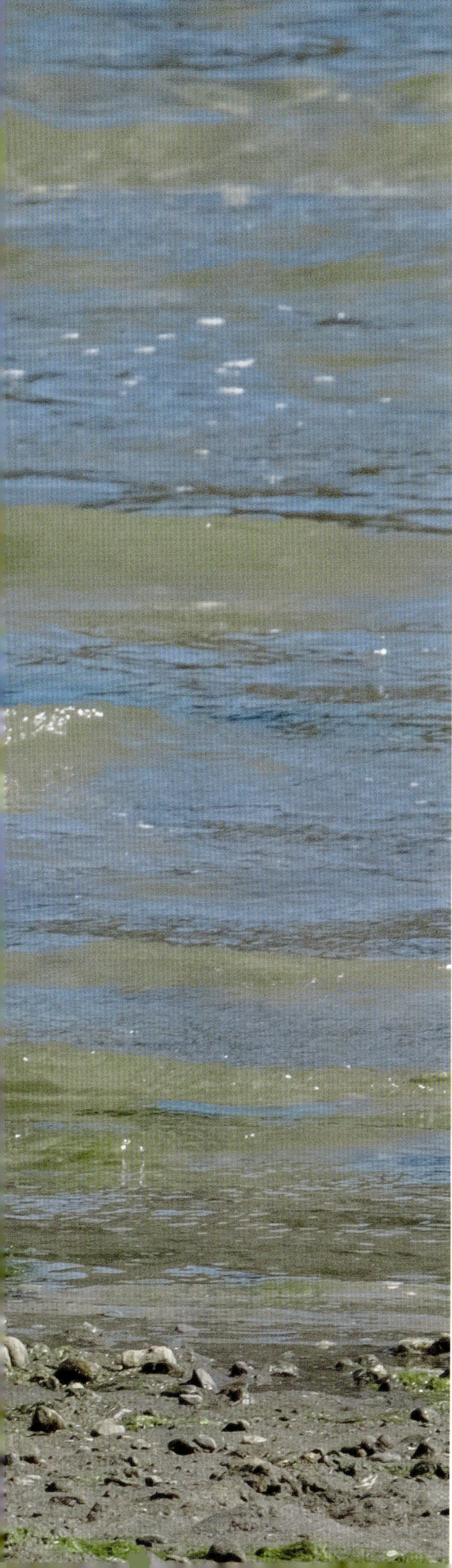

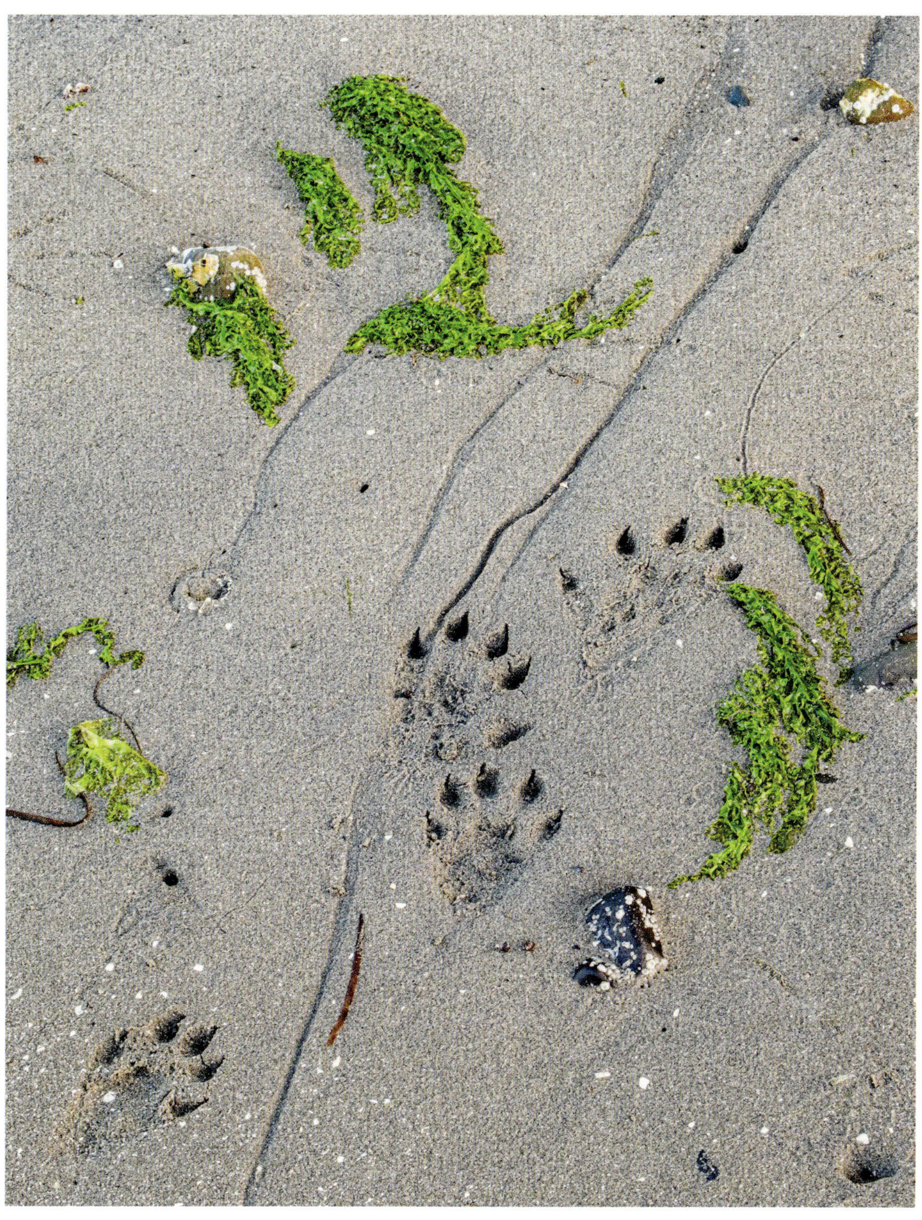

River otters and their tracks are commonly seen by the seaside.

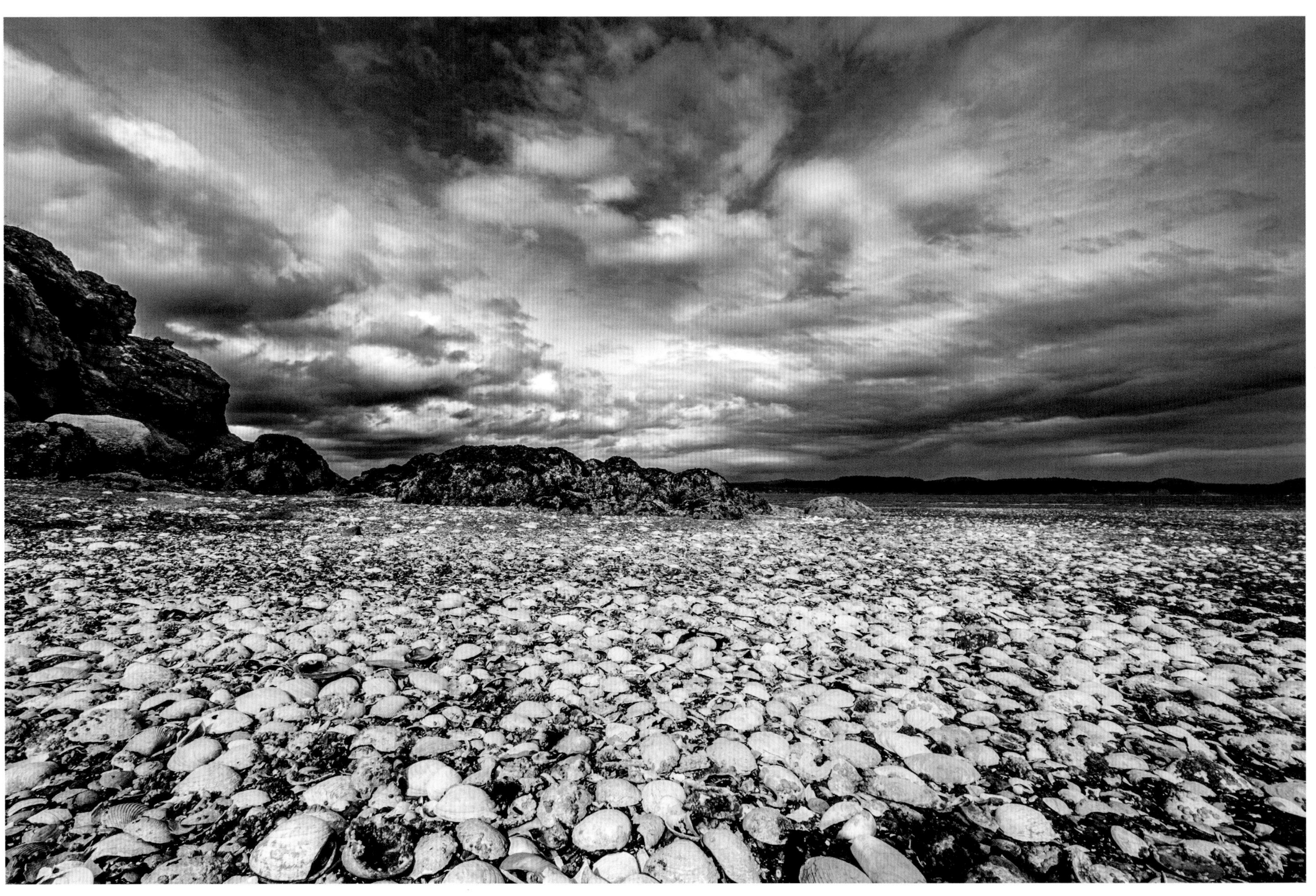

Seashells cover the flats at low tide at the mouth of Cusheon Creek near Beddis Beach.

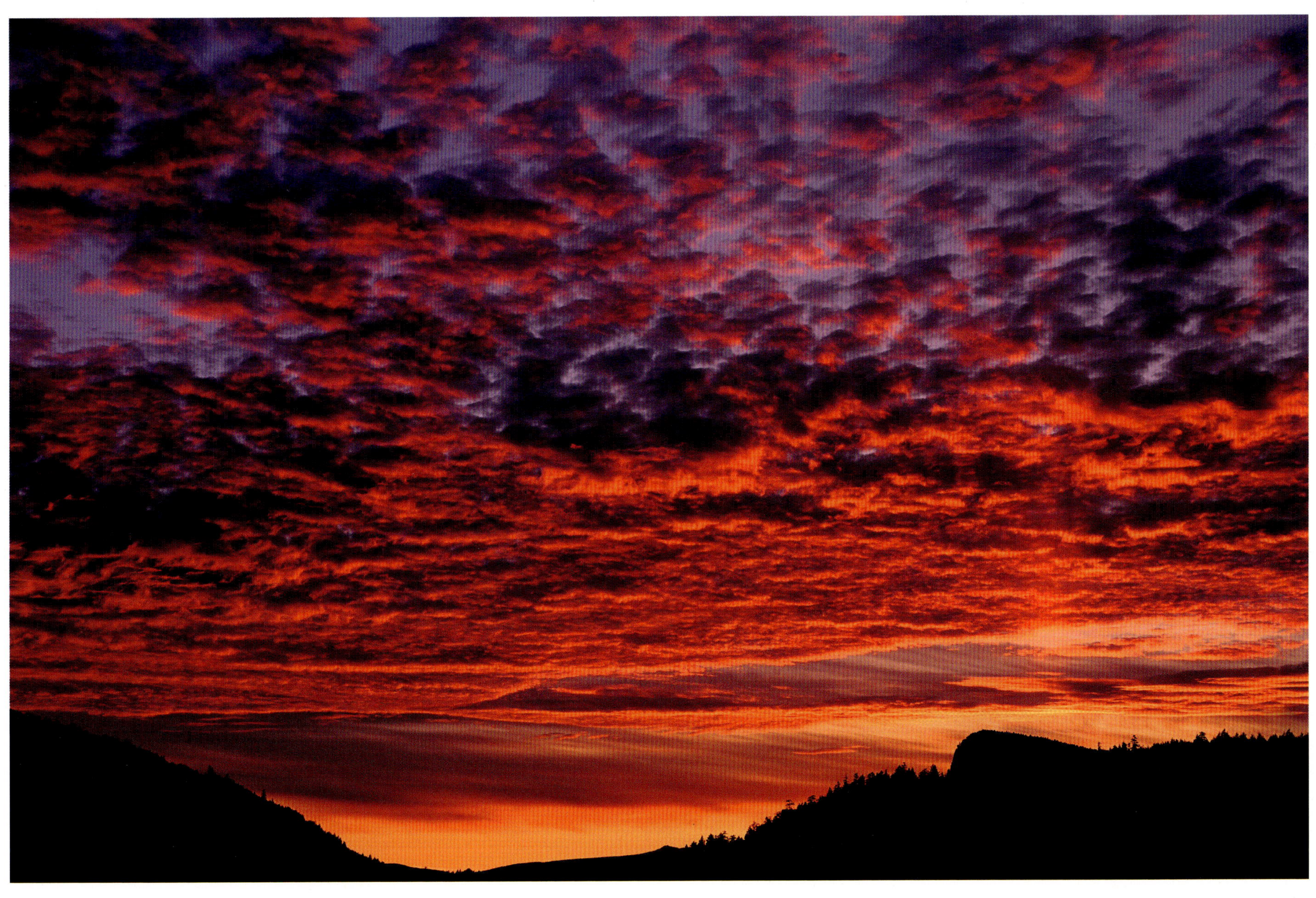

A fiery midsummer sunset over Fulford Valley.

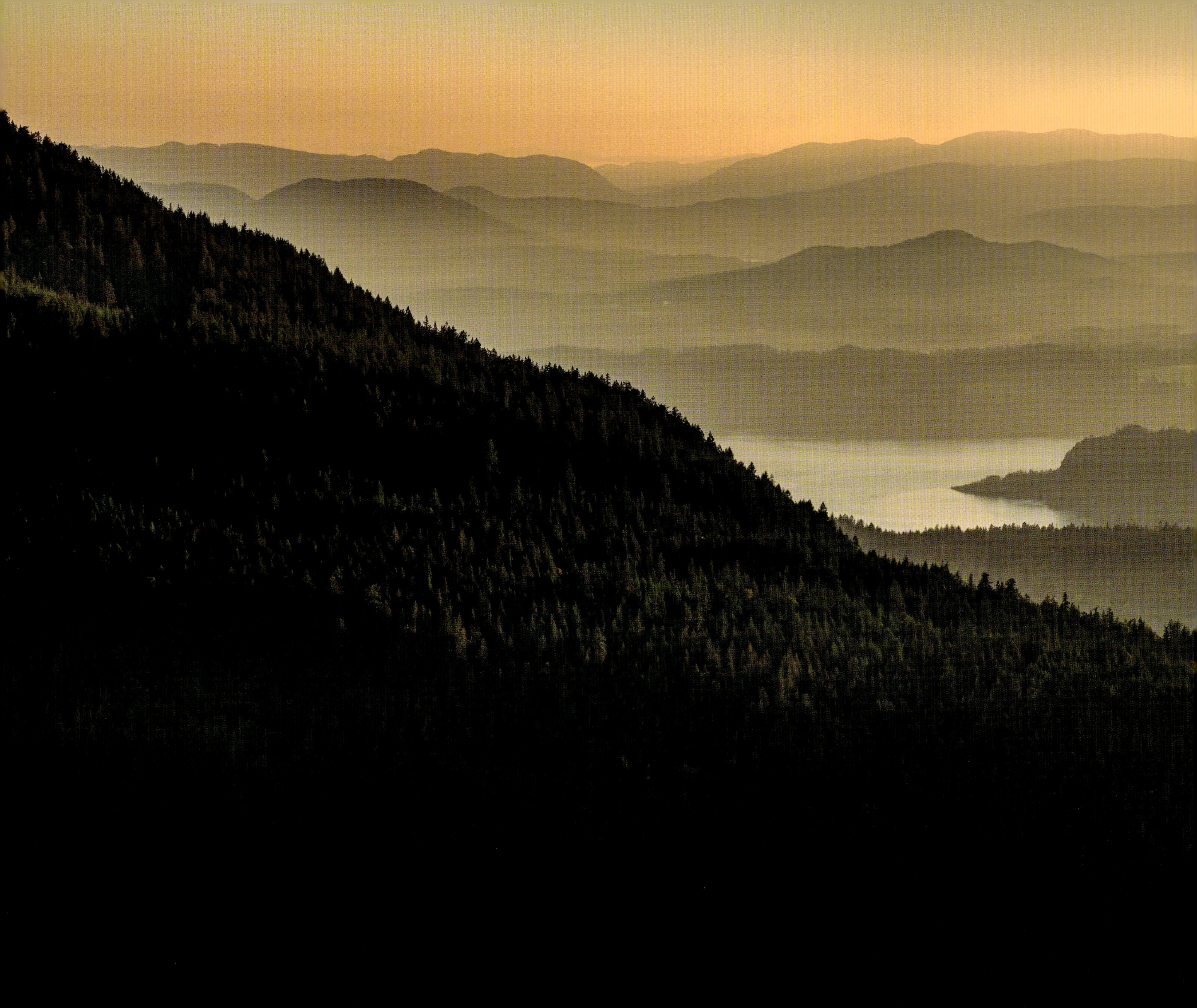

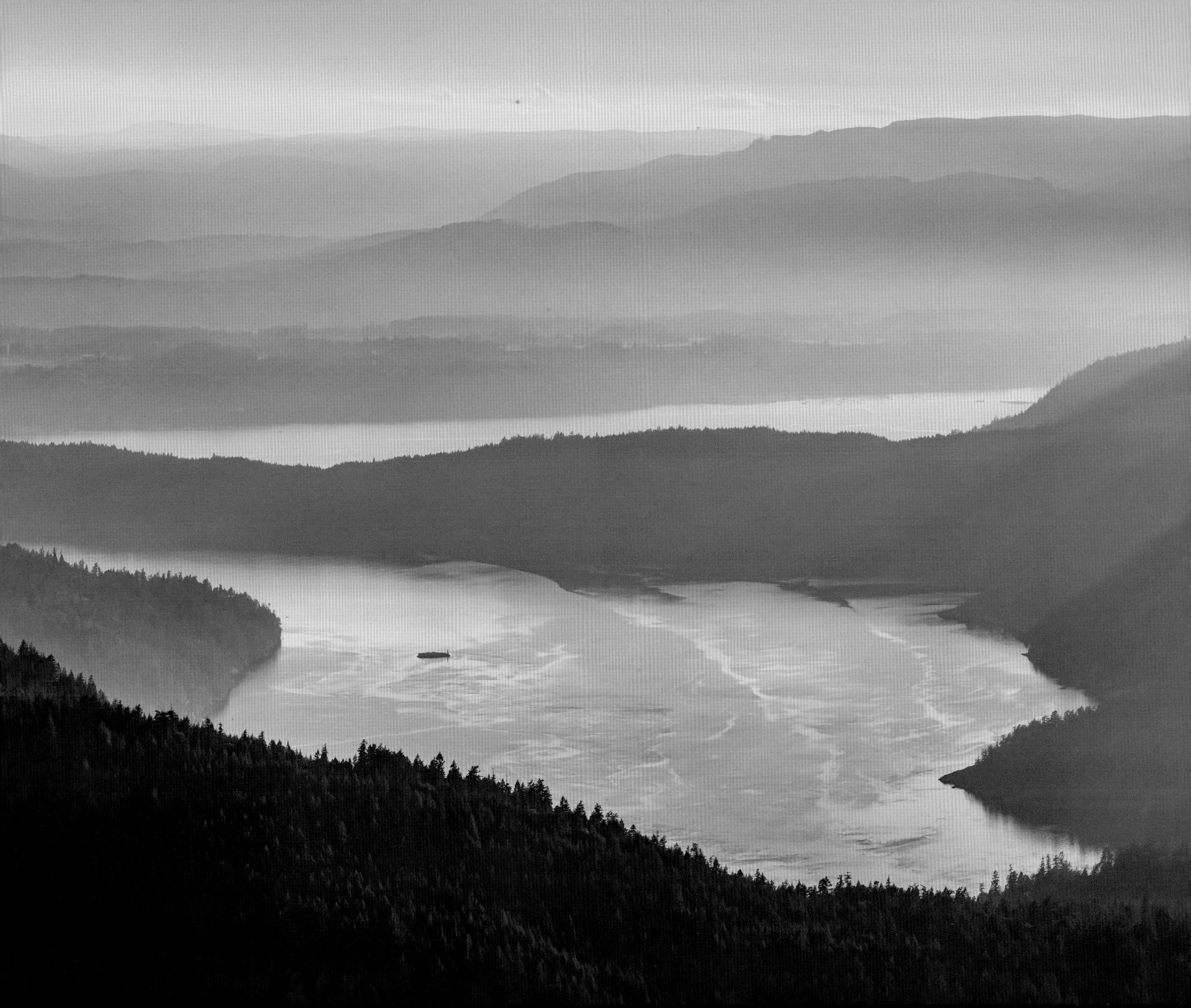

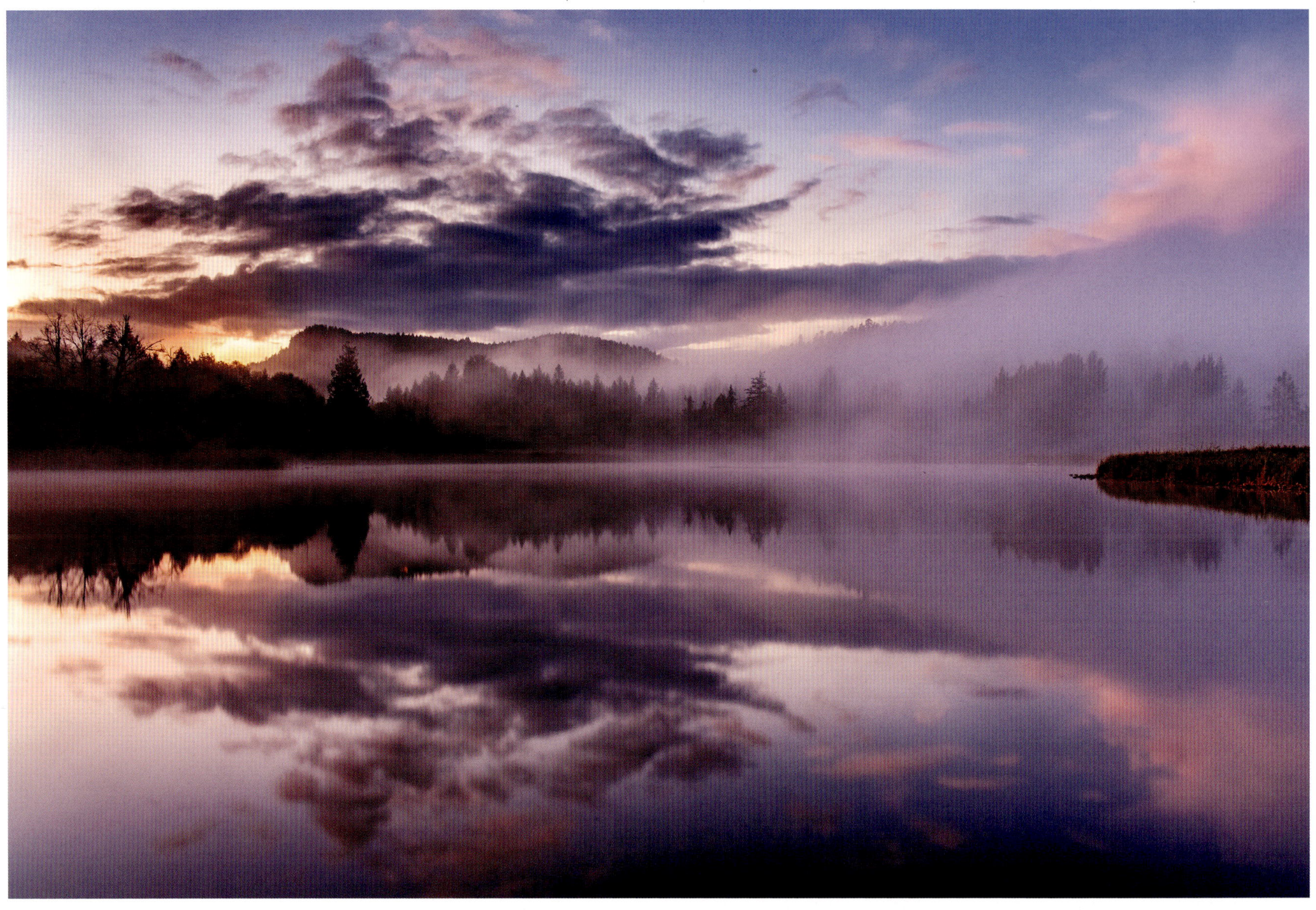

(Previous page) A panorama from Mount Maxwell across the Sansum Narrows and Cowichan Bay to the rugged landscape of Vancouver Island on an October evening.

Dusk at Blackburn Lake in October (above).

Looking towards the head of Fulford Harbour at sunset in April (right).

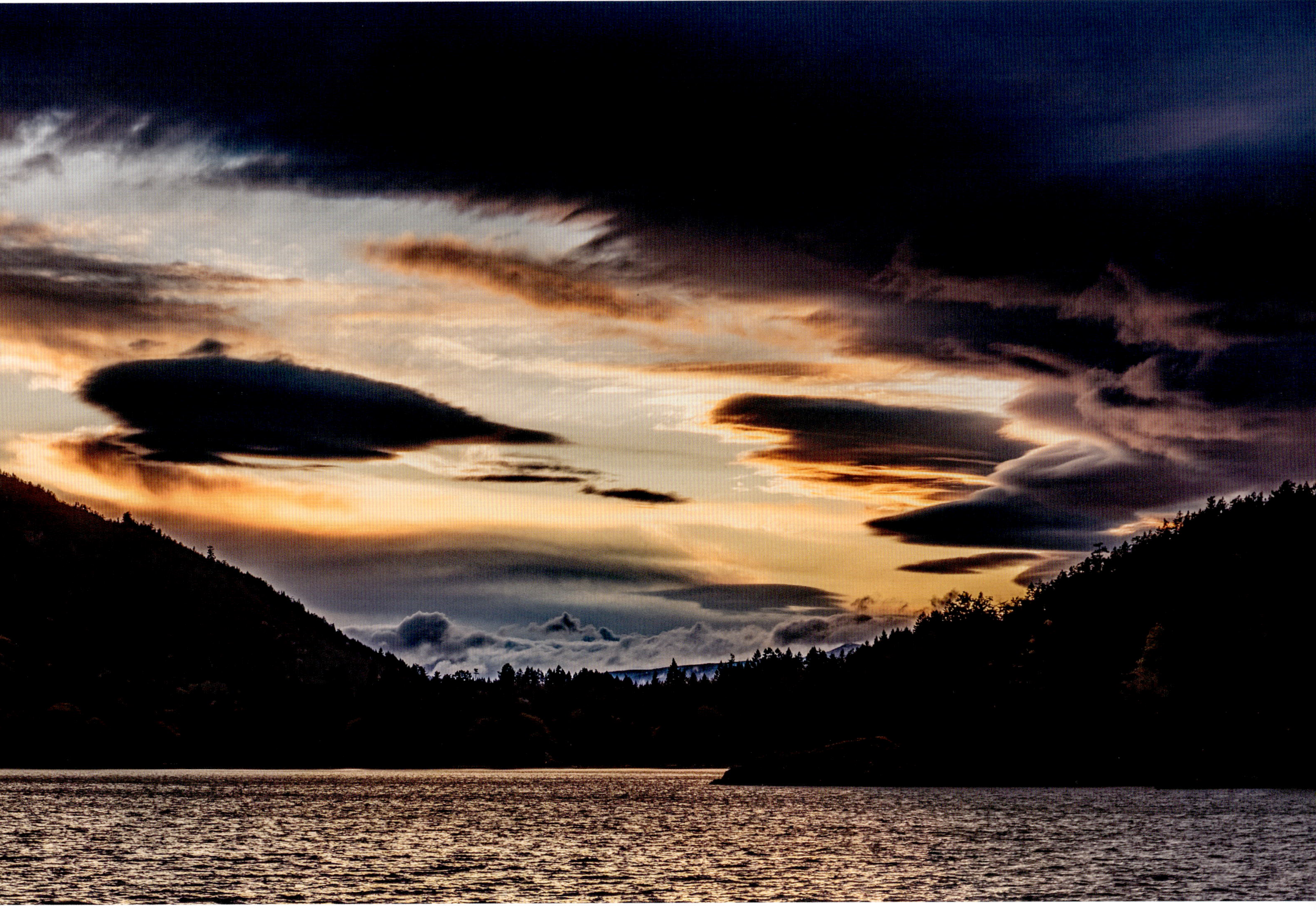

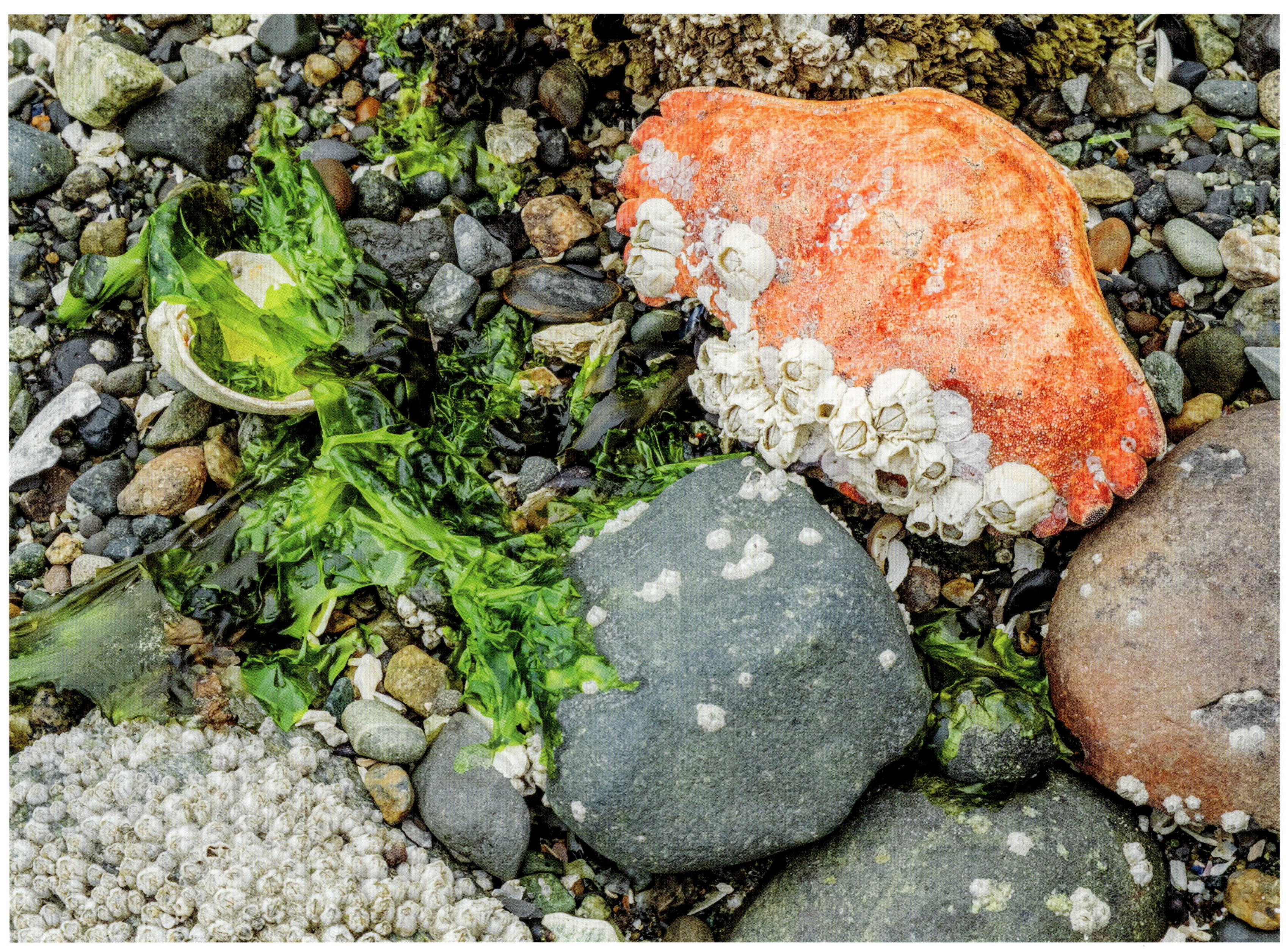

Seaweed and the shell of a red rock crab (above), and purple varnish clams exposed at low tide near Drummond Park (right).

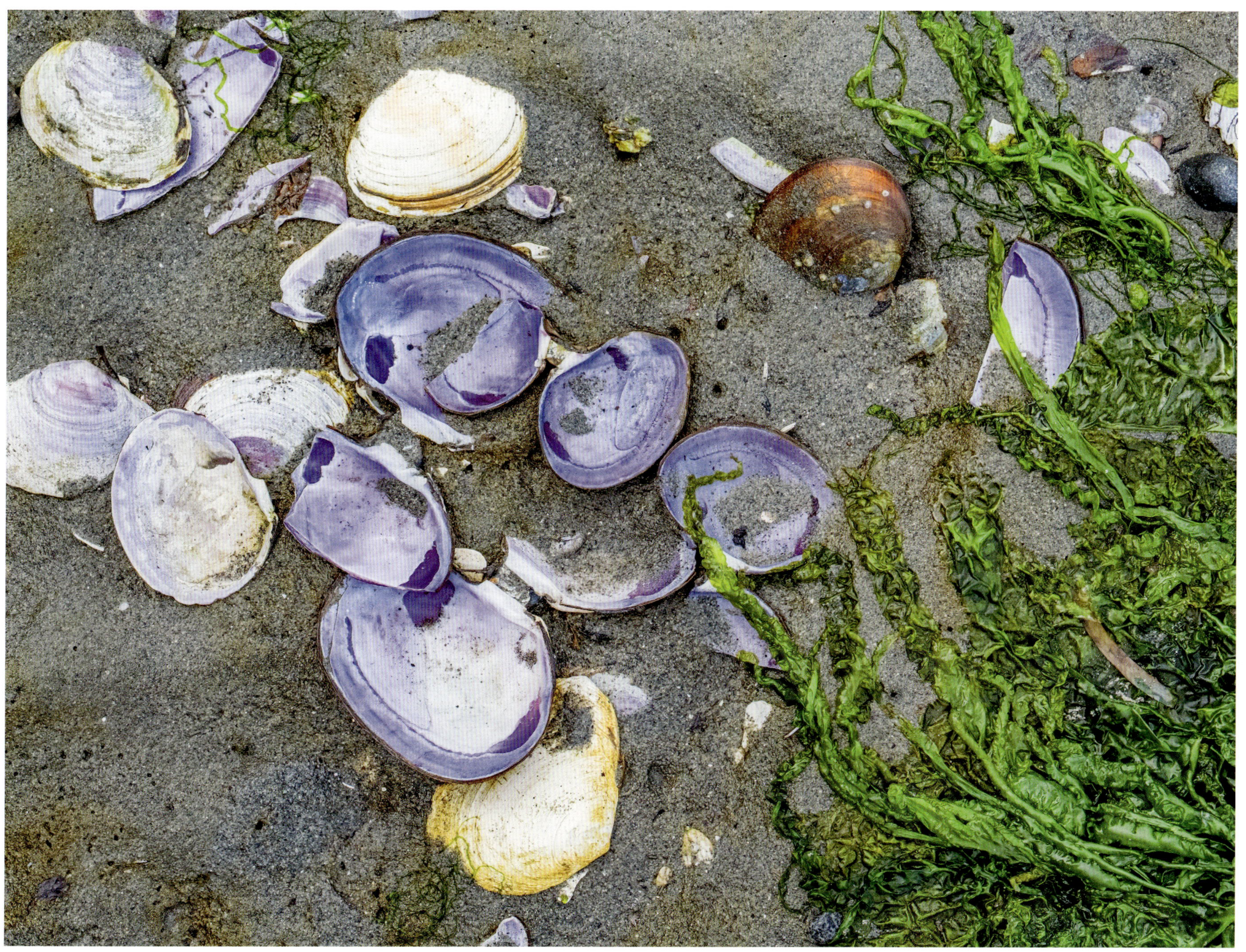

Idol Island, a First Nations burial site, from Zach Beach (right).

Seaweed on the three-kilometre stretch of beach that is exposed at low tide along the west shore of Fulford Harbour (far right).

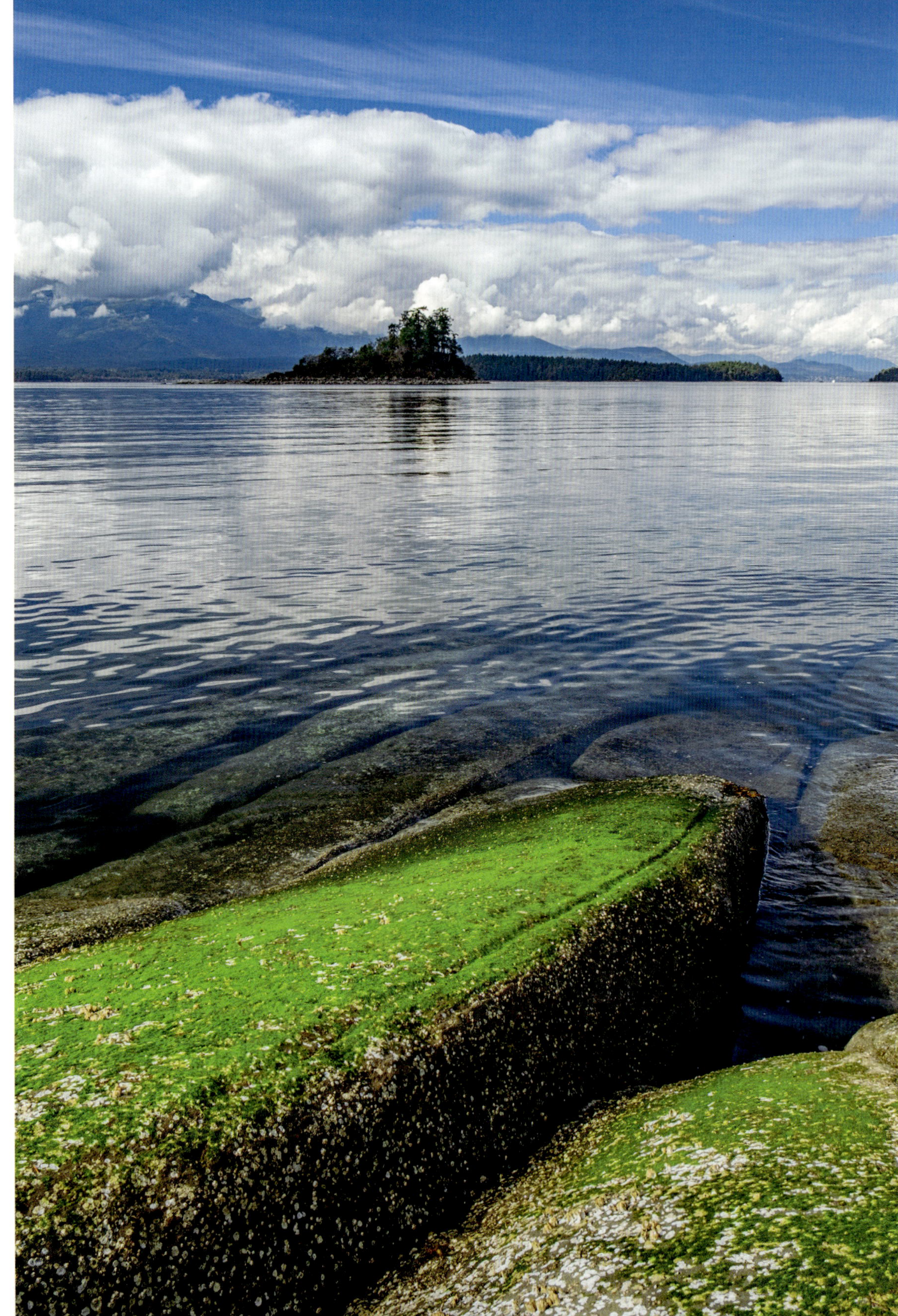

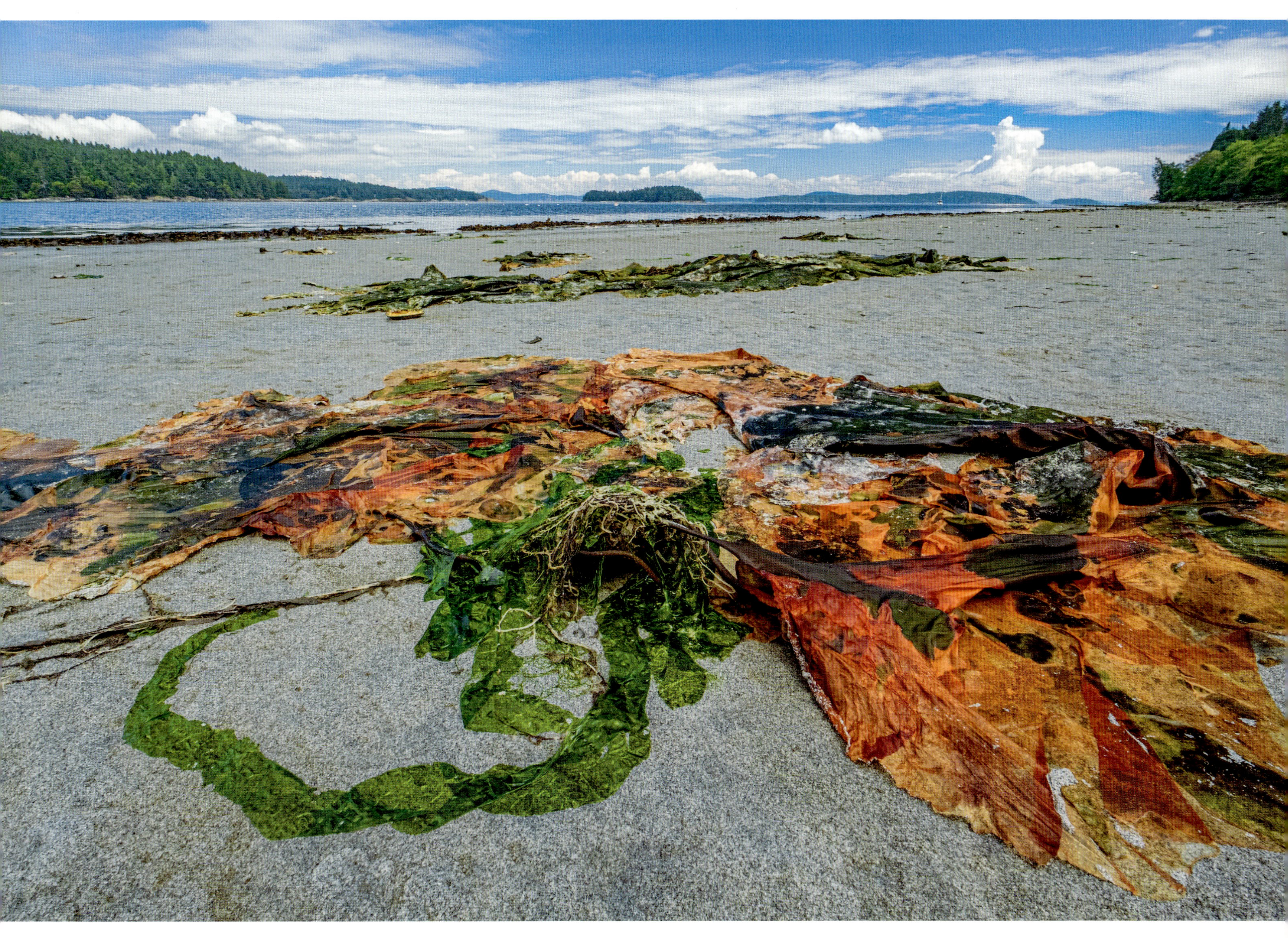

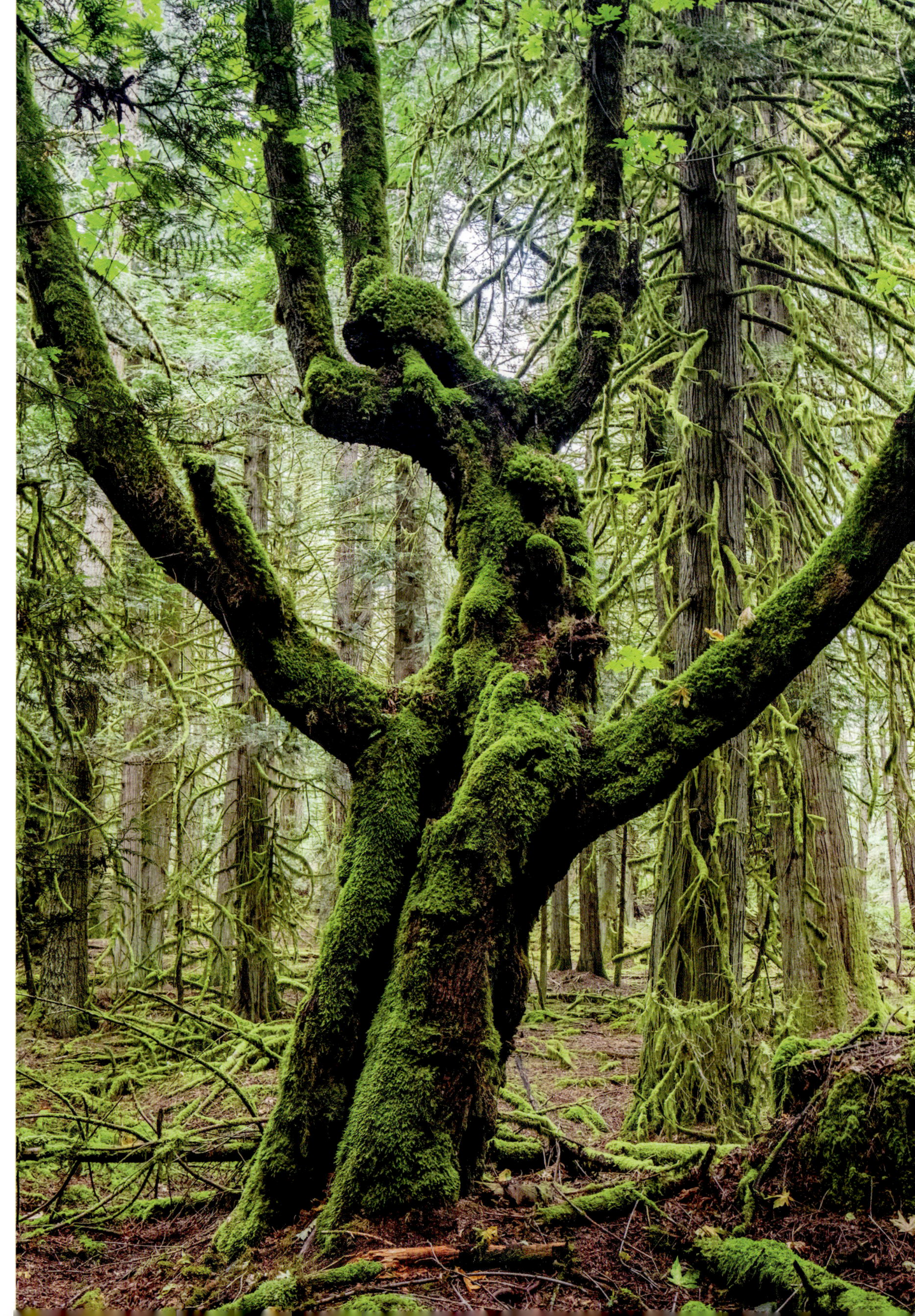

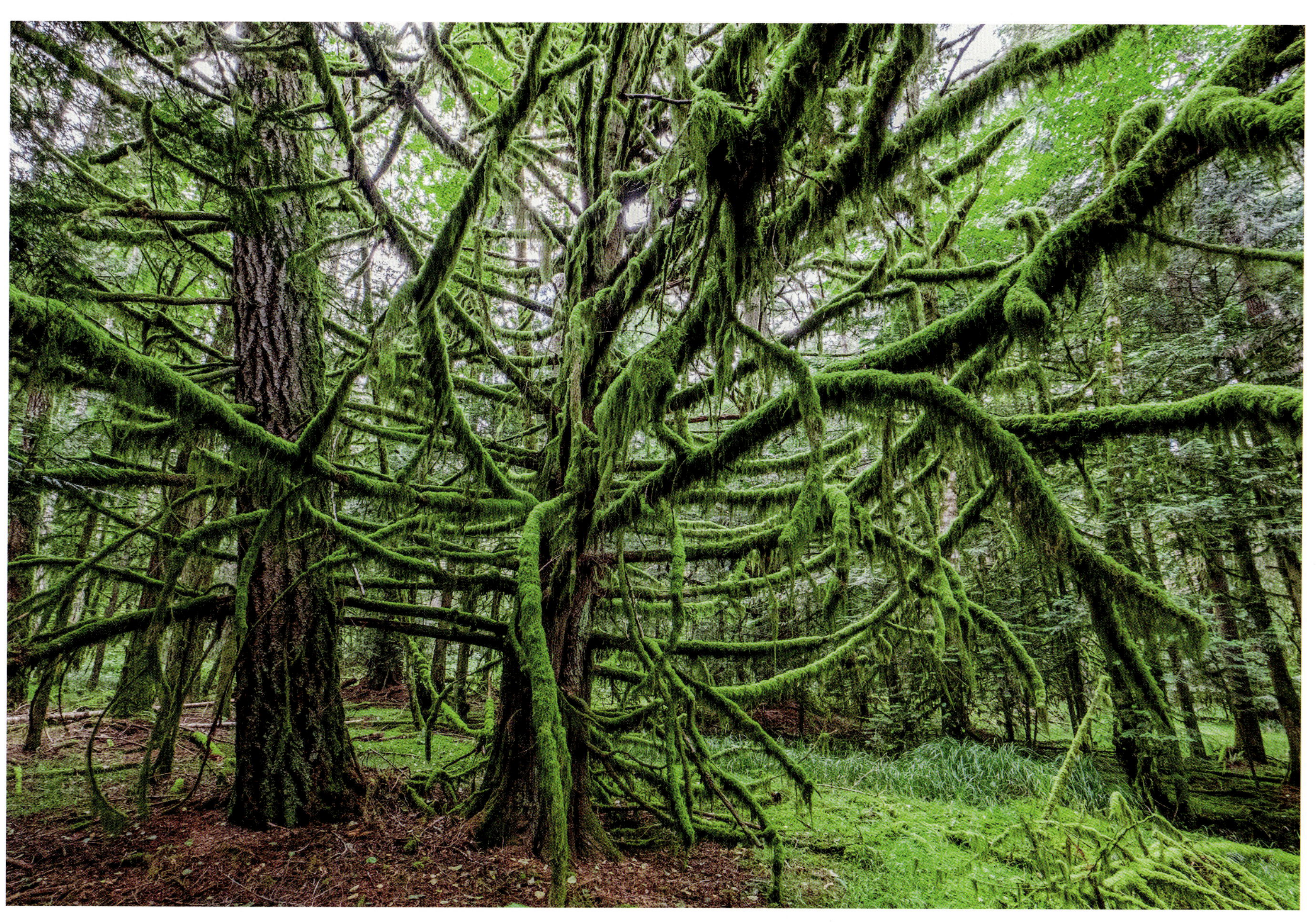

The mossy forest along the Hilltop Trail near Merganser Pond in the remote centre of Ruckle Provincial Park in August.

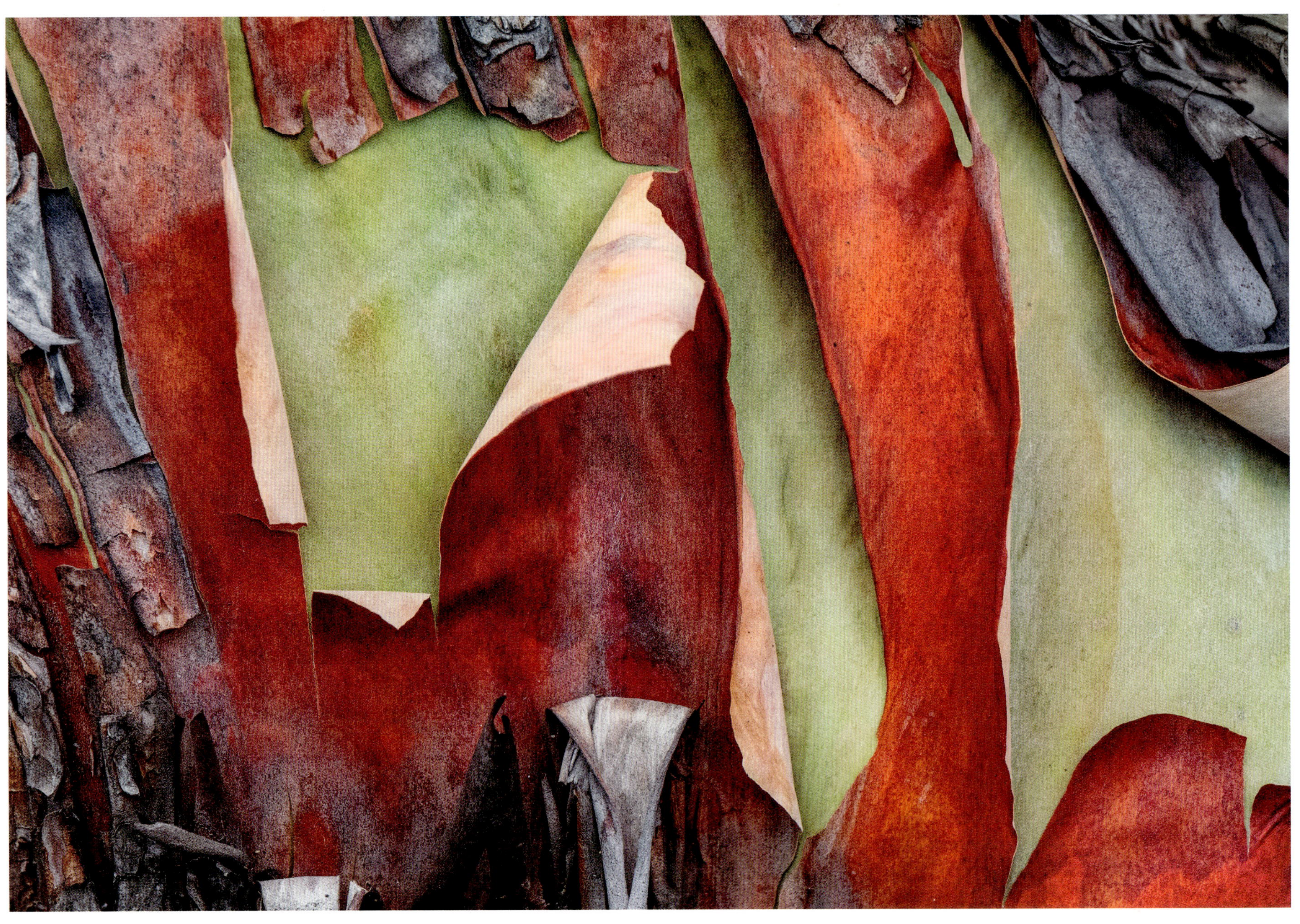

Details on an arbutus trunk.

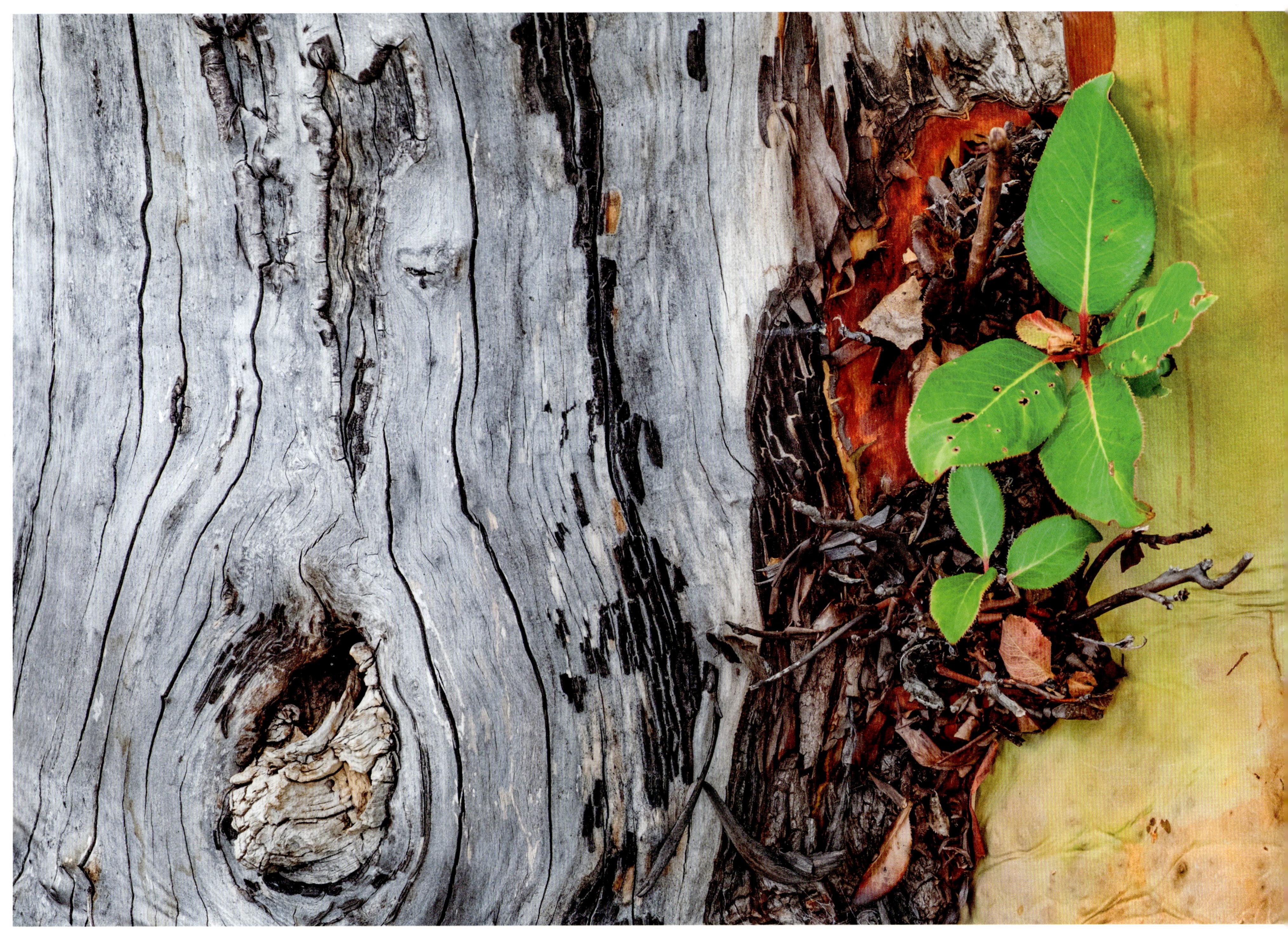

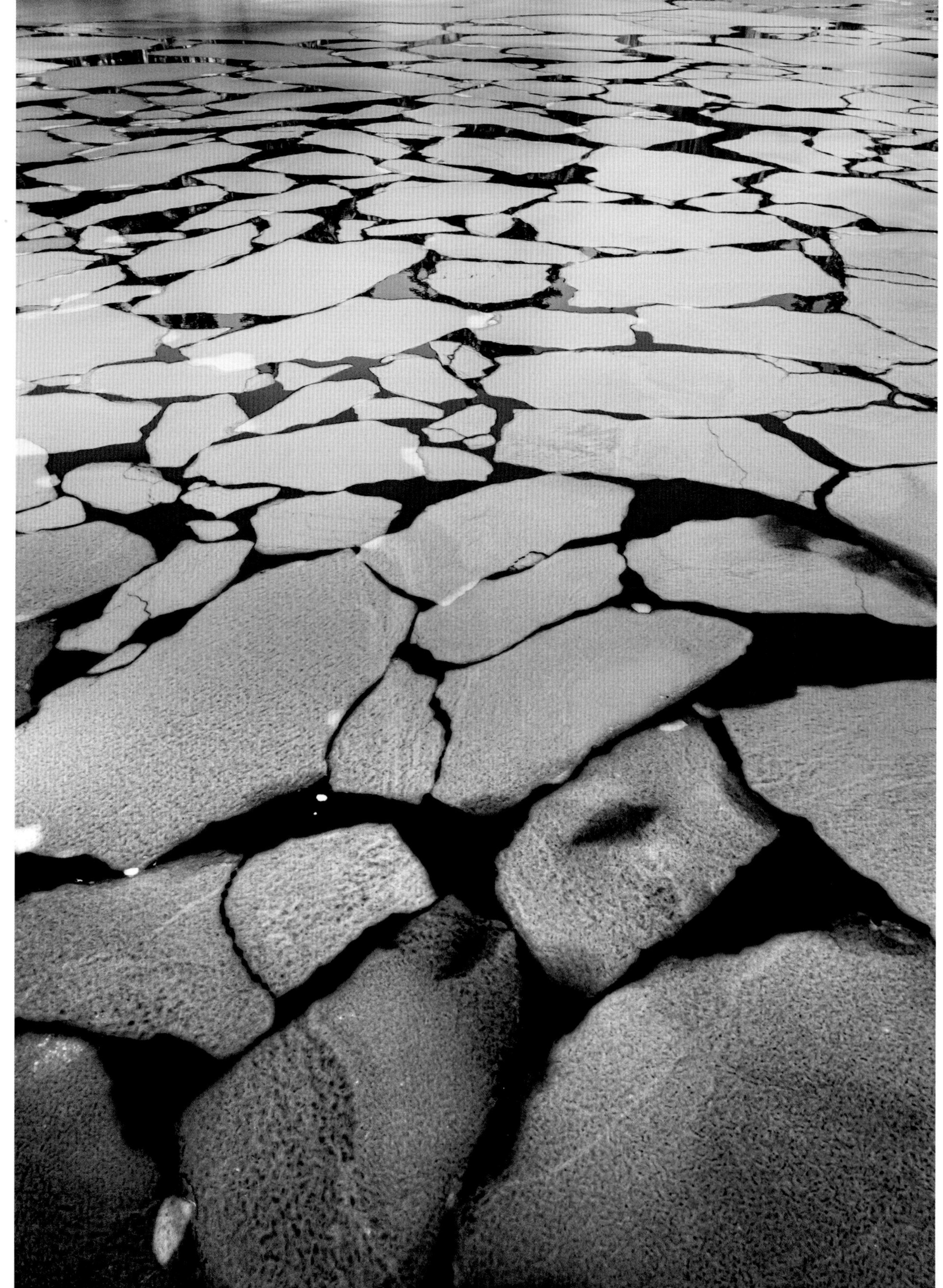

Pans of frozen snow in Fulford Harbour (right), and icicles below a frozen seep on Mount Erskine (far right), both in January.

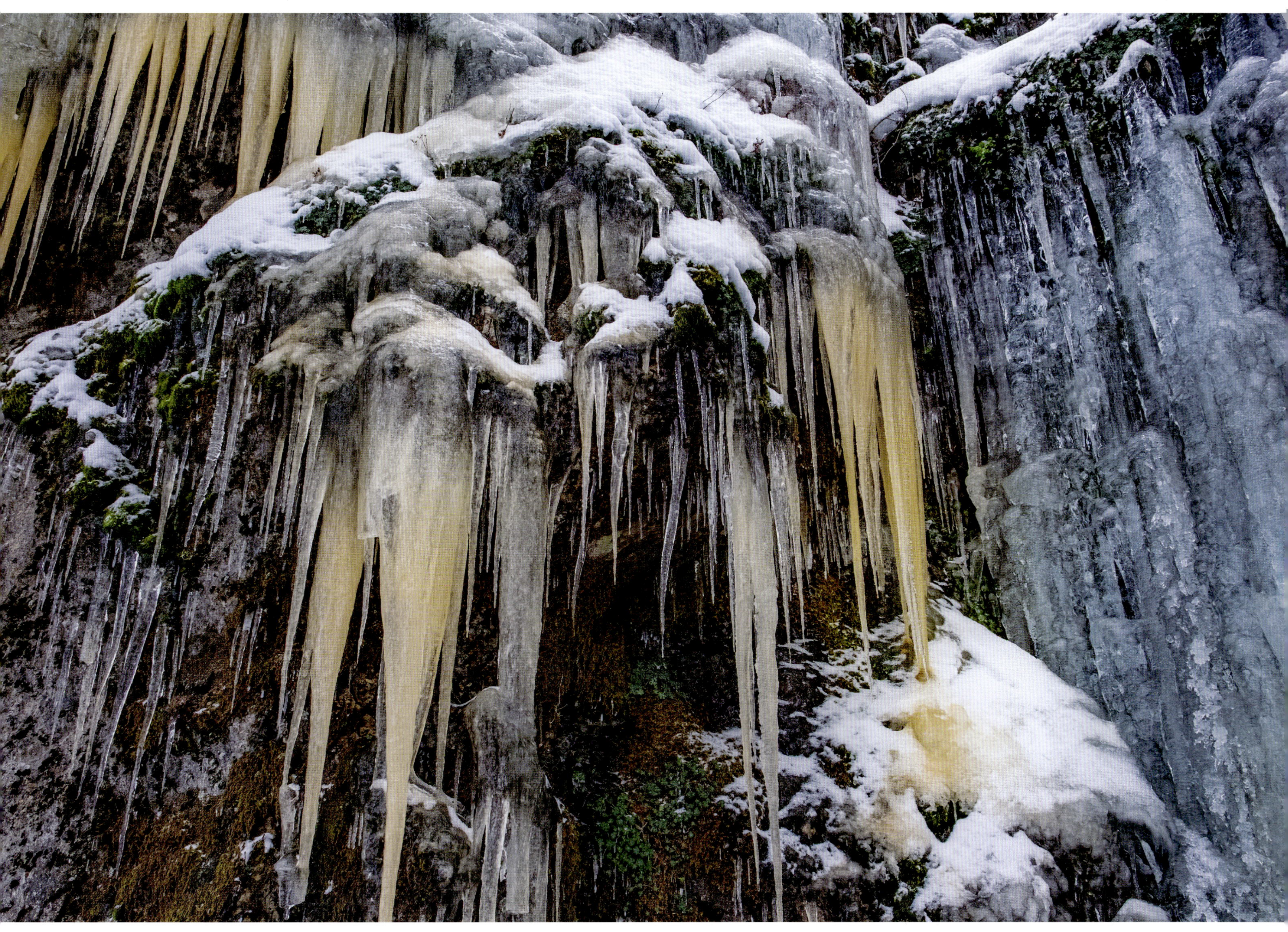

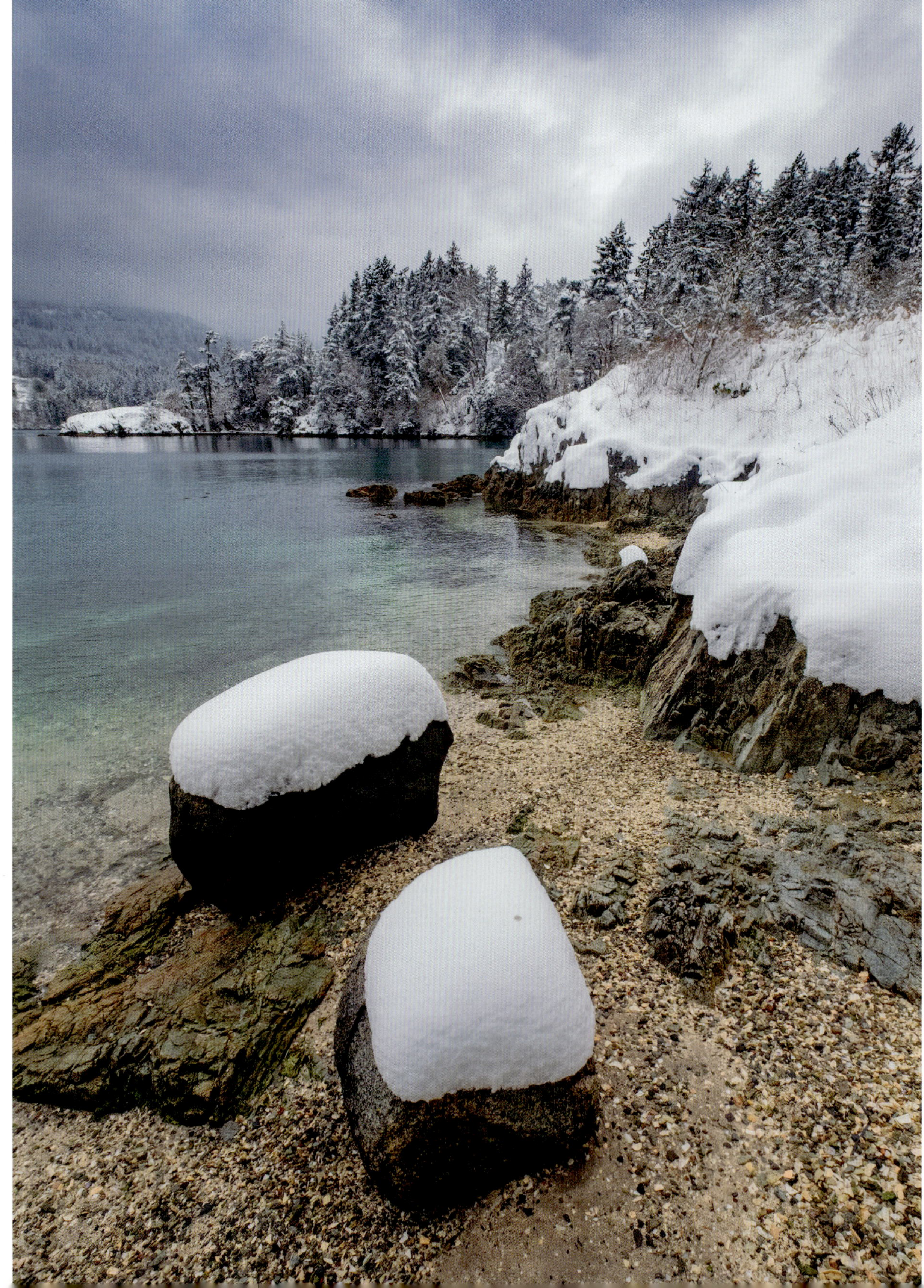

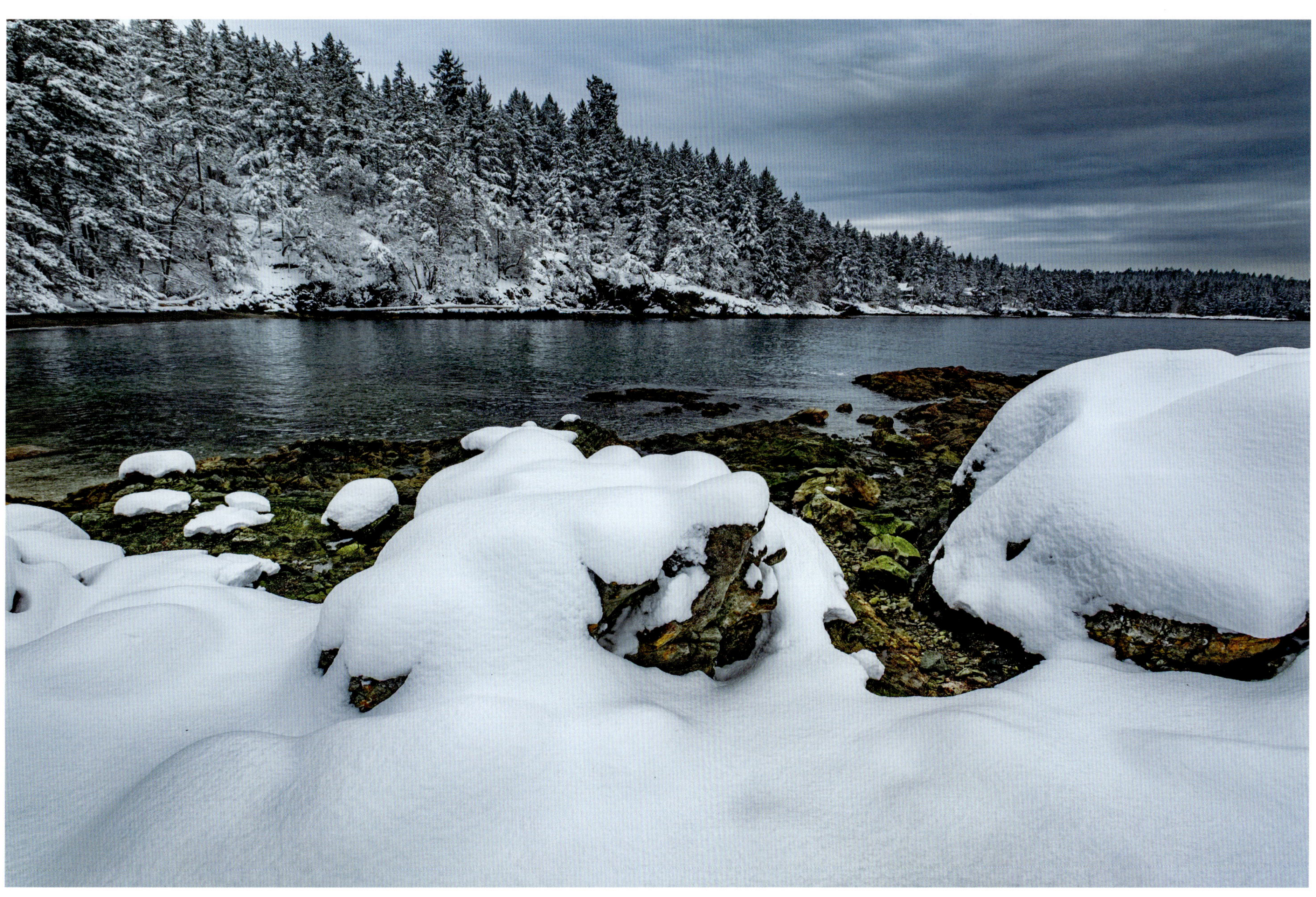

Snowfall is a rare occasion each winter on Salt Spring. The retreating tide exposes bare ground in a small cove off Morningside Road in January (left), and in the Tsawout Reserve in February a year earlier (above).

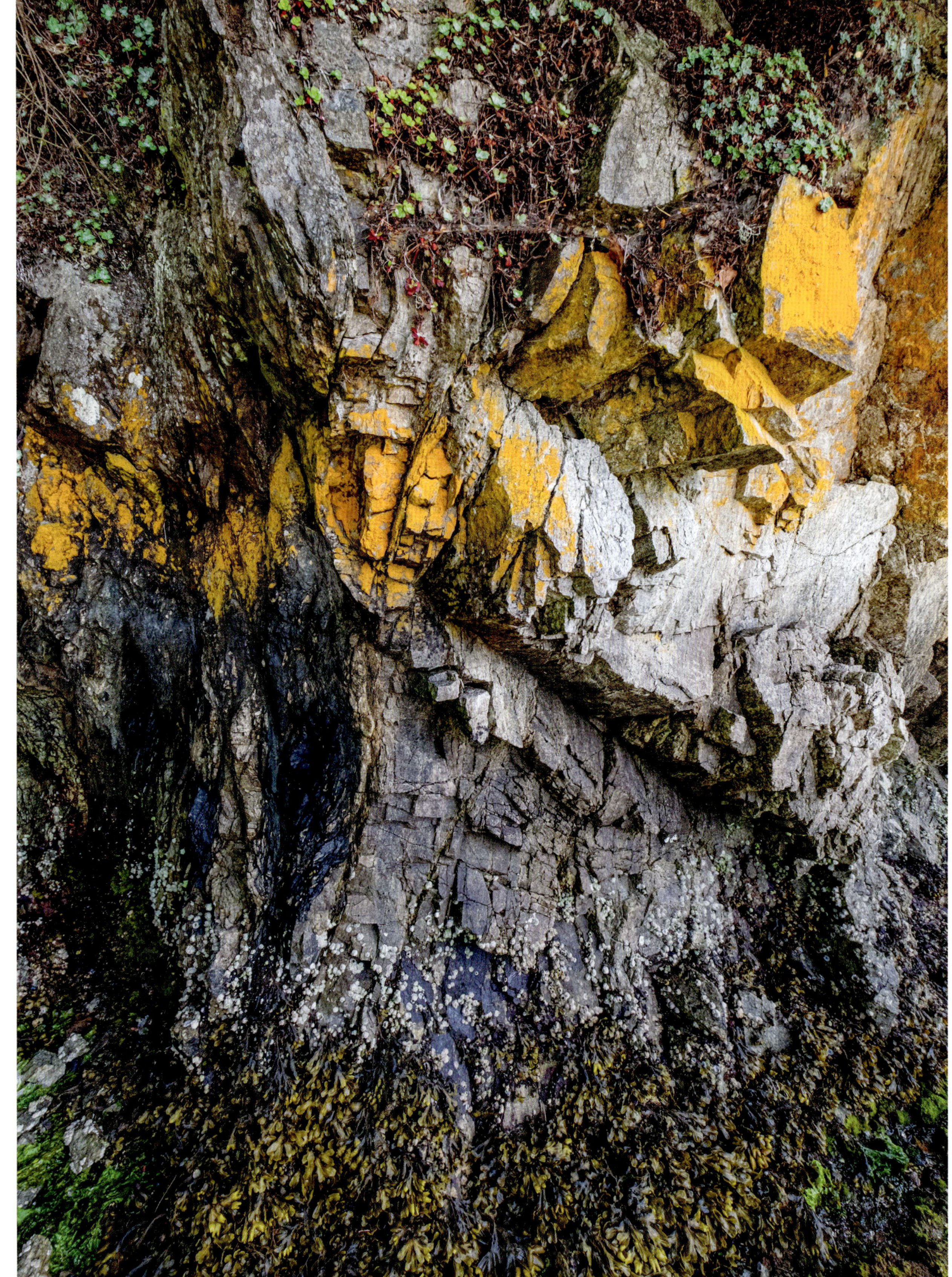

Colourful and varied geology along the shoreline in Fulford Harbour (right), and at Beaver Point in Ruckle Provincial Park (far right).

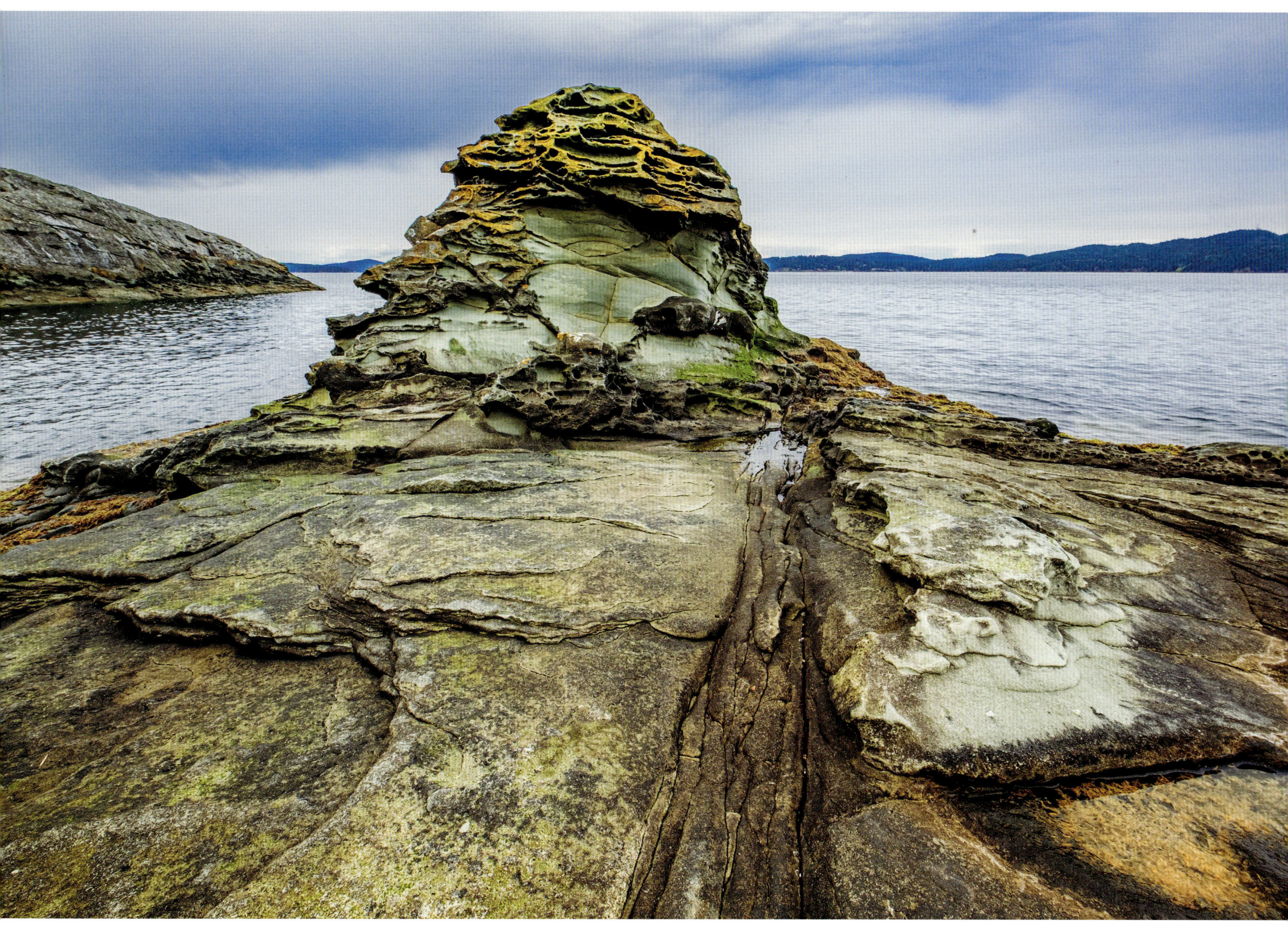

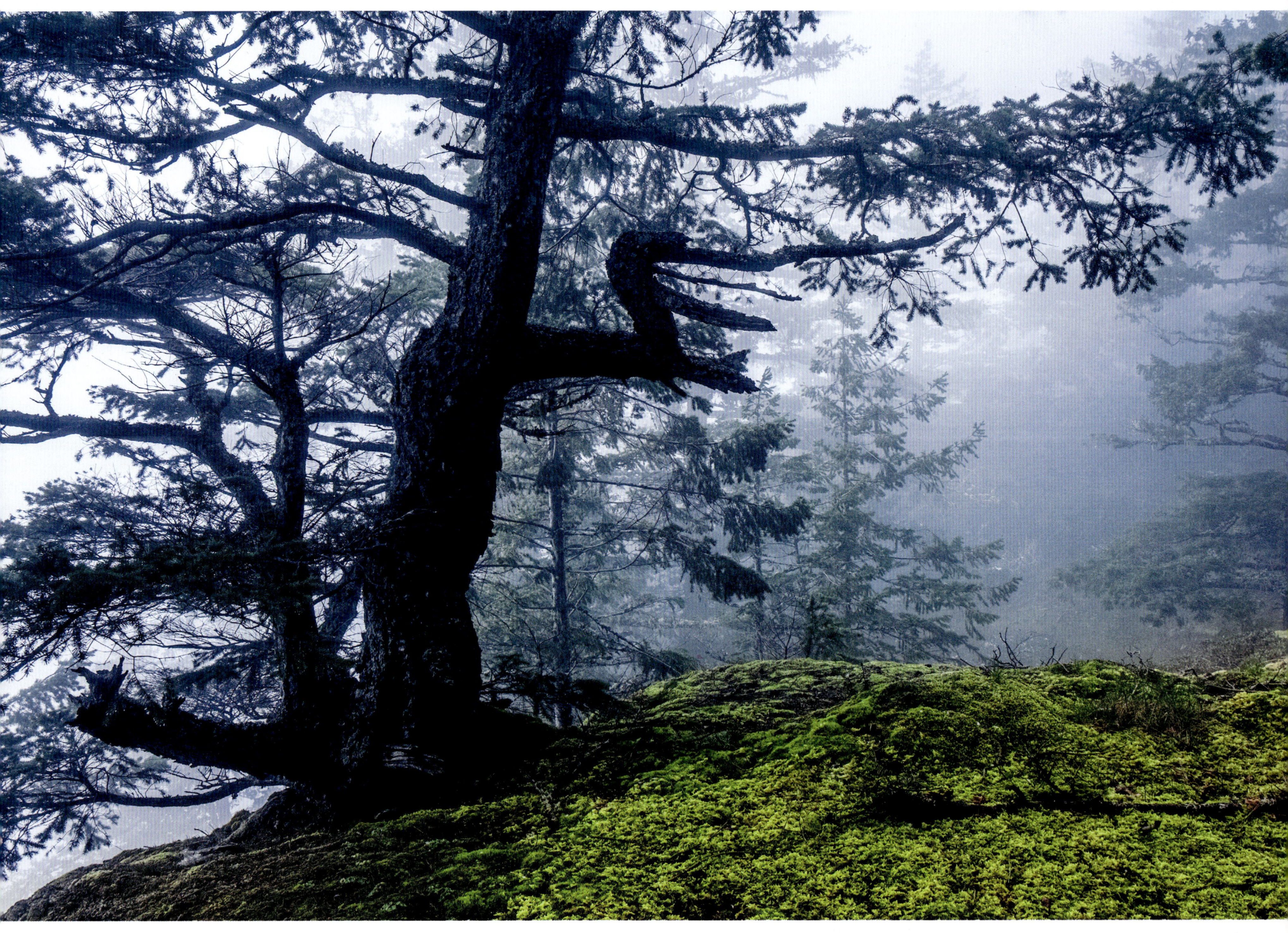

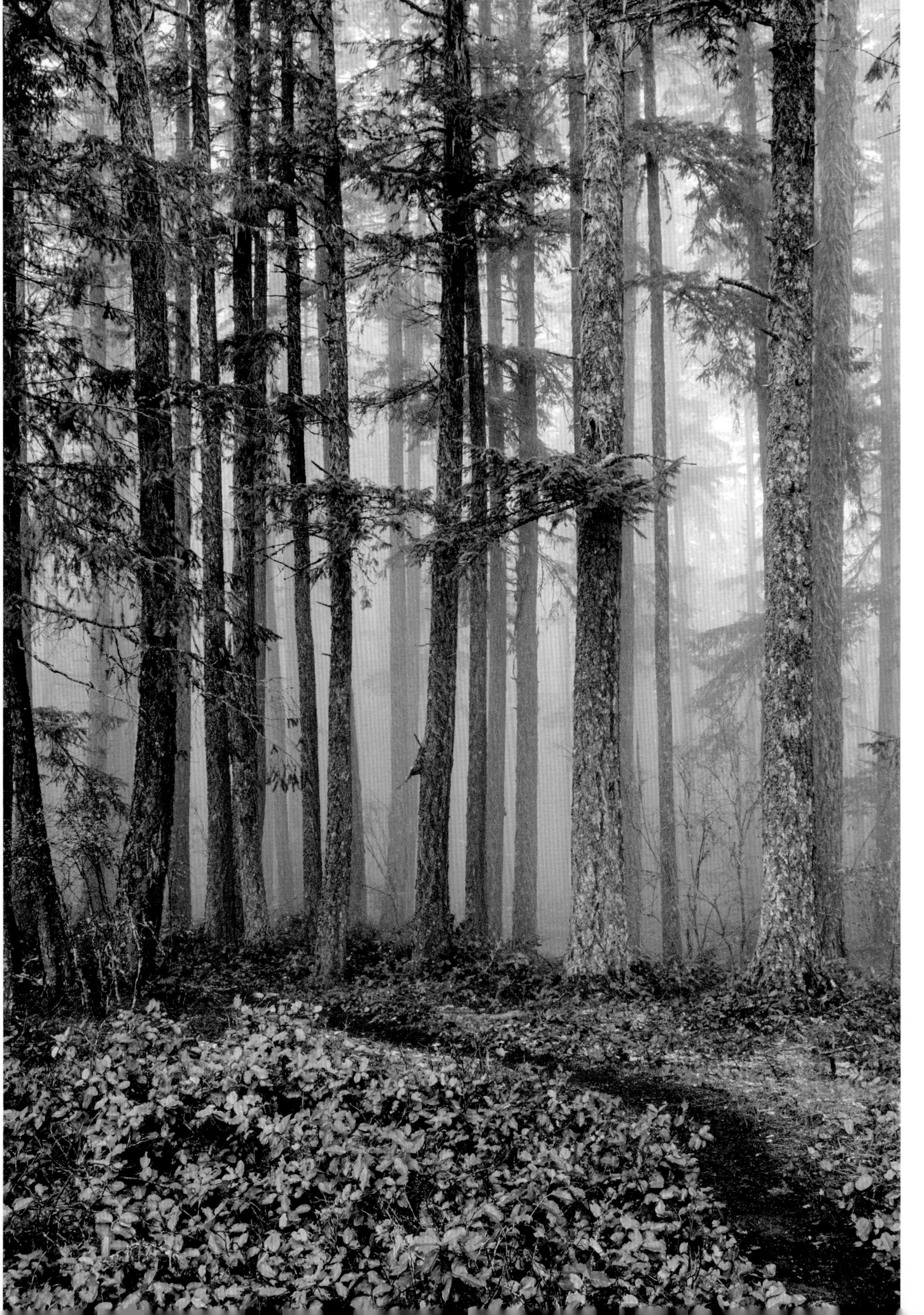

Cloud enshrouds the forest at the top of Mount Maxwell in April.

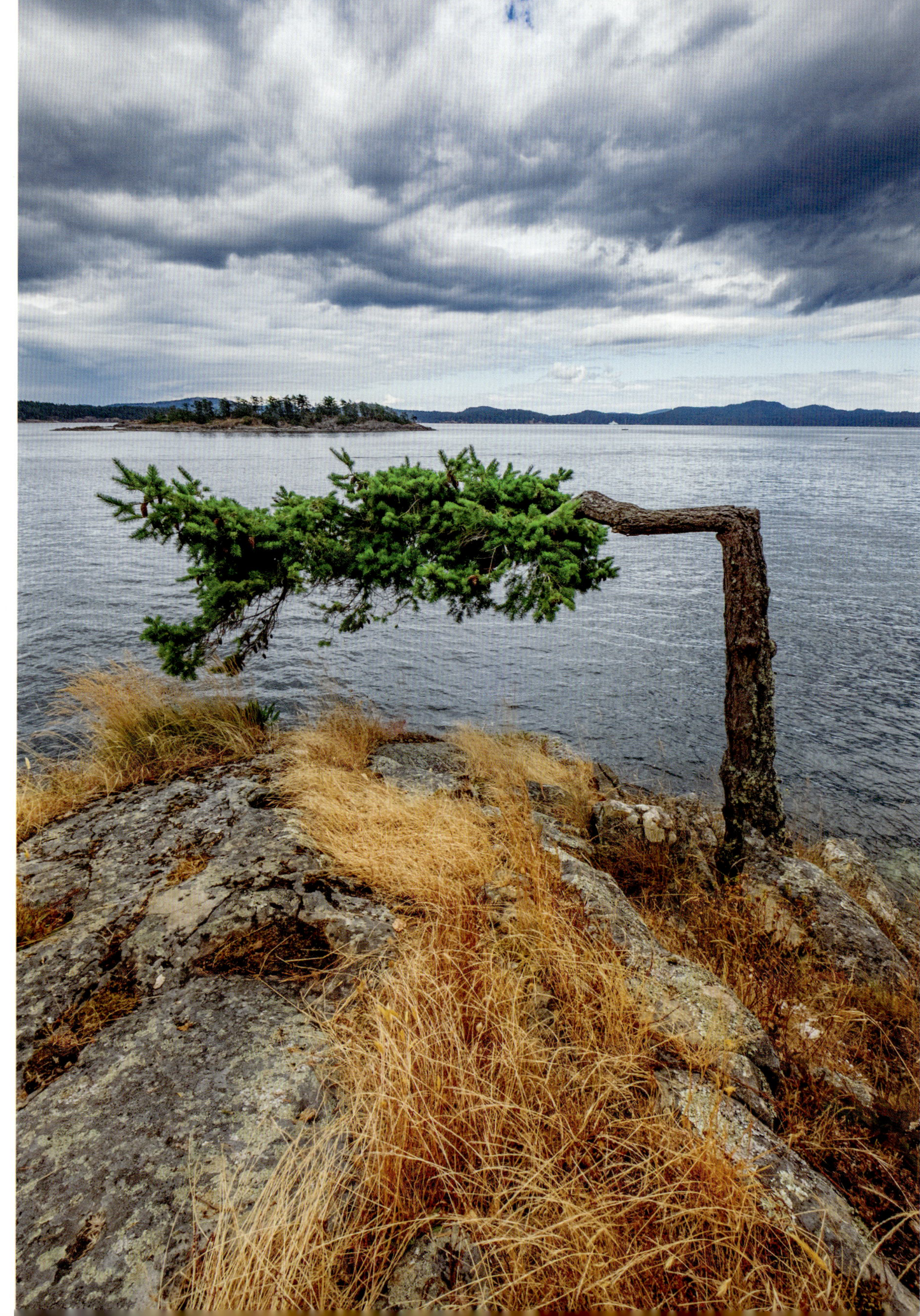

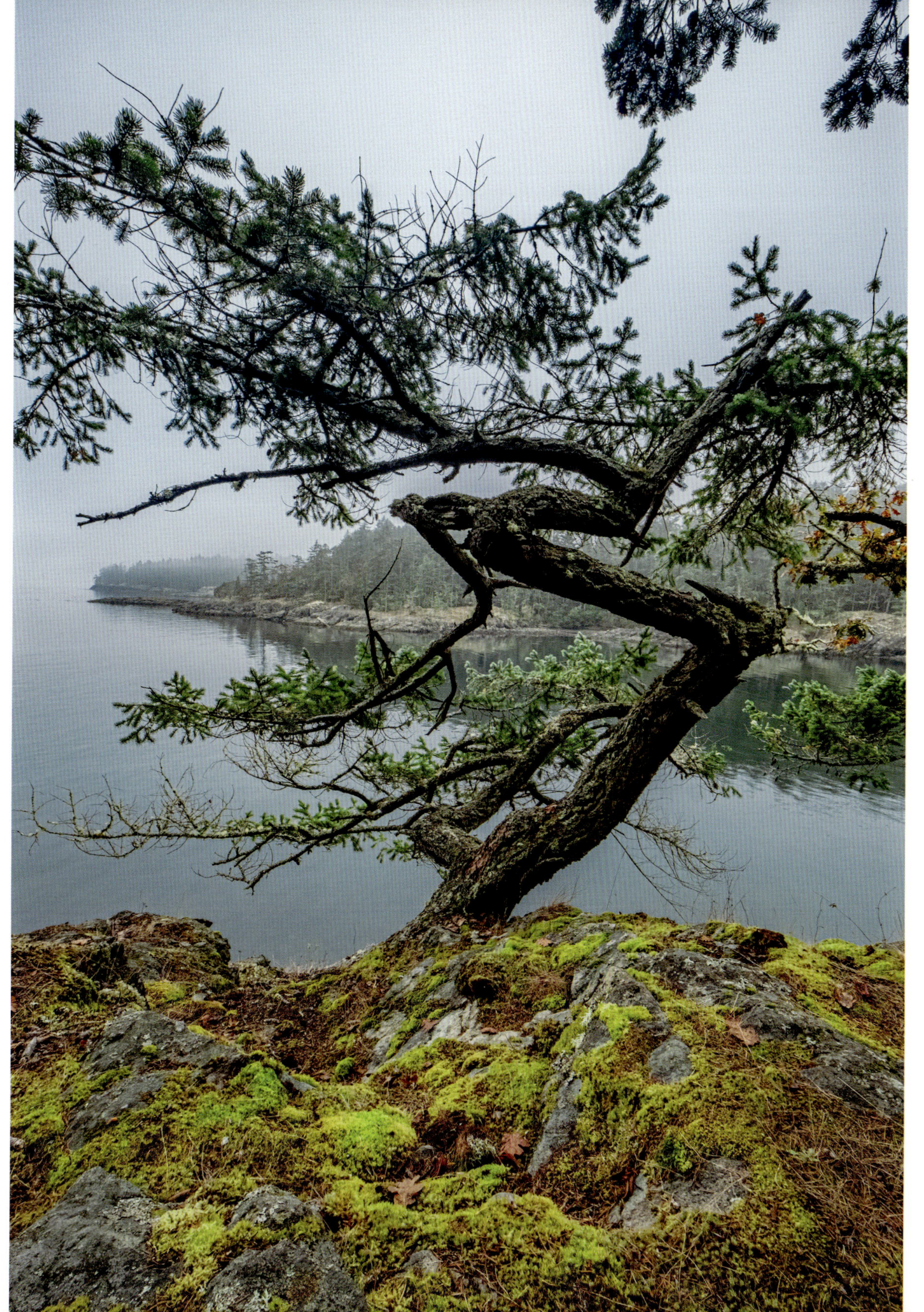

Small wind-beaten Douglas fir trees at Yeo Point (far left), and near Grandma's Beach in Ruckle Provincial Park (left).

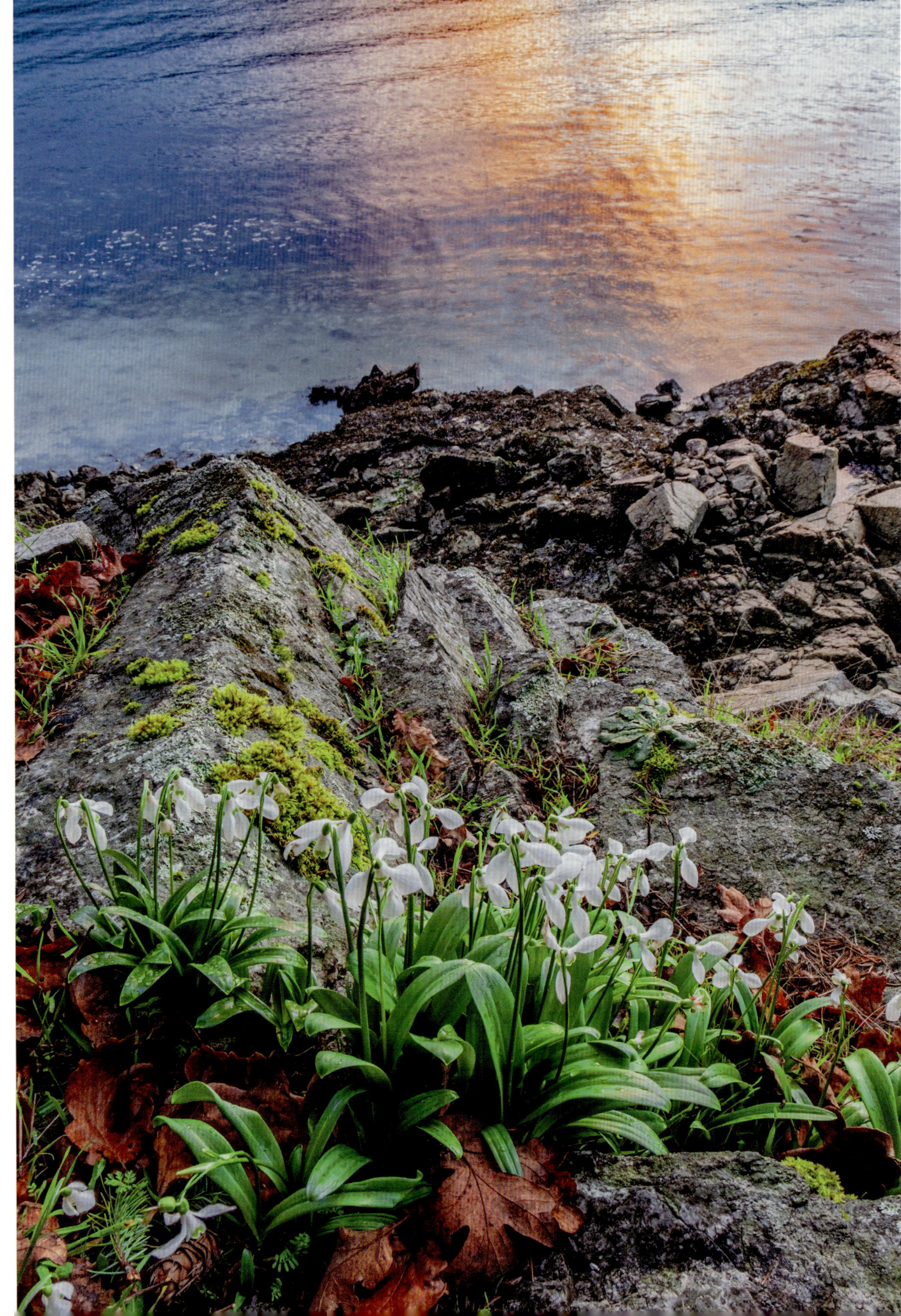

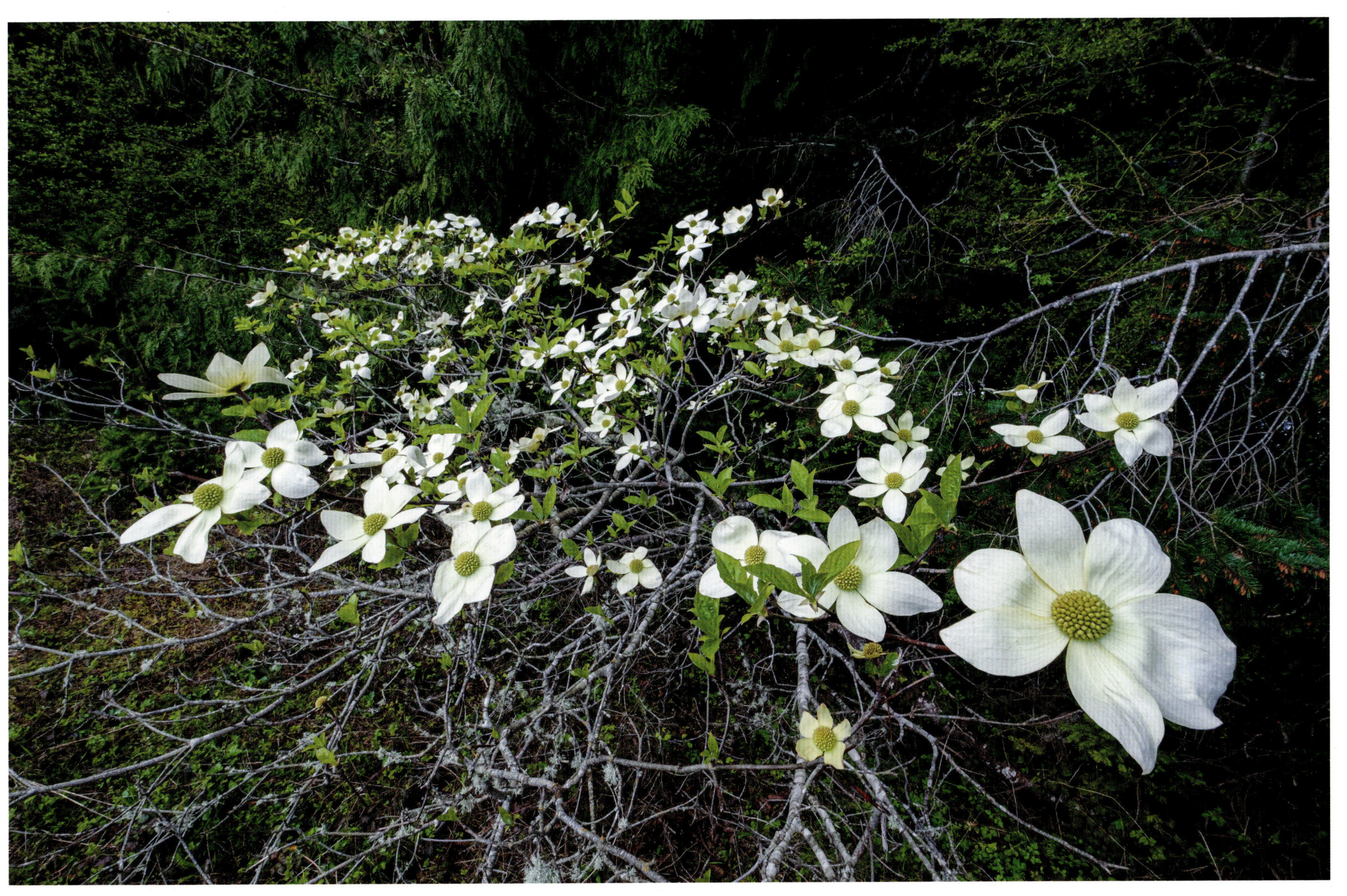

Snowdrops, the first flowers to bloom and often as early as in January, along the shore with sunset clouds reflected in the water (left).

Pacific dogwood in Burgoyne Bay in April (above).

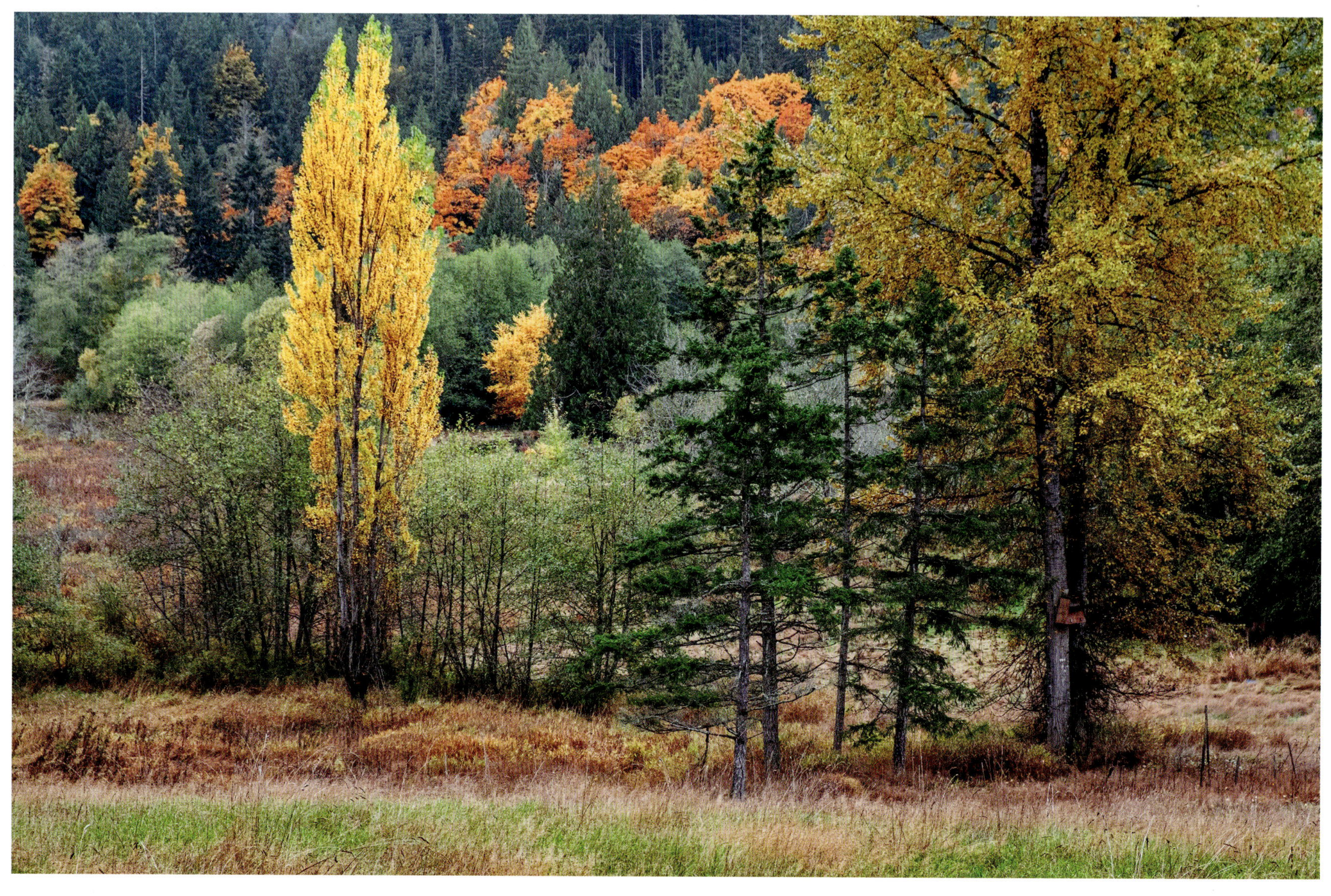

Autumn colours in October at Blackburn Lake Nature Reserve (above), and at the Salt Spring Island golf course (right).

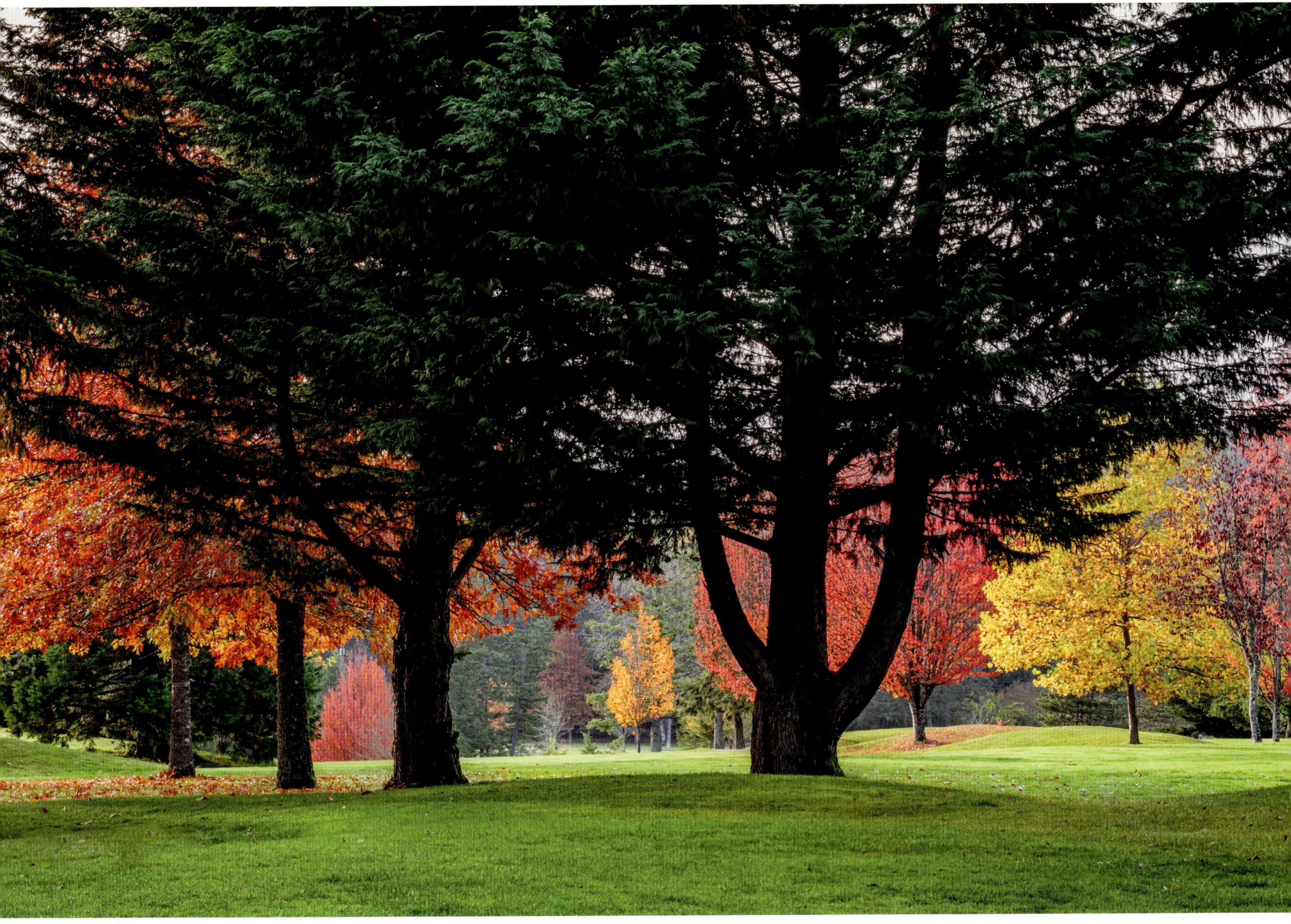

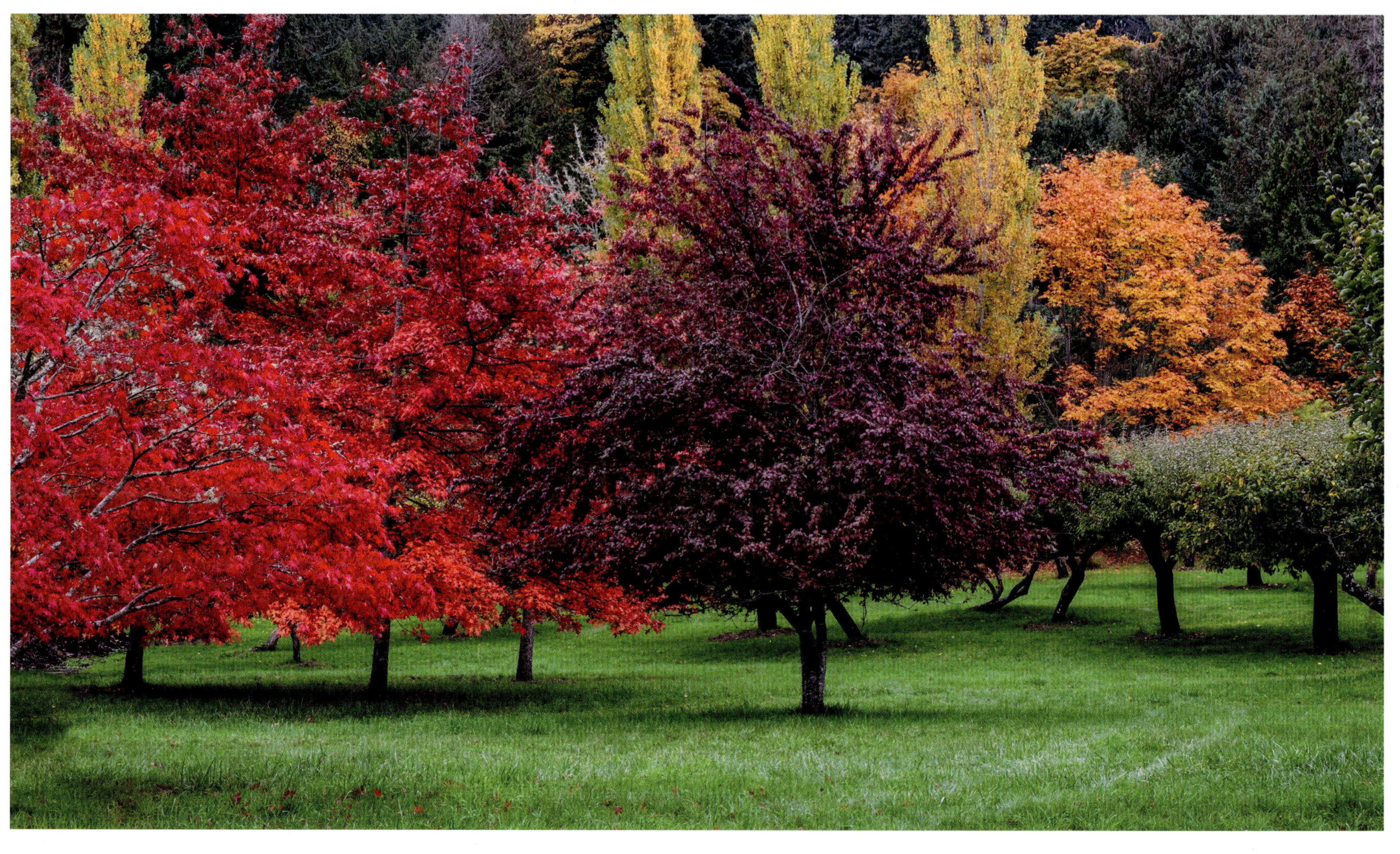

Autumn colours at Lionel Crescent in October (above), and along Morningside Road in November (right).

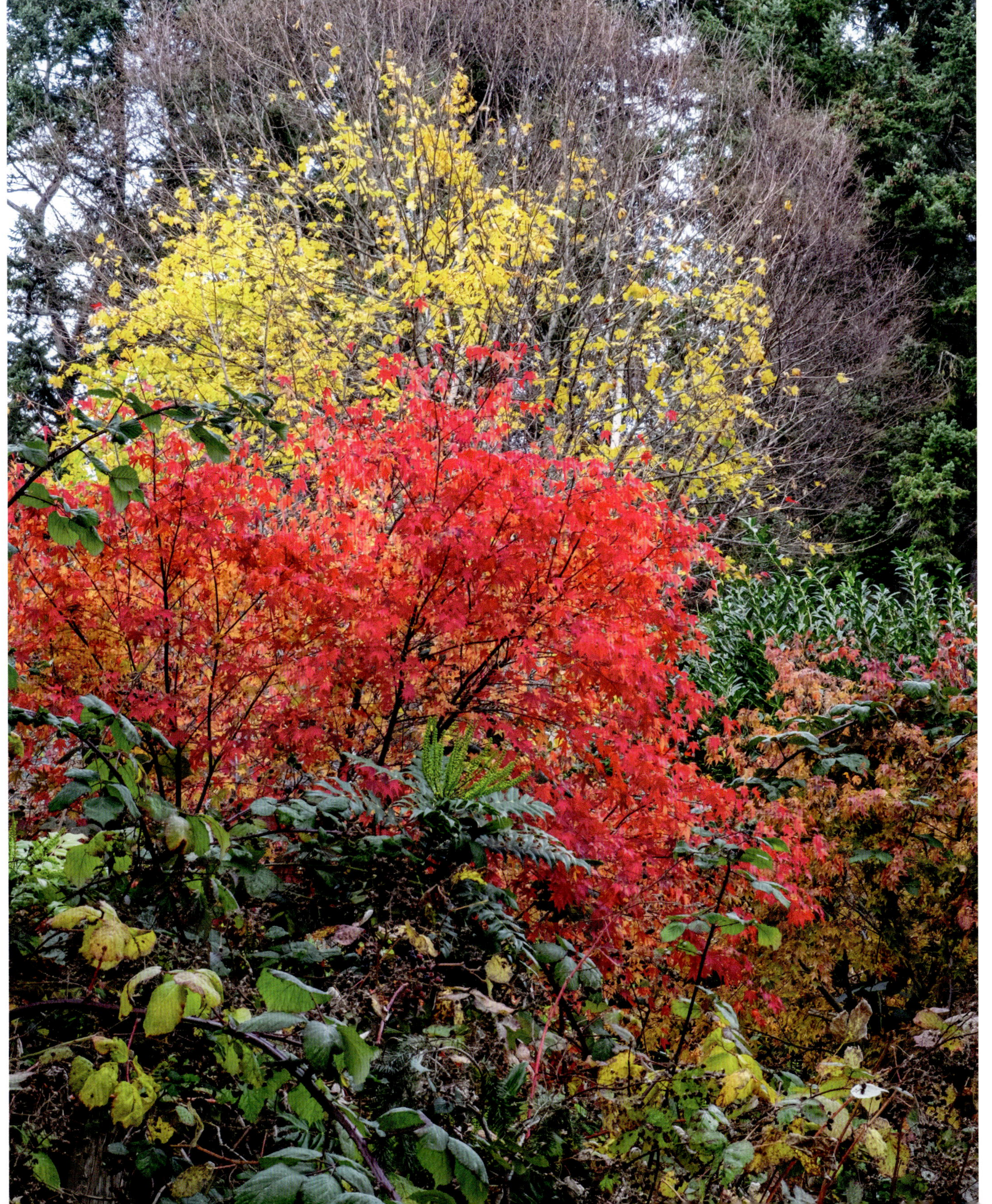

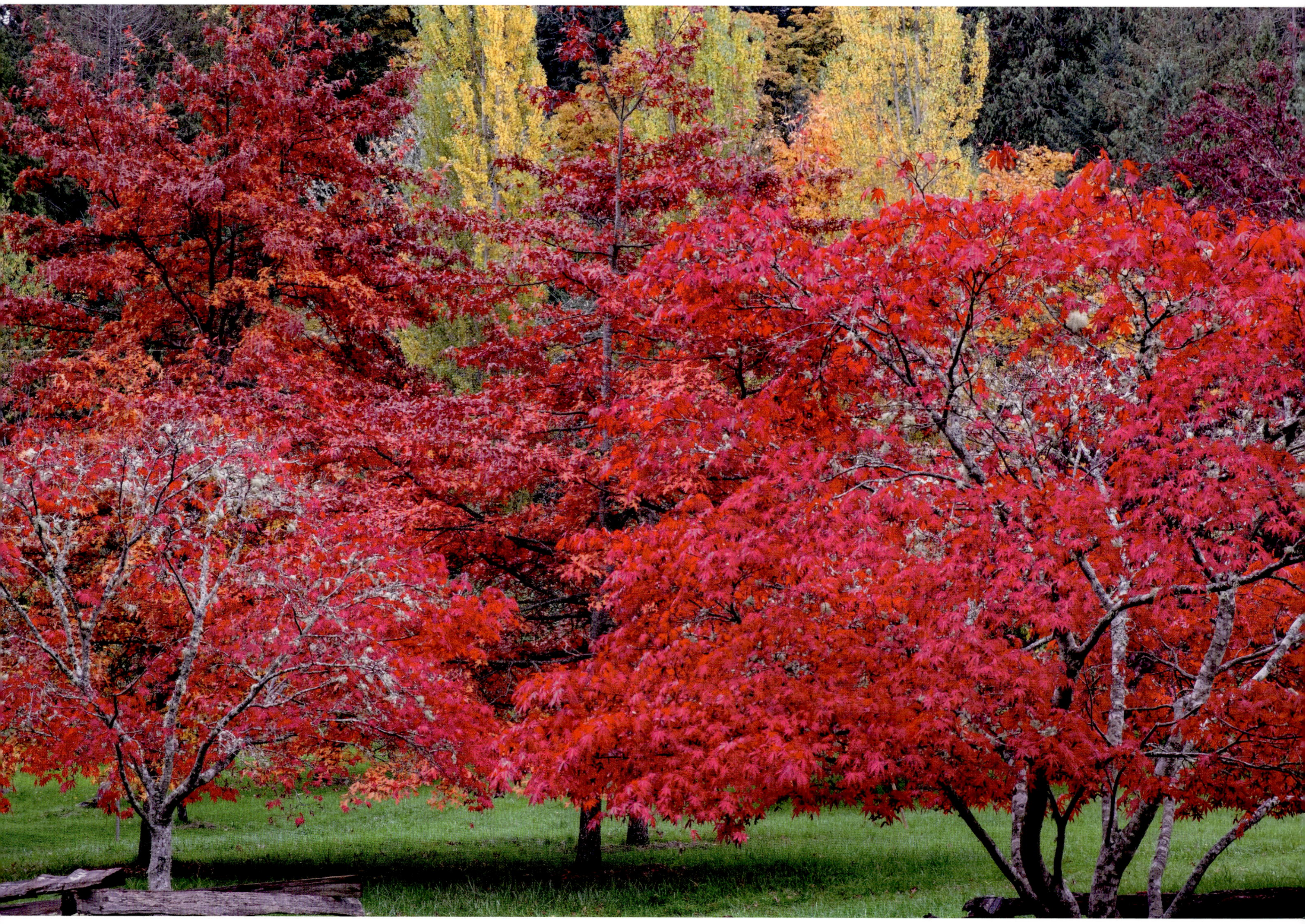

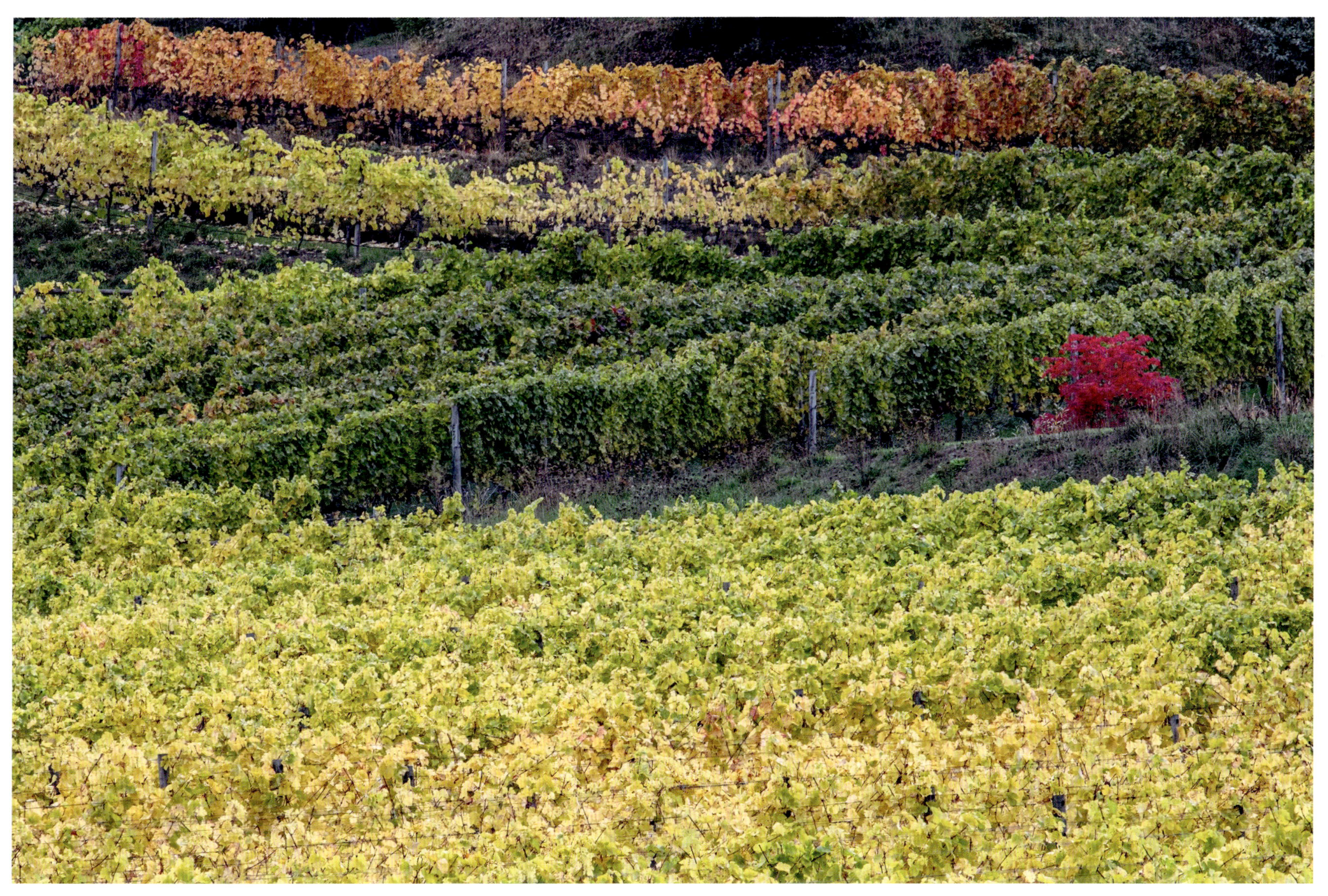

October colour at Lionel Crescent near Beddis Beach (left), and in the vineyard of the Garry Oaks Winery on Lee's Hill (above).

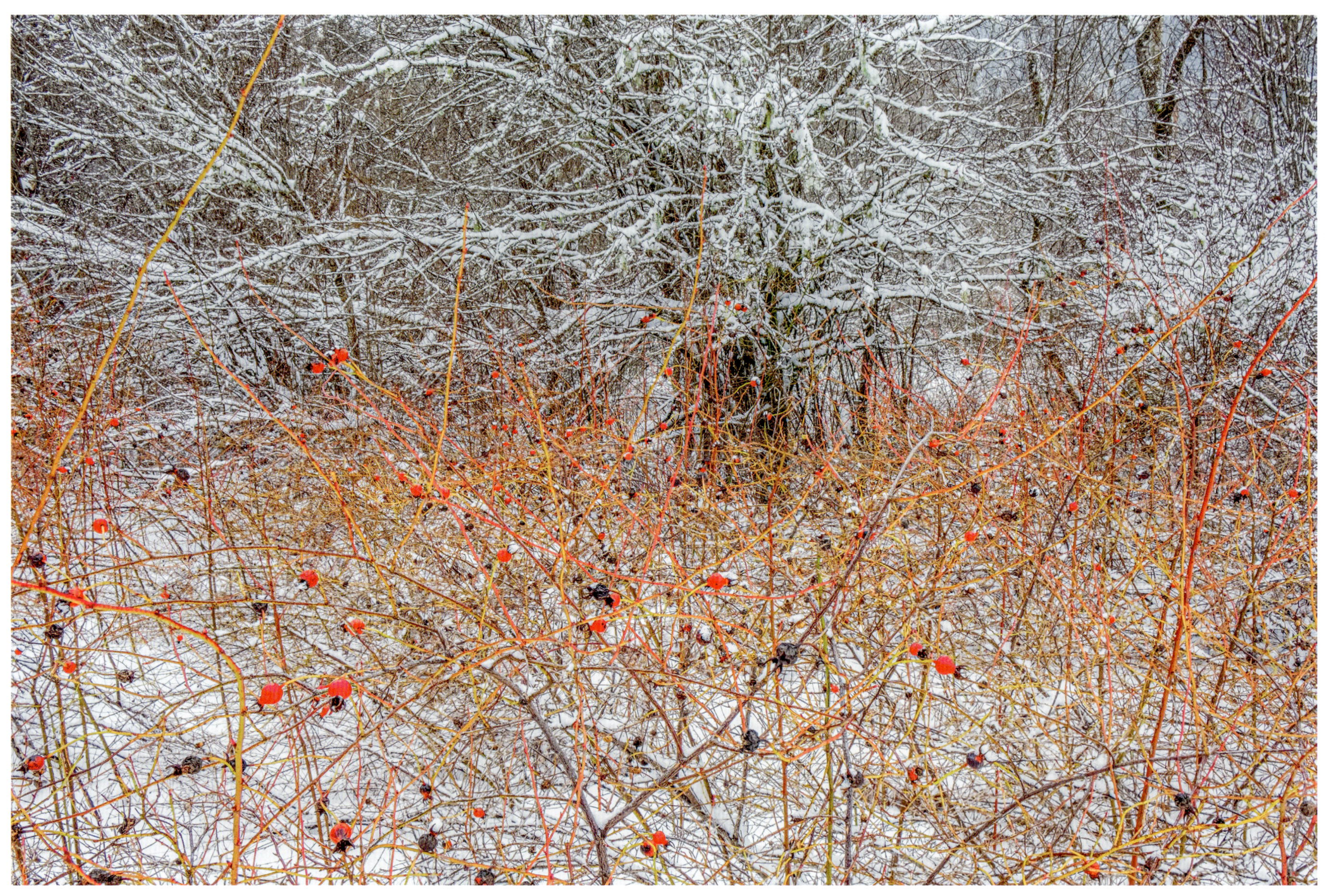

Wild rose hips after a February snowfall in Burgoyne Bay Provincial Park (above).

Tafoni, honeycomb-shaped weathering caused by salt, is an attractive feature in sandstone shoreline rock throughout the Gulf Islands, here at Zach Beach below Sunset Drive (right).

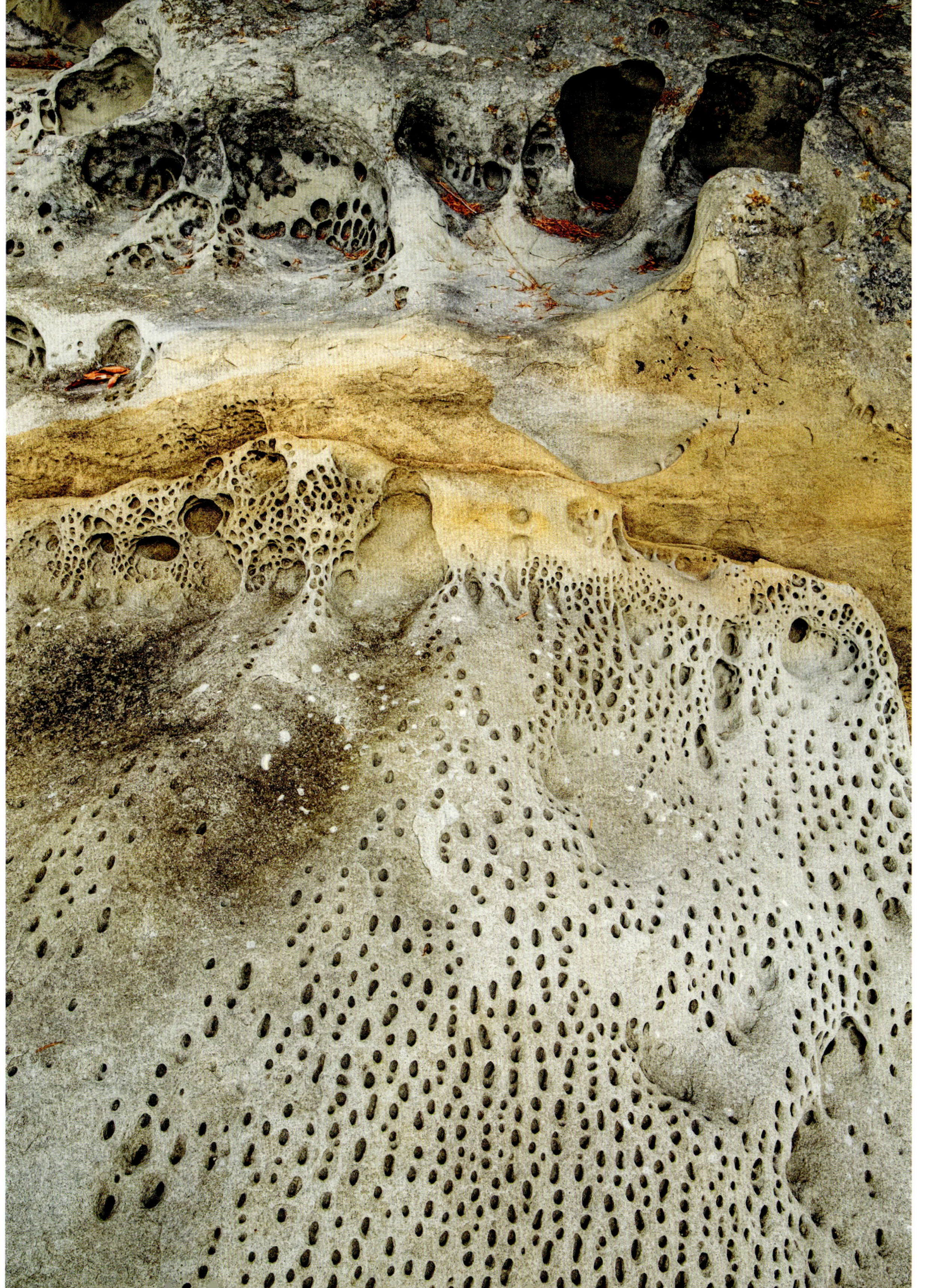

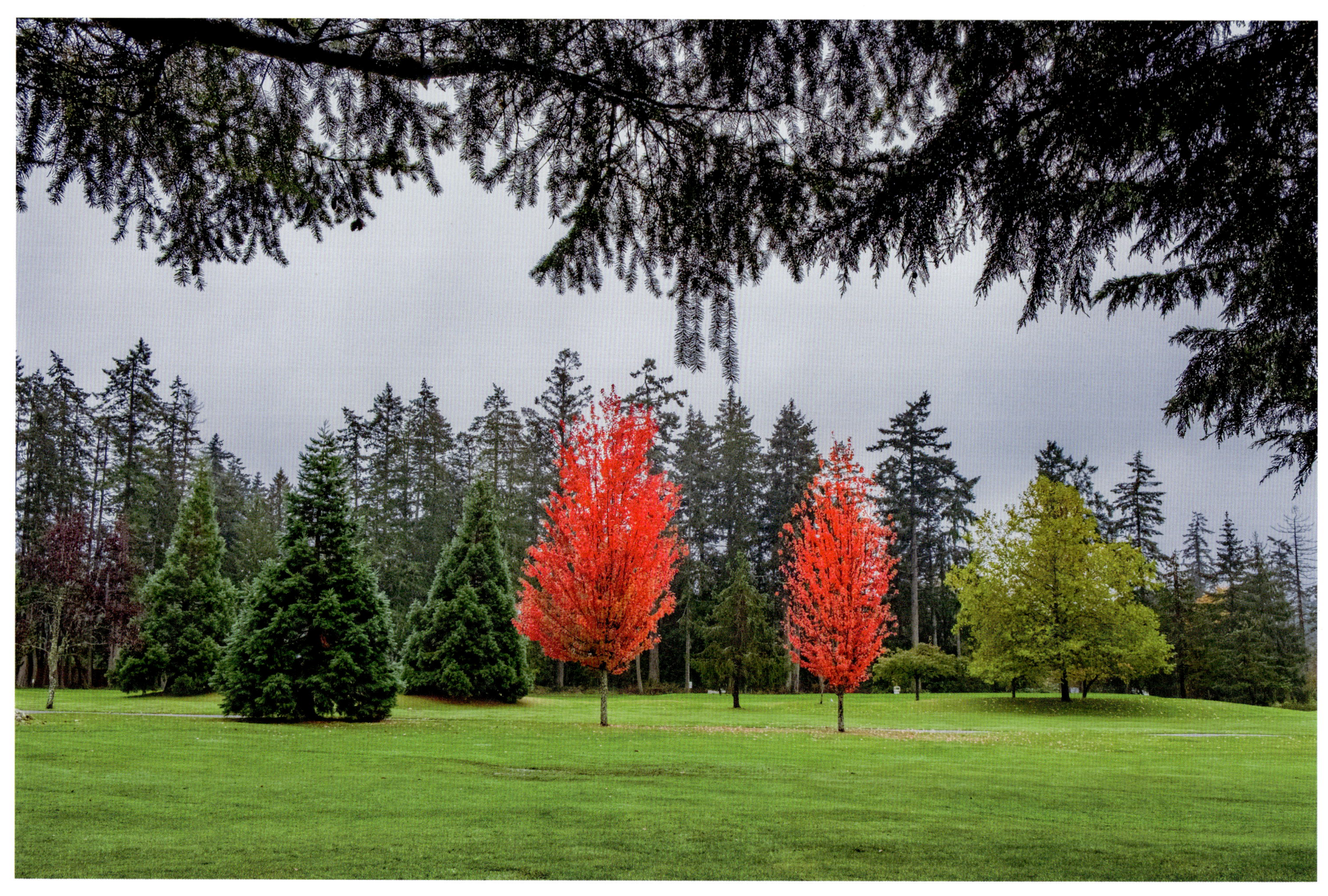

Red maples on the golf course beside Upper Ganges Road in October.

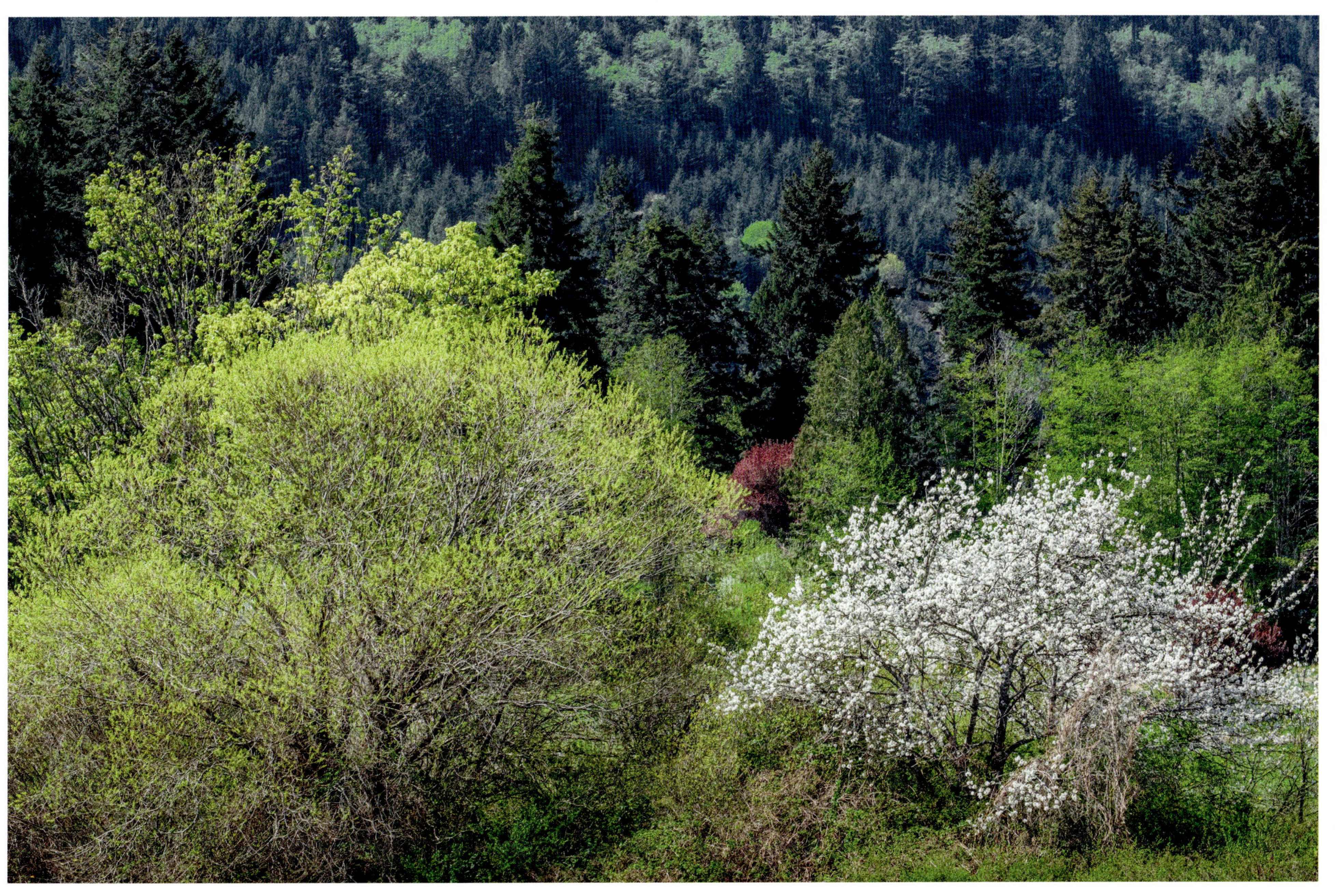

Spring forest in the Fulford Valley in April.

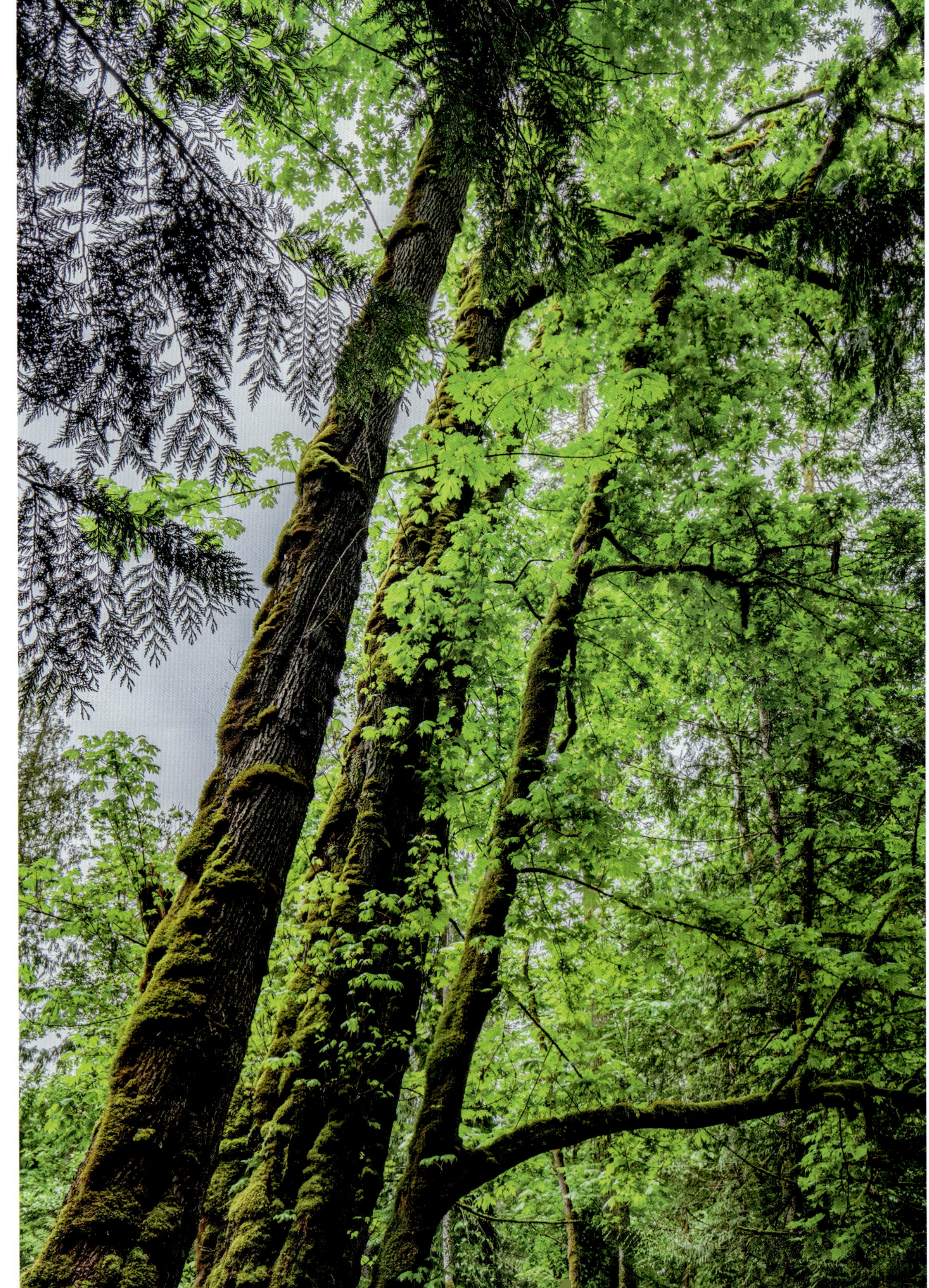

The forest in Mouat Regional Park in Ganges in May.

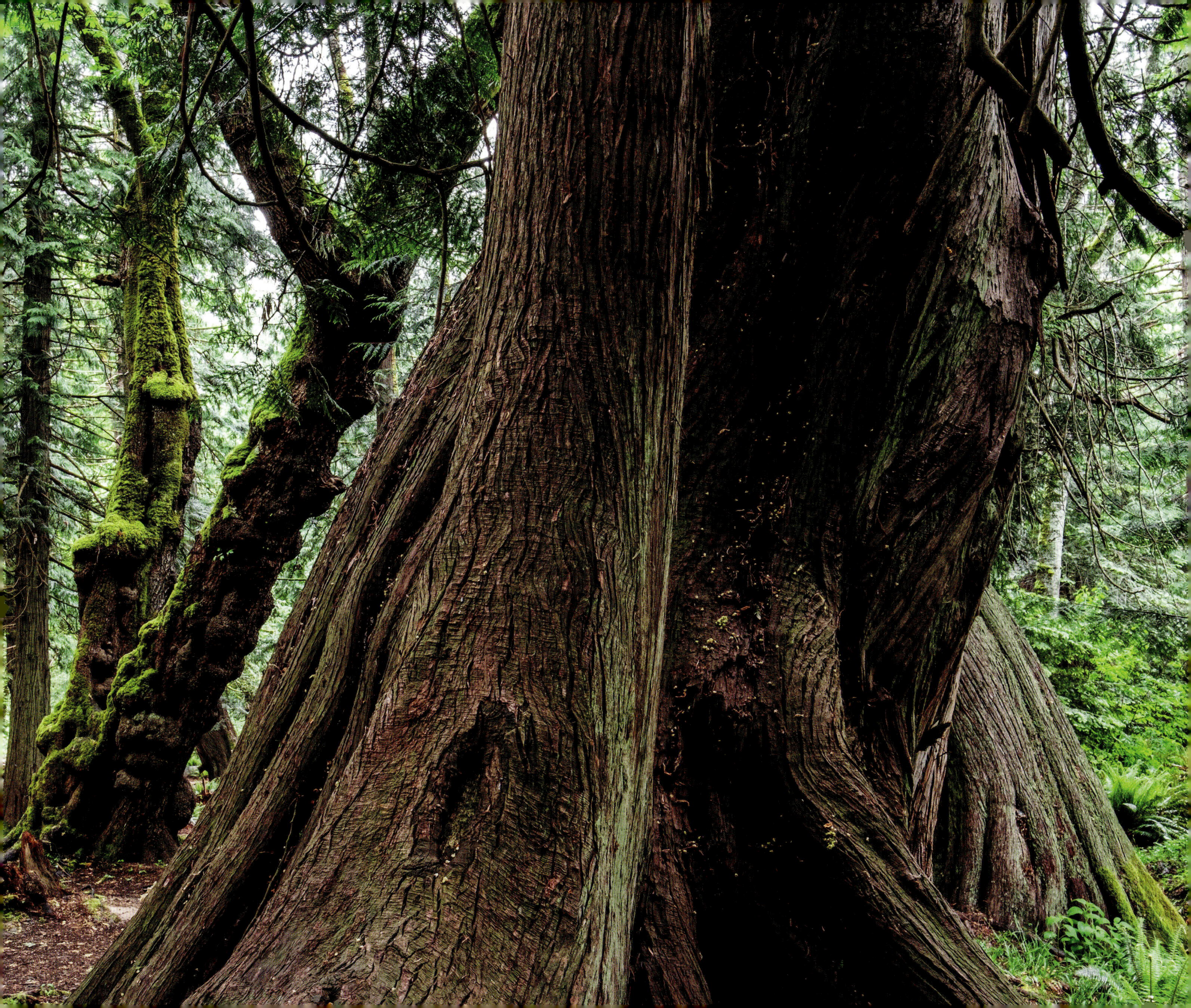

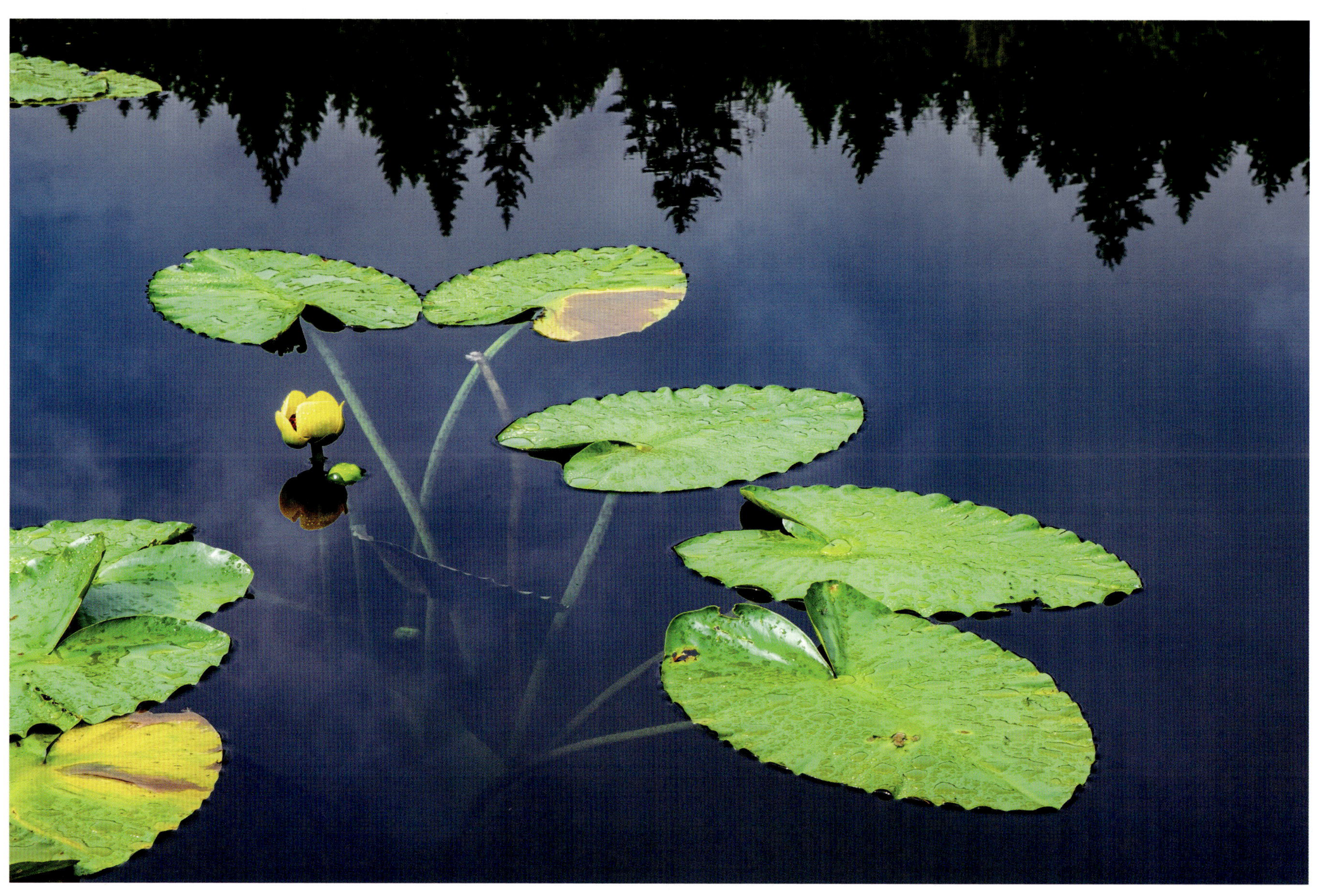

Yellow water-lily in Blackburn Lake and a profusion of flowers along Furness Road, both in June.

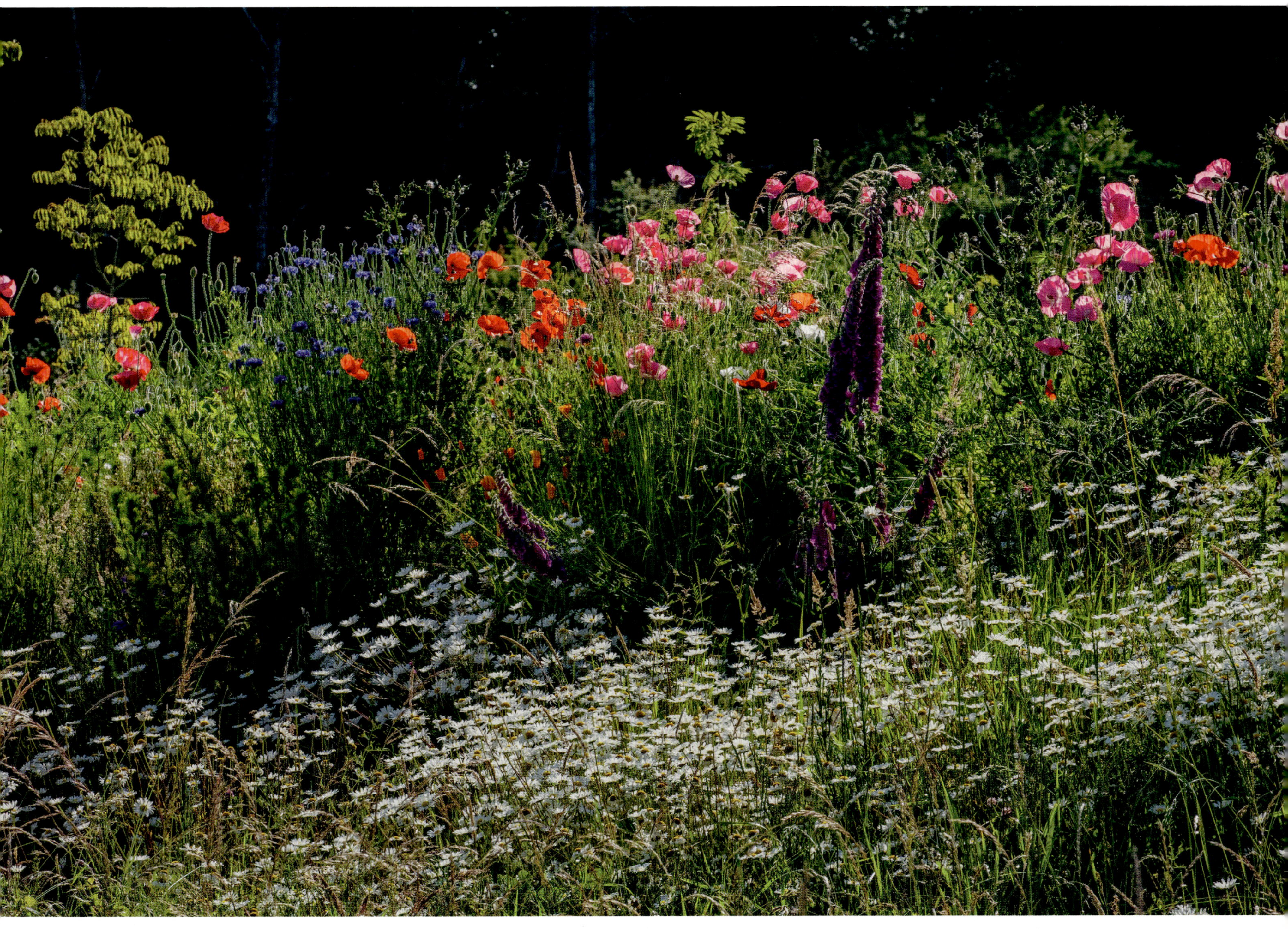

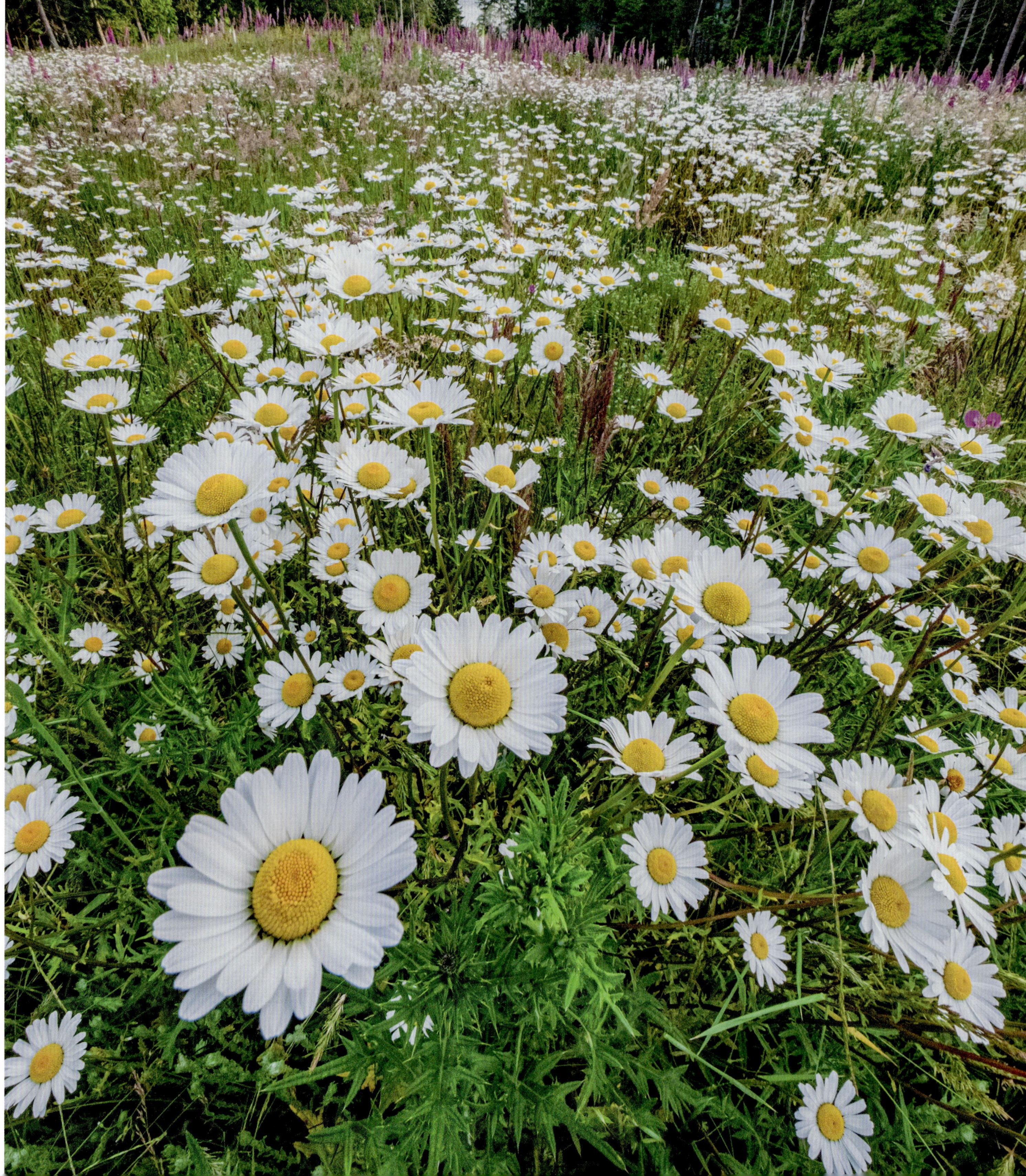

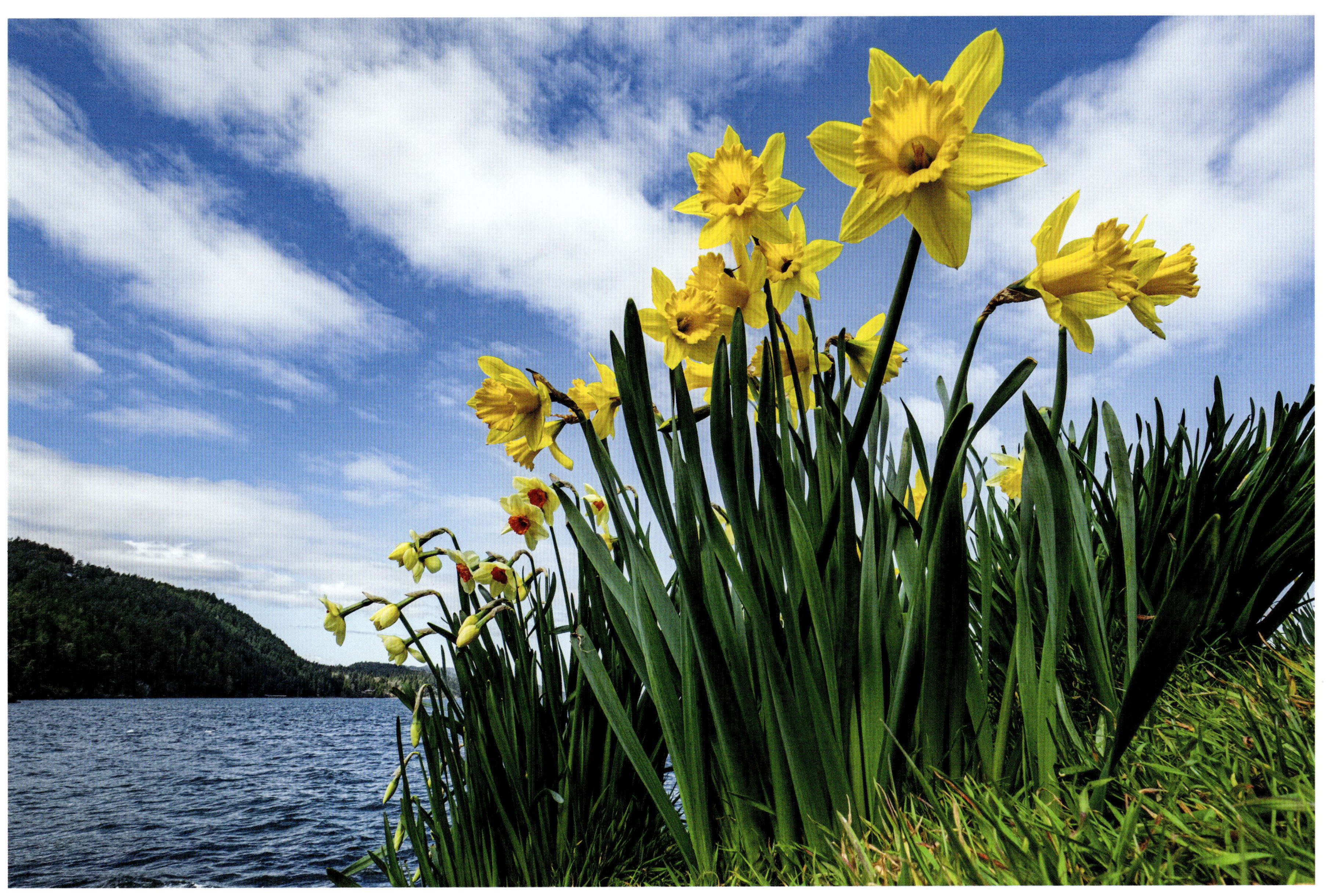

An invasive but attractive plant of European origin, the ubiquitous daisy was quick to colonize this clearcut (left).

Also non-native but growing wild, daffodils beautify the landscape in March, here at Cusheon Cove (above).

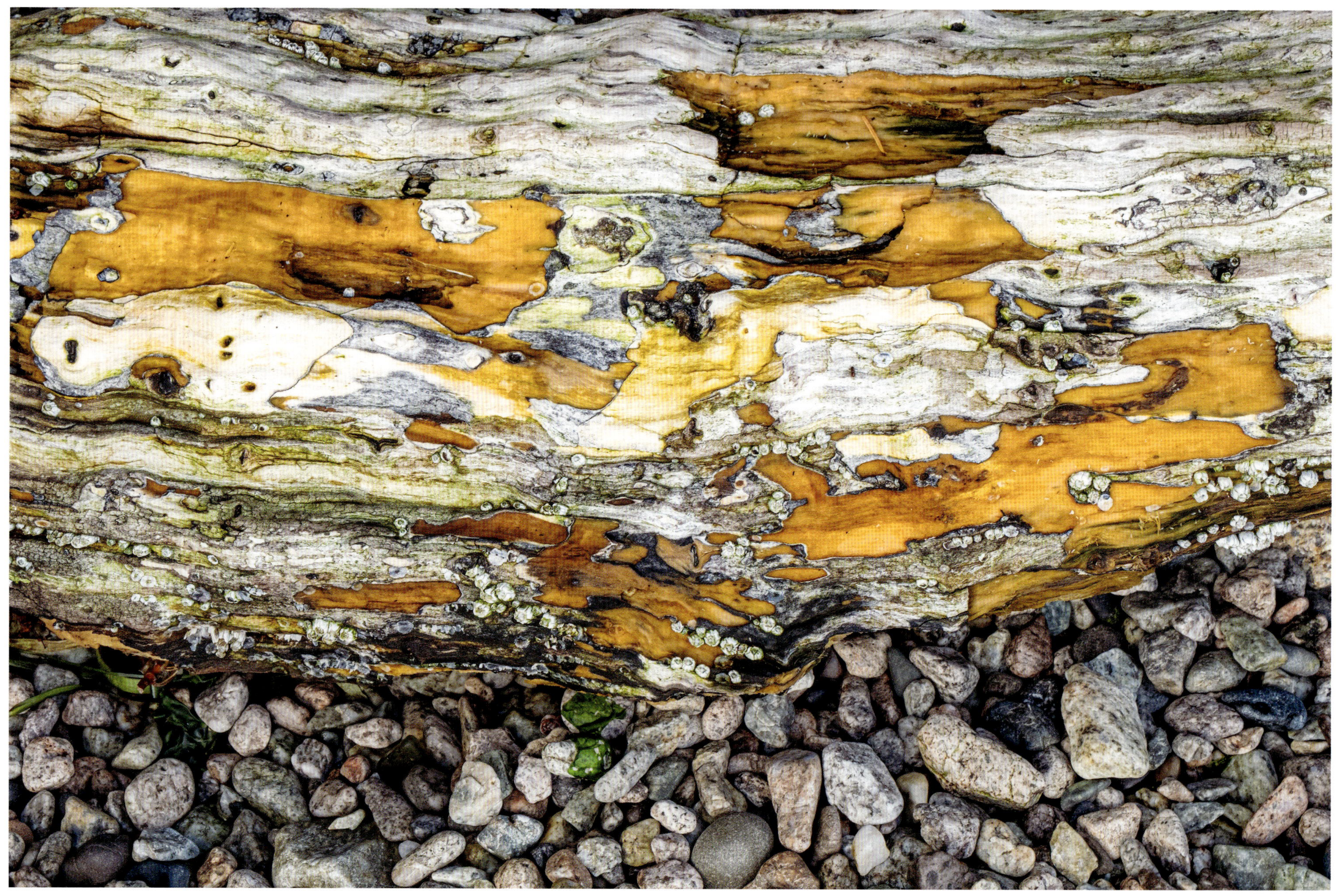

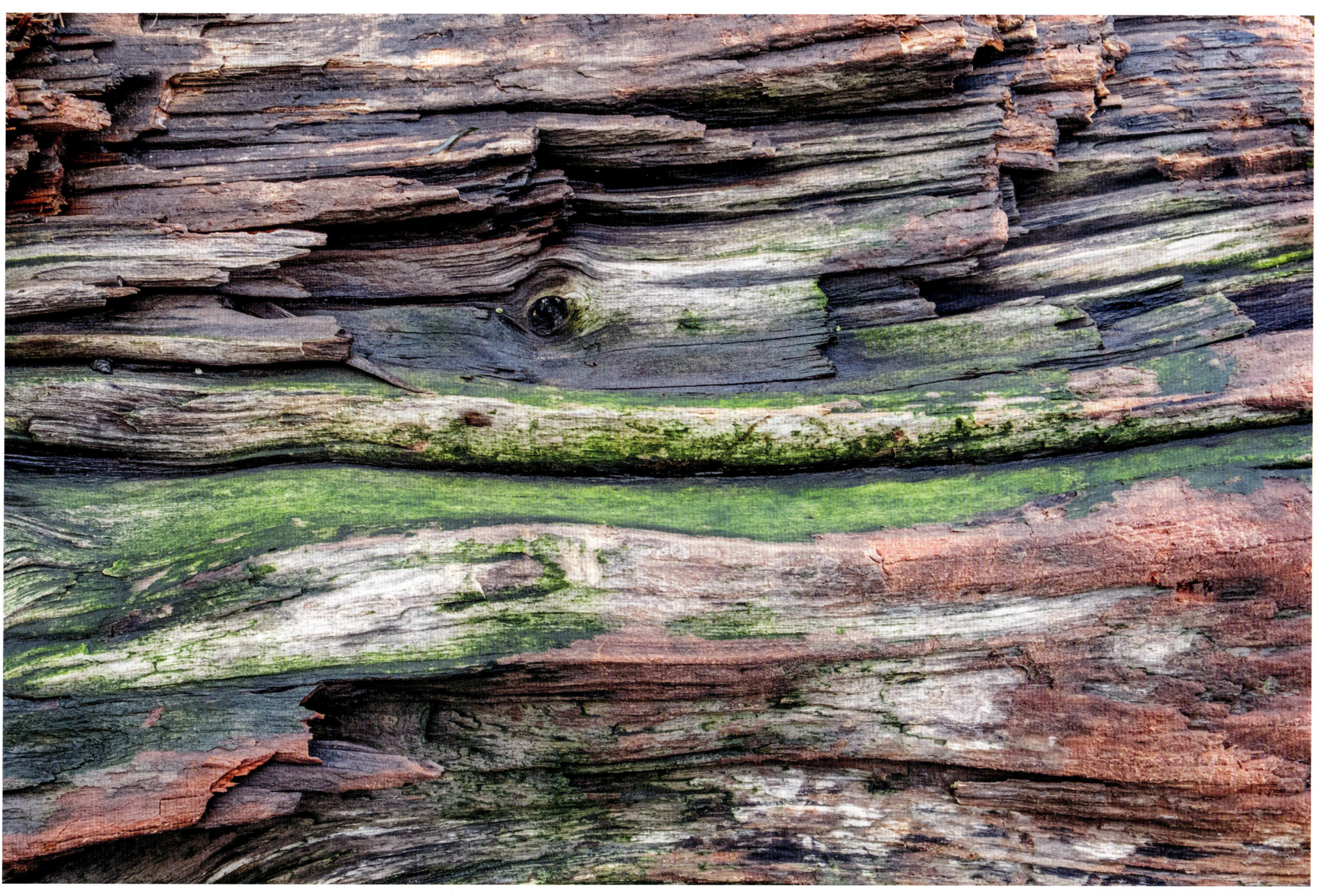

Details of driftwood logs on the beach in the Tsawout Reserve.

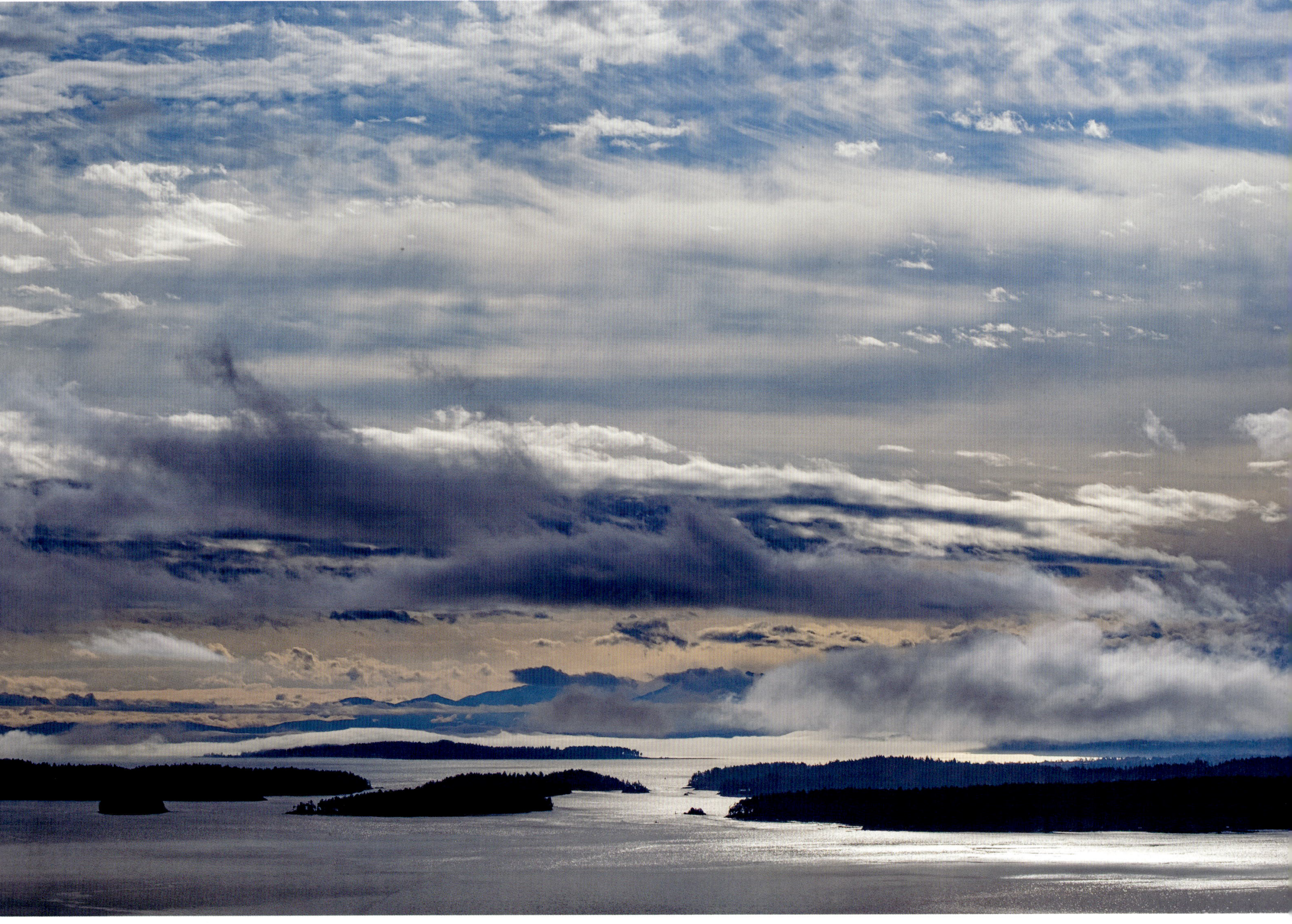

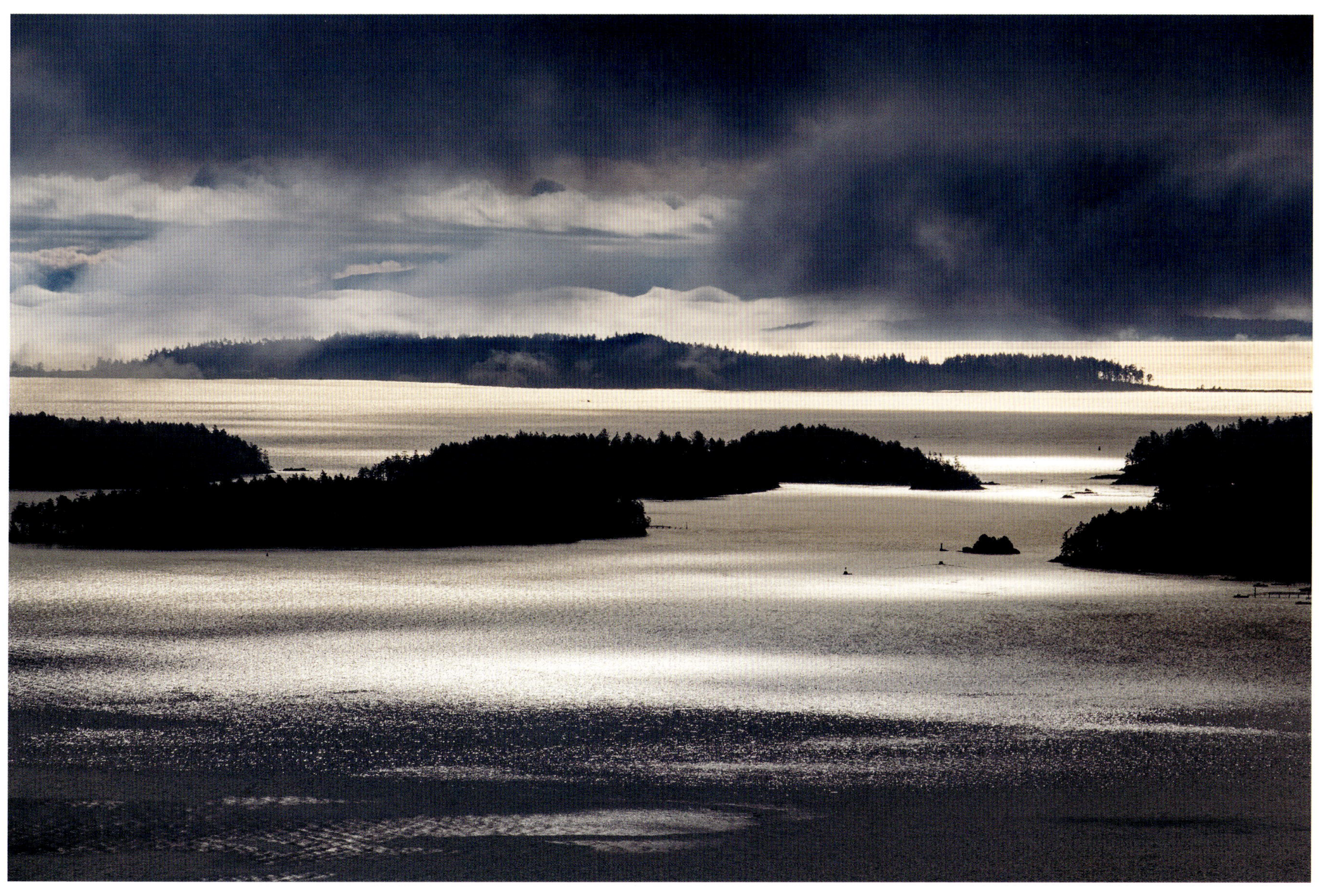

From one of several viewpoints on Reginald Hill looking towards Gosse Passage and the islands around Swartz Bay in early November.

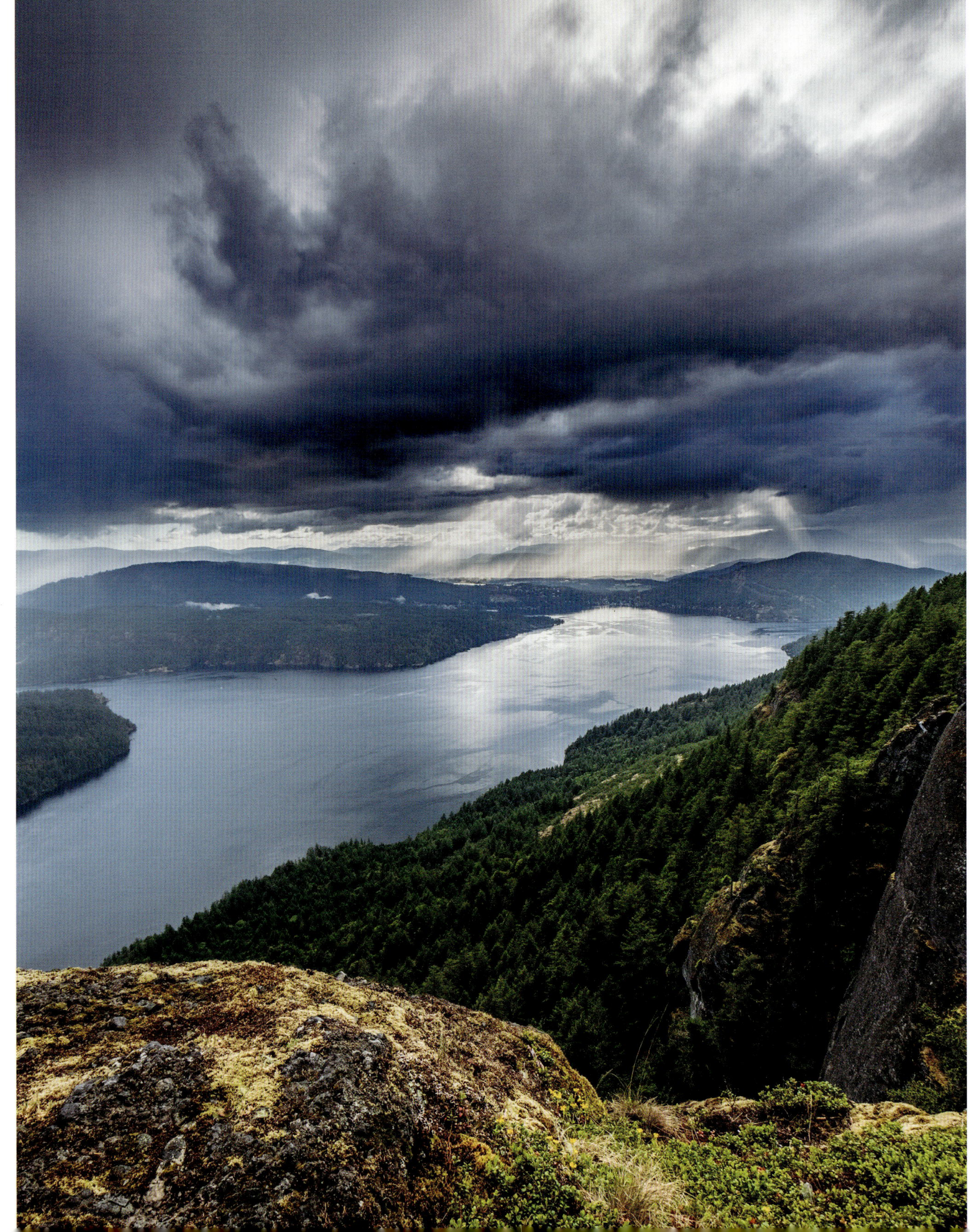

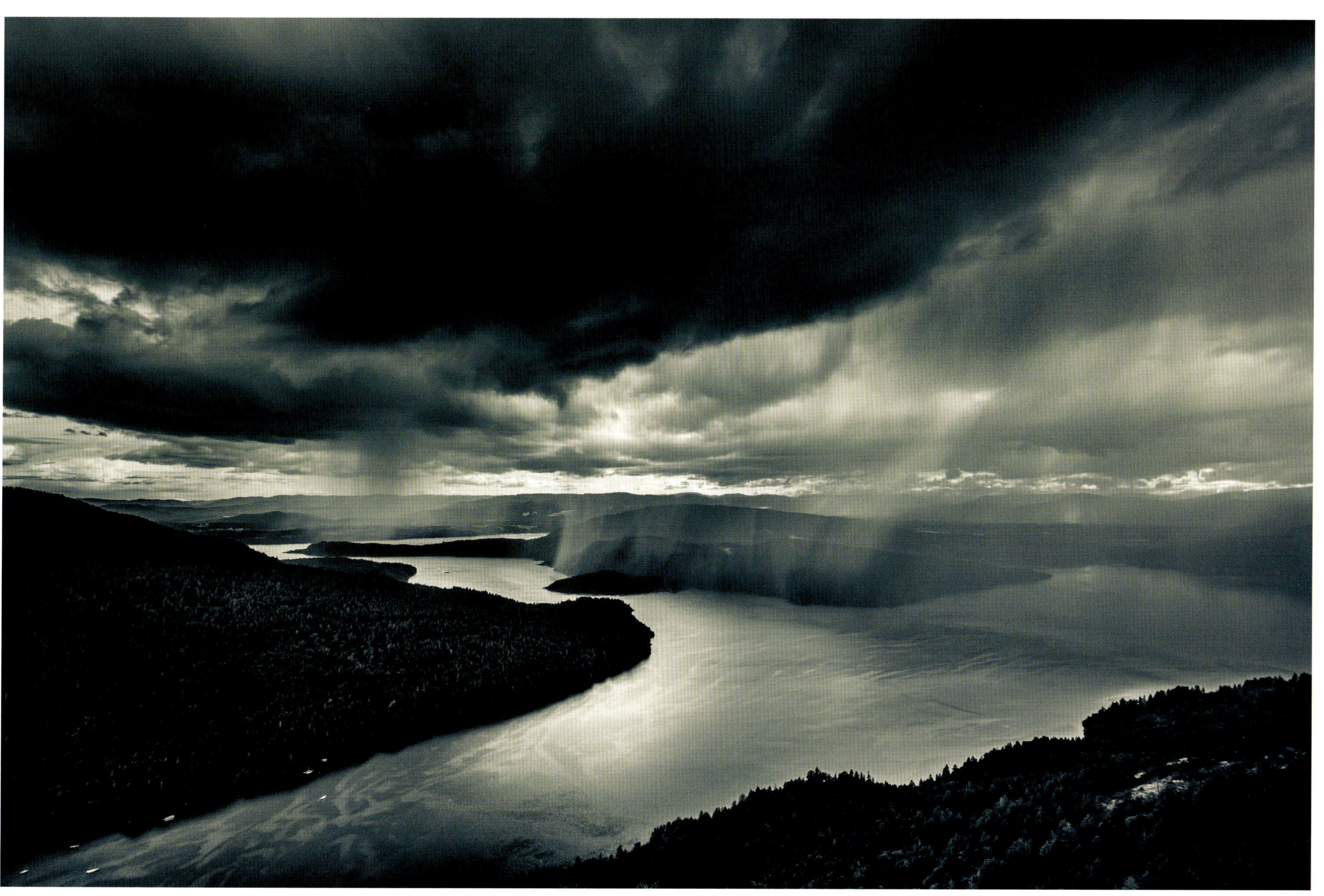

Stormy weather from Baynes Peak, Mount Maxwell Provincial Park, in June, looking west towards the Sansum Narrows and Maple Bay.

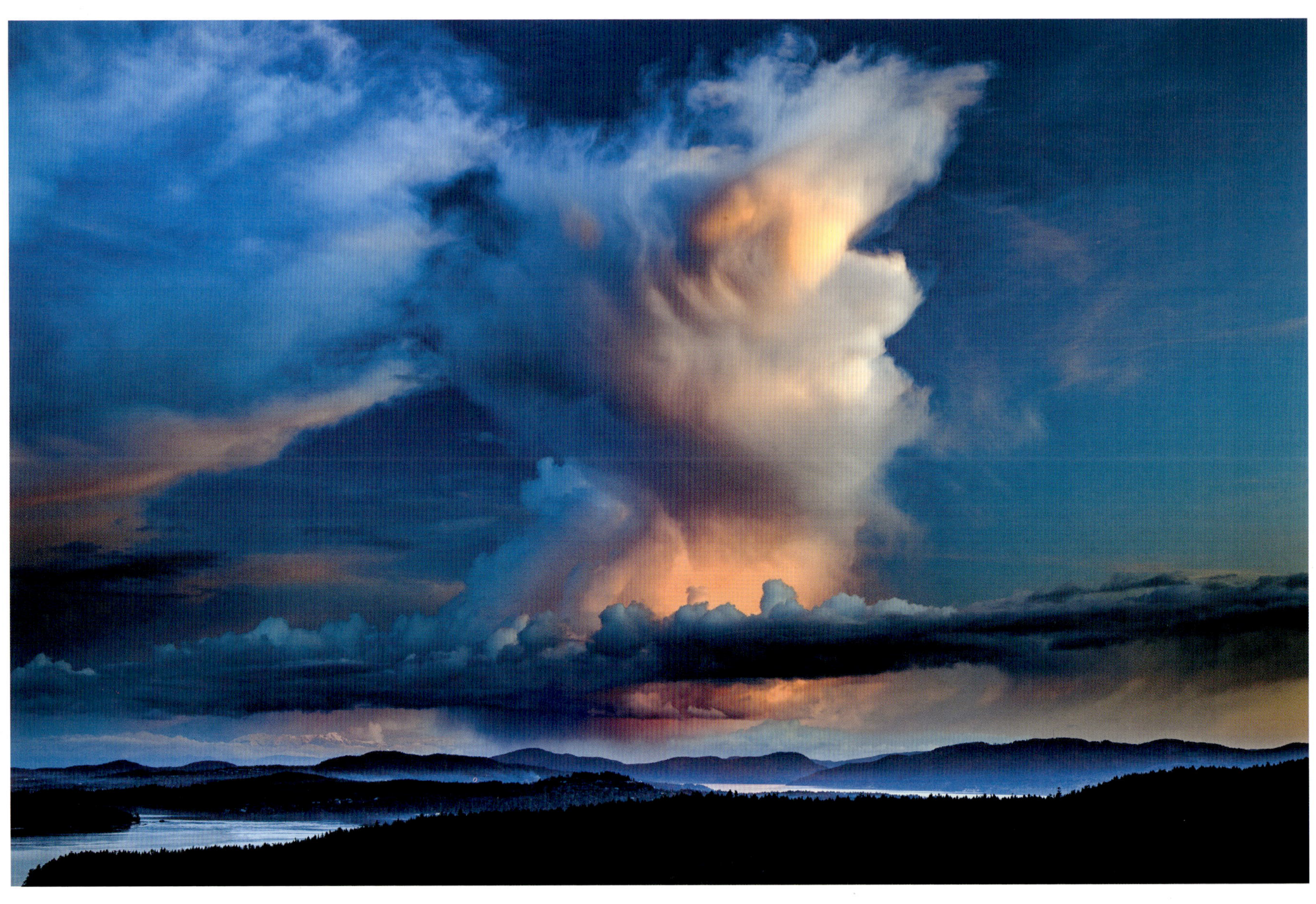

Sunset illuminates a thundercloud in April.

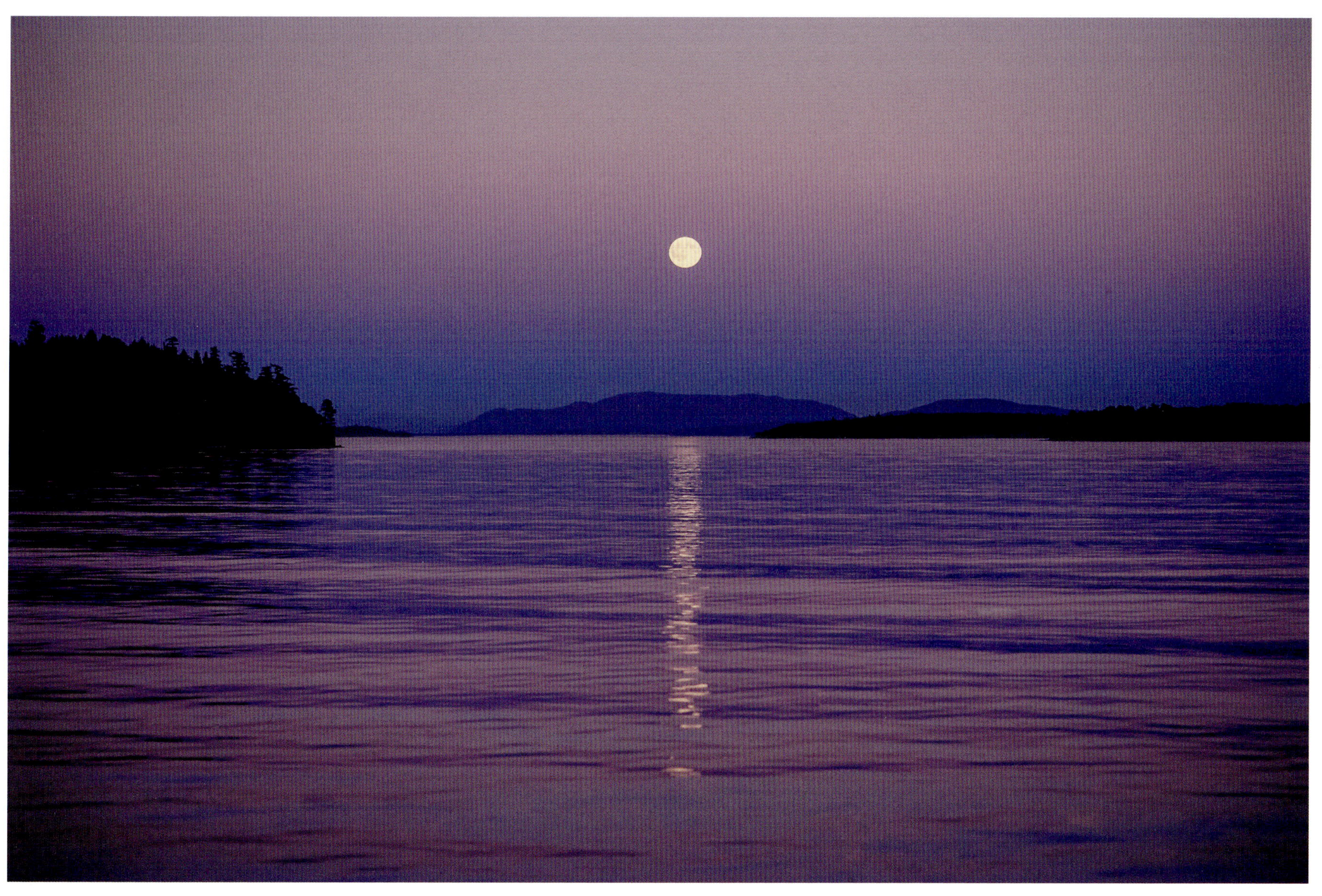

Moonrise from the waters of Fulford Harbour at dusk.

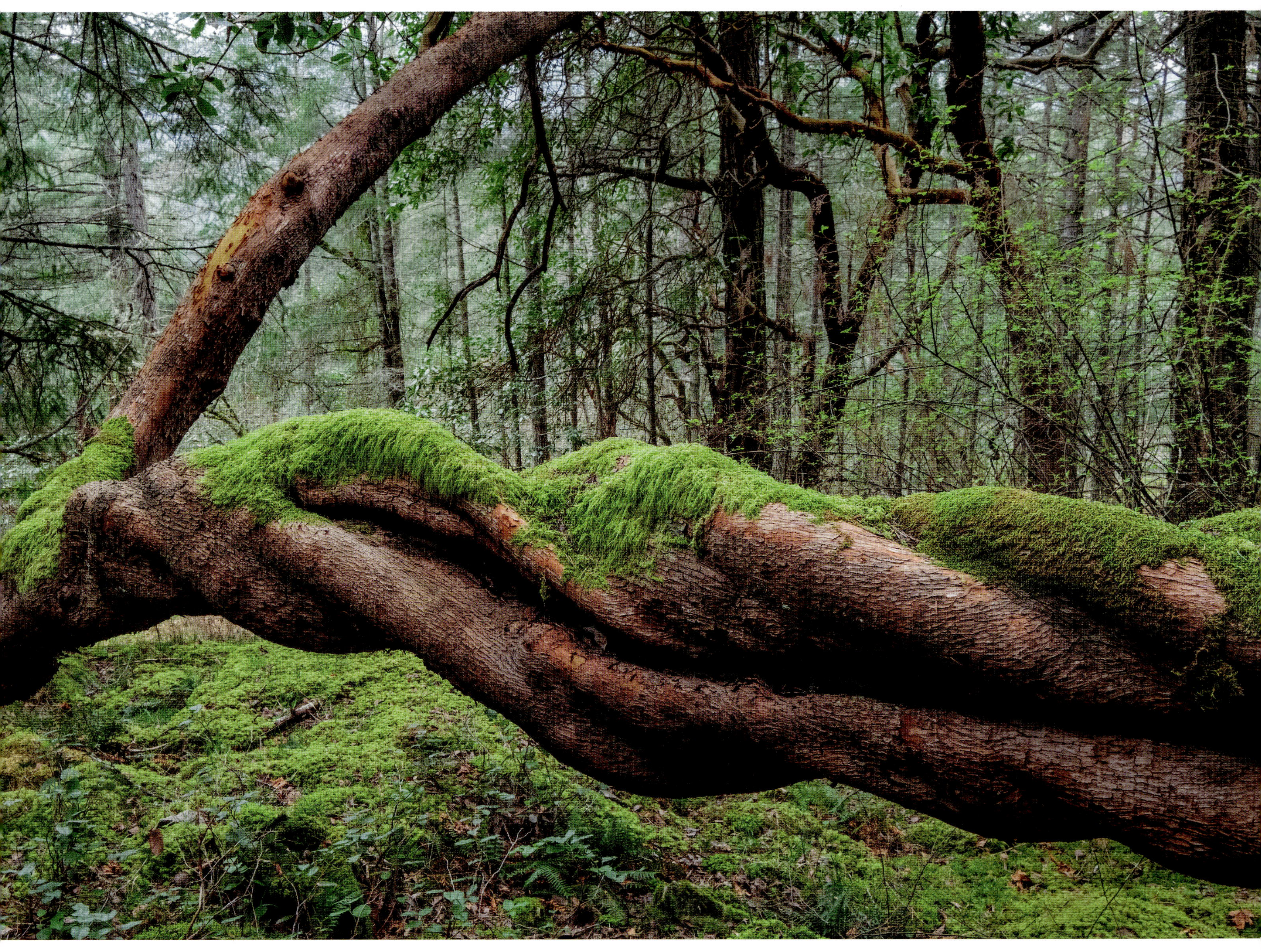

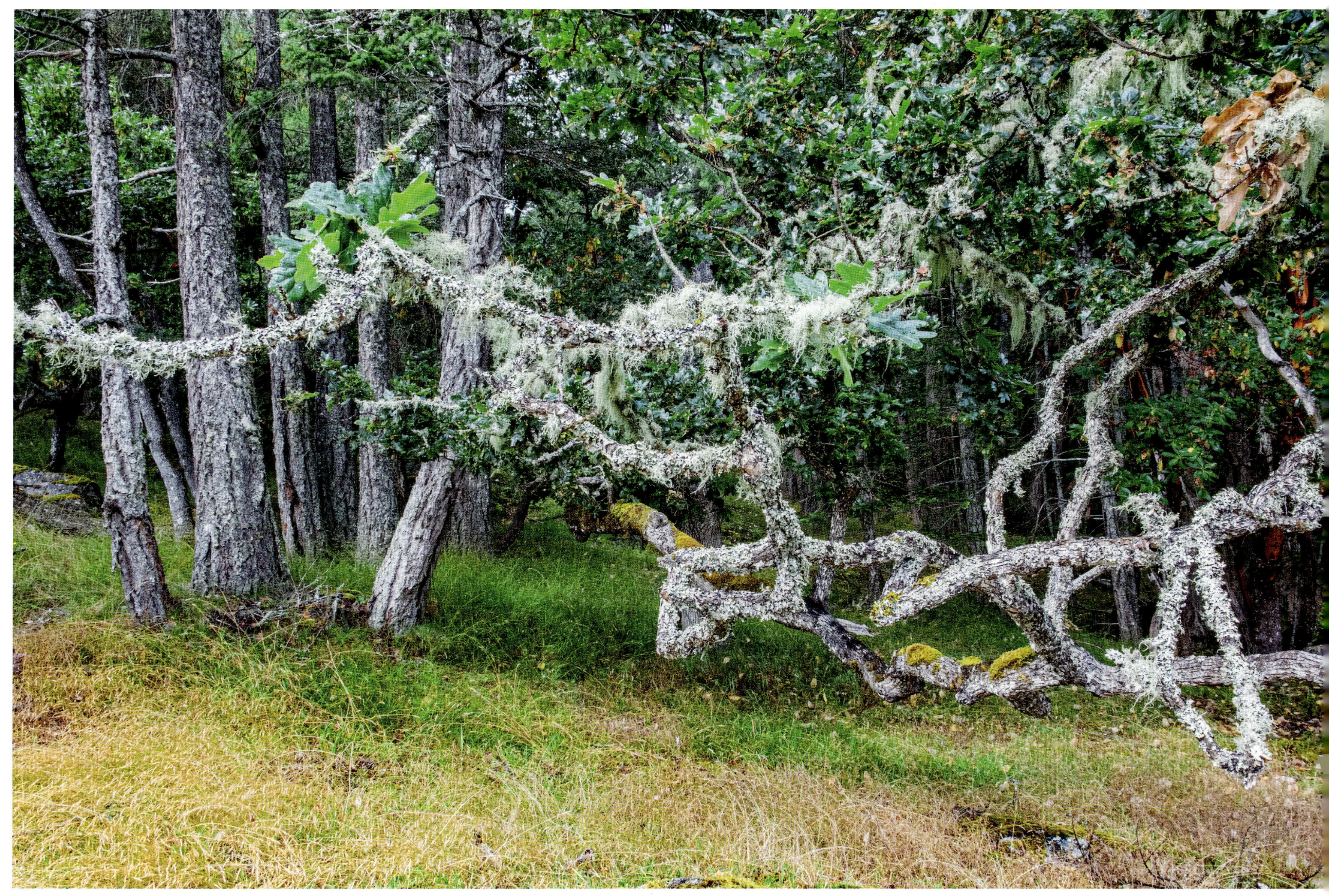

The most picturesque of the Island's trees are the arbutus (left) and the Garry oak (above) with their freeform twisted limbs.

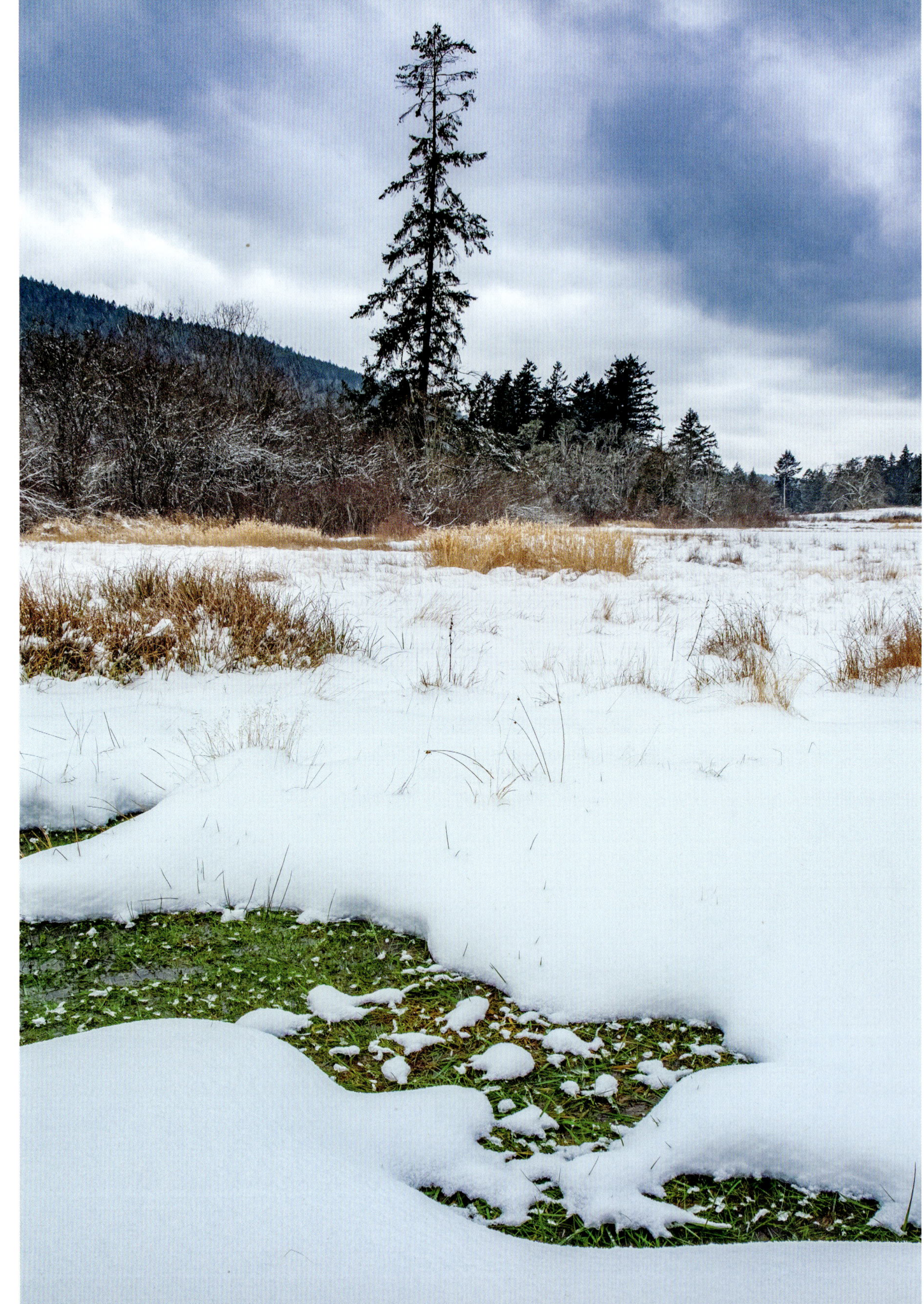

Burgoyne Bay Provincial Park after a mid-February snowfall (right).

Bulrushes line a duck pond beside Sunset Drive in February (far right).

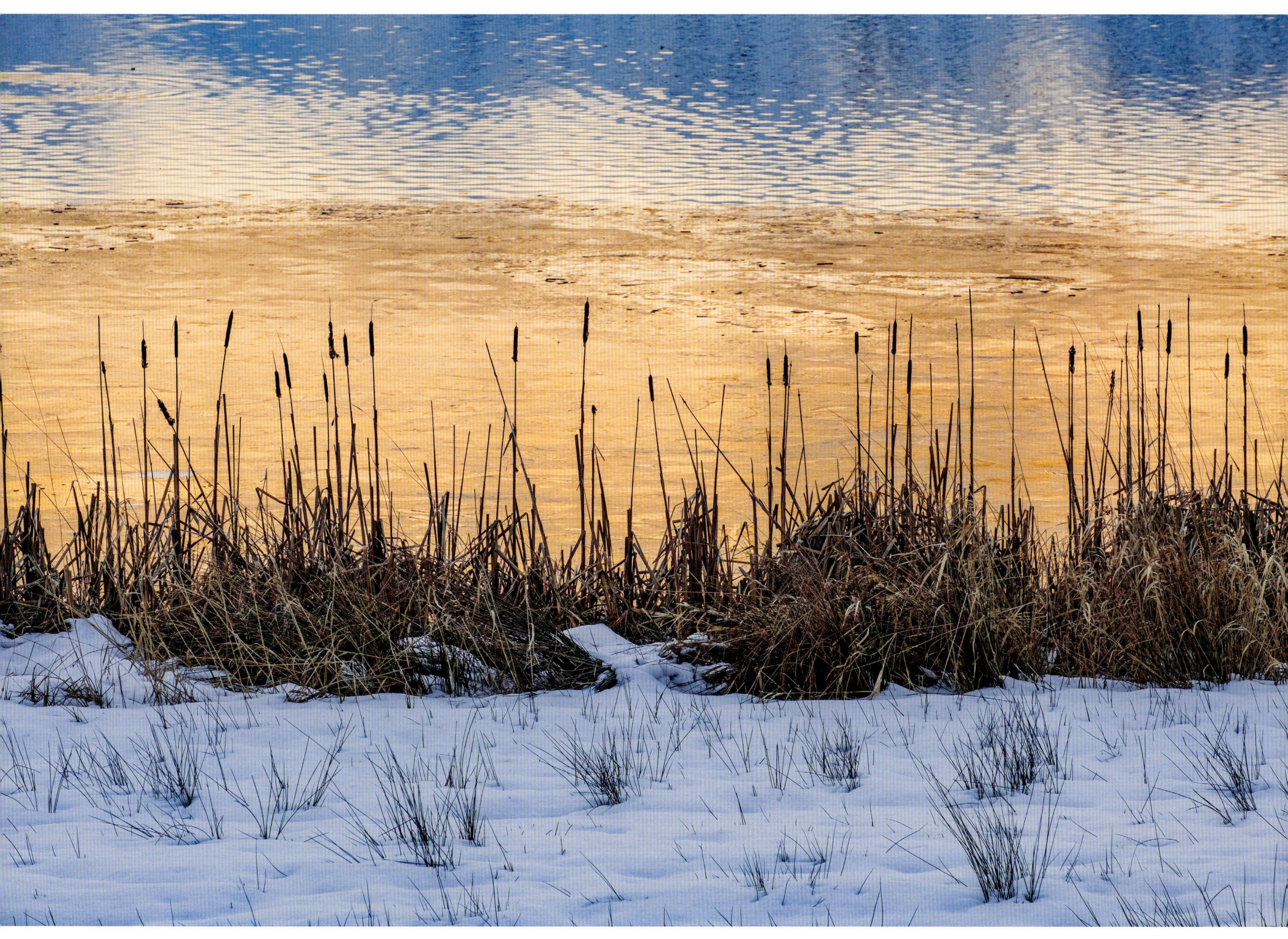

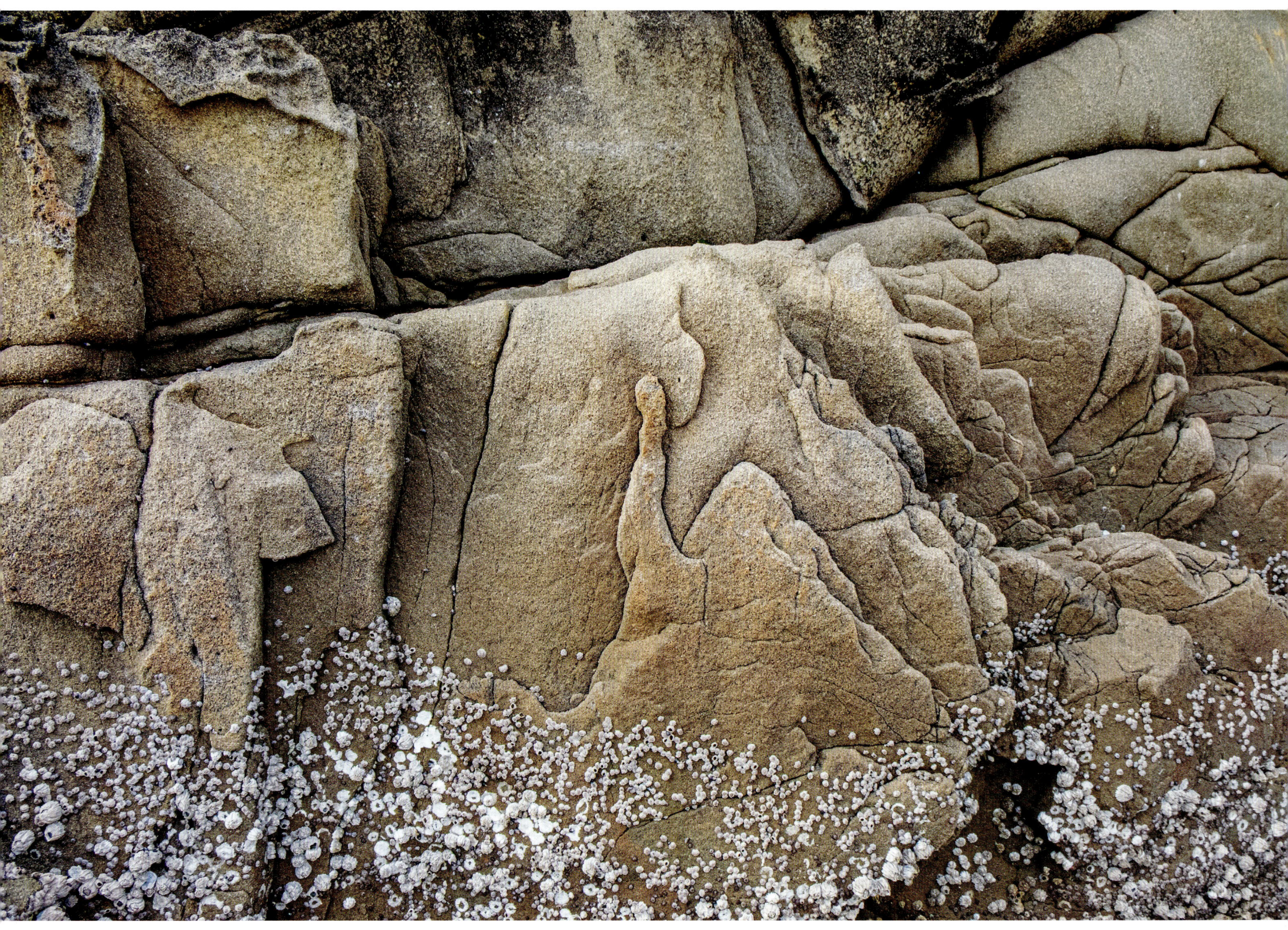

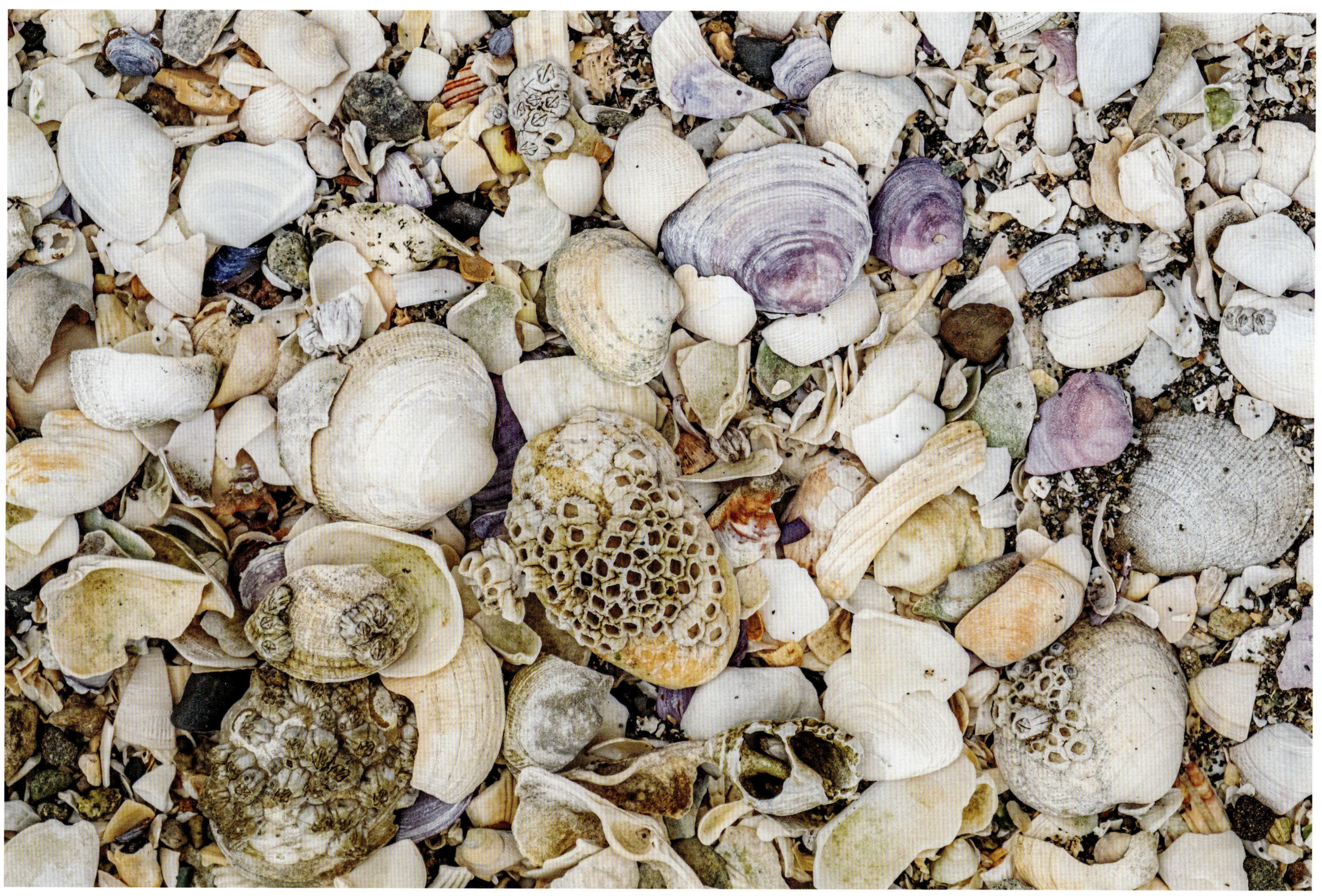

A rock detail at the high-tide mark at Grace Point in Ganges Harbour (left).

Shell deposits are common on the beaches of the island (above).

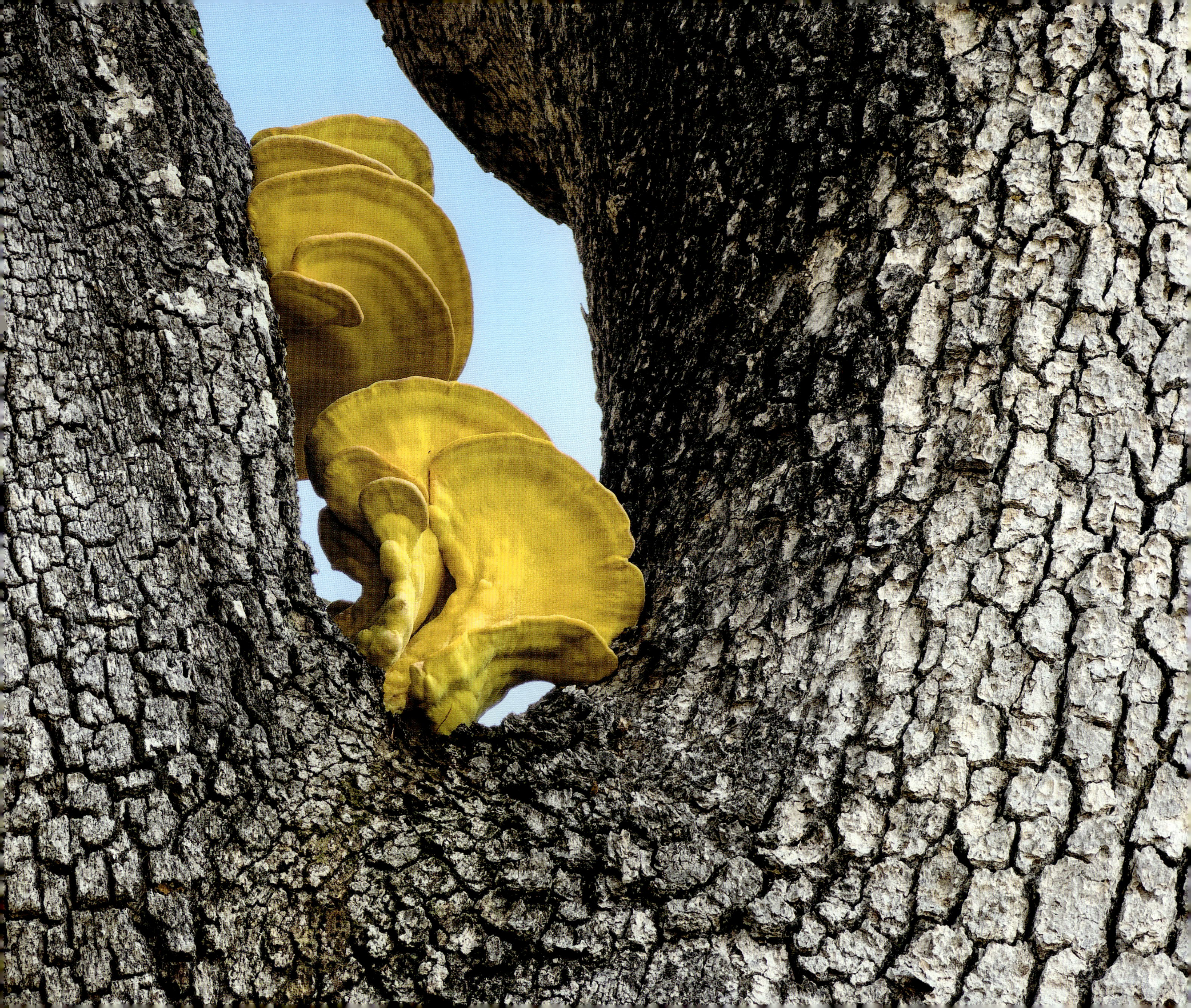

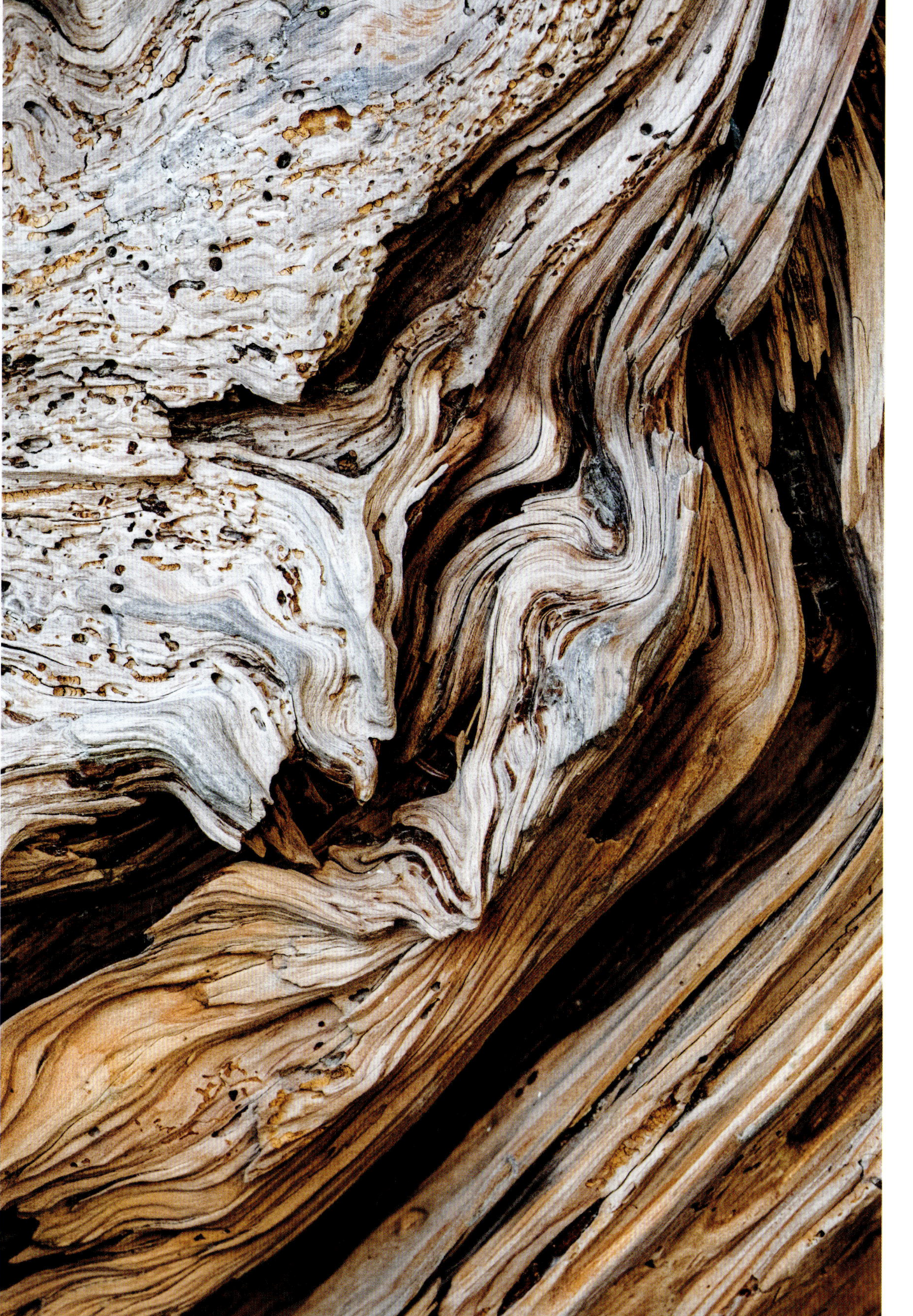

Sulfur shelf fungus (chicken of the woods) on a mature Garry oak (far left).

Driftwood detail along the shore of Ganges Harbour (left).

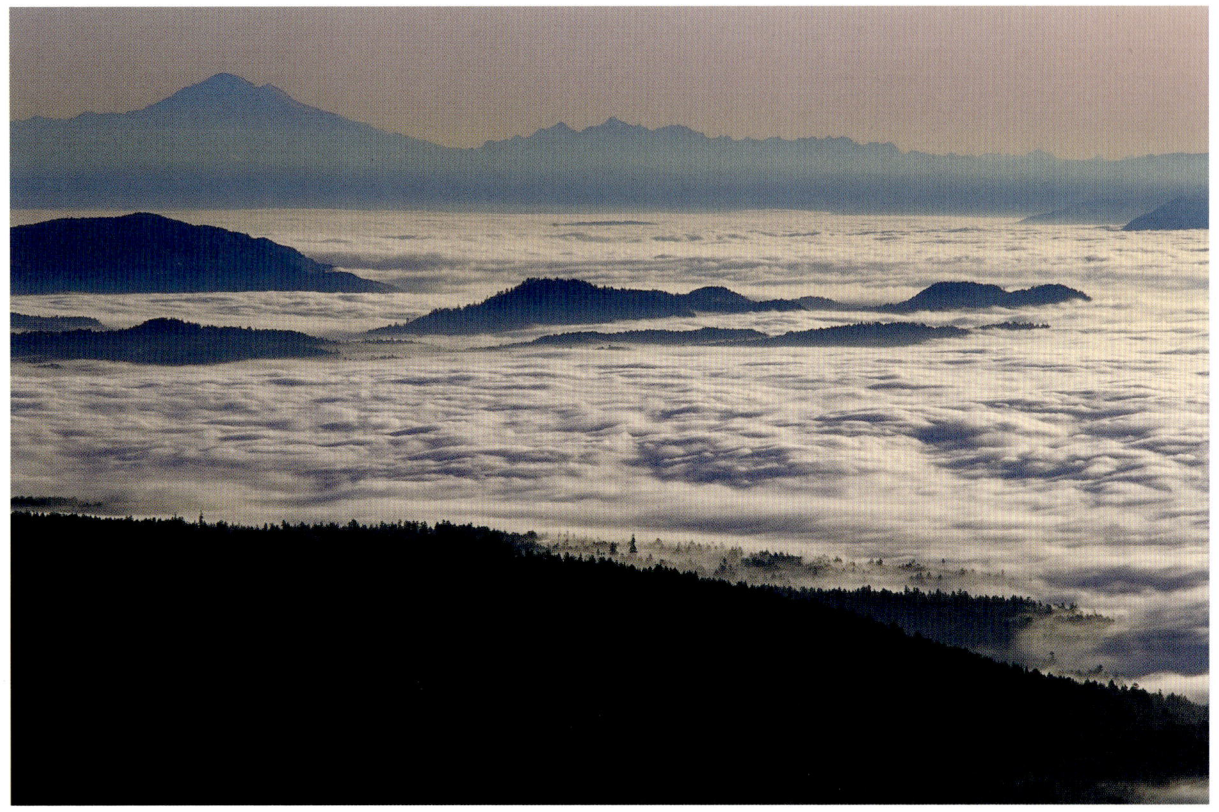

Fog covers the entire Salish Sea at sunrise in February, viewed from the summit of Mount Bruce, the highest point on Salt Spring. On the horizon to the east are Mount Baker and the North Cascades (above), and to the northeast, the Coast Mountains (right).

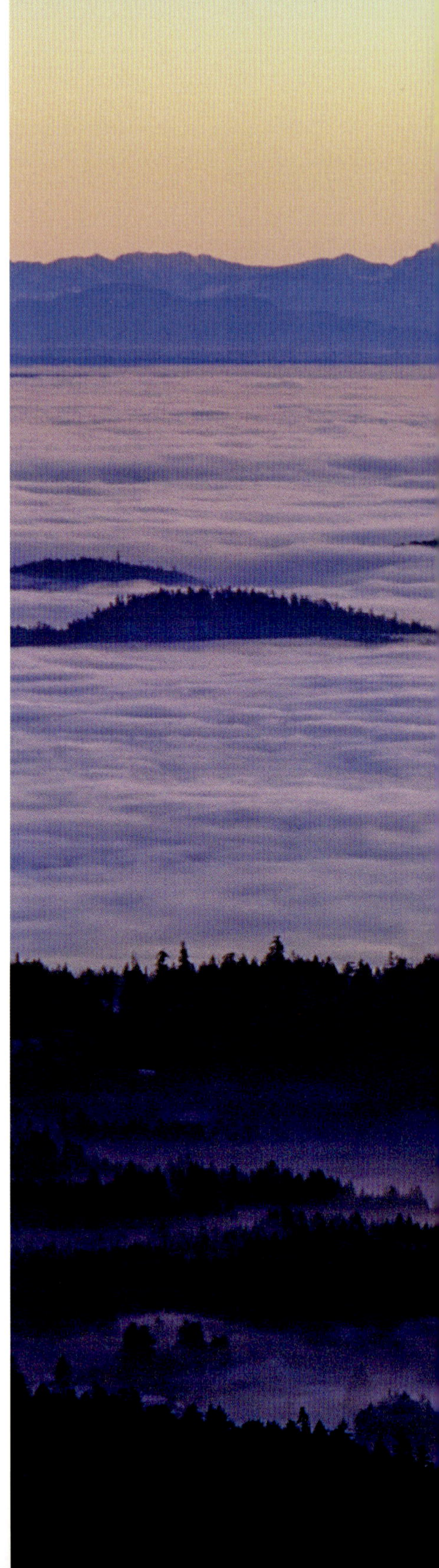

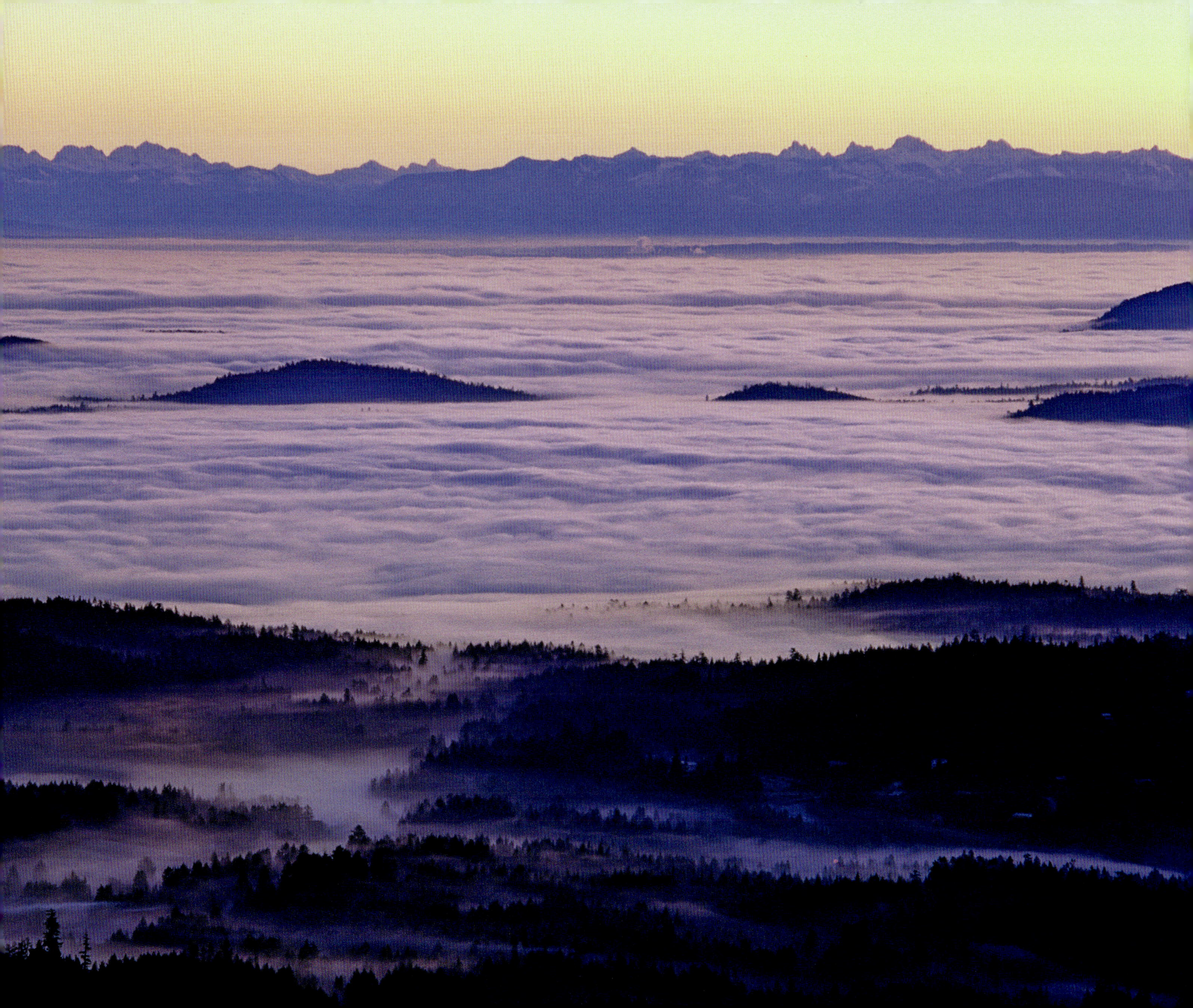

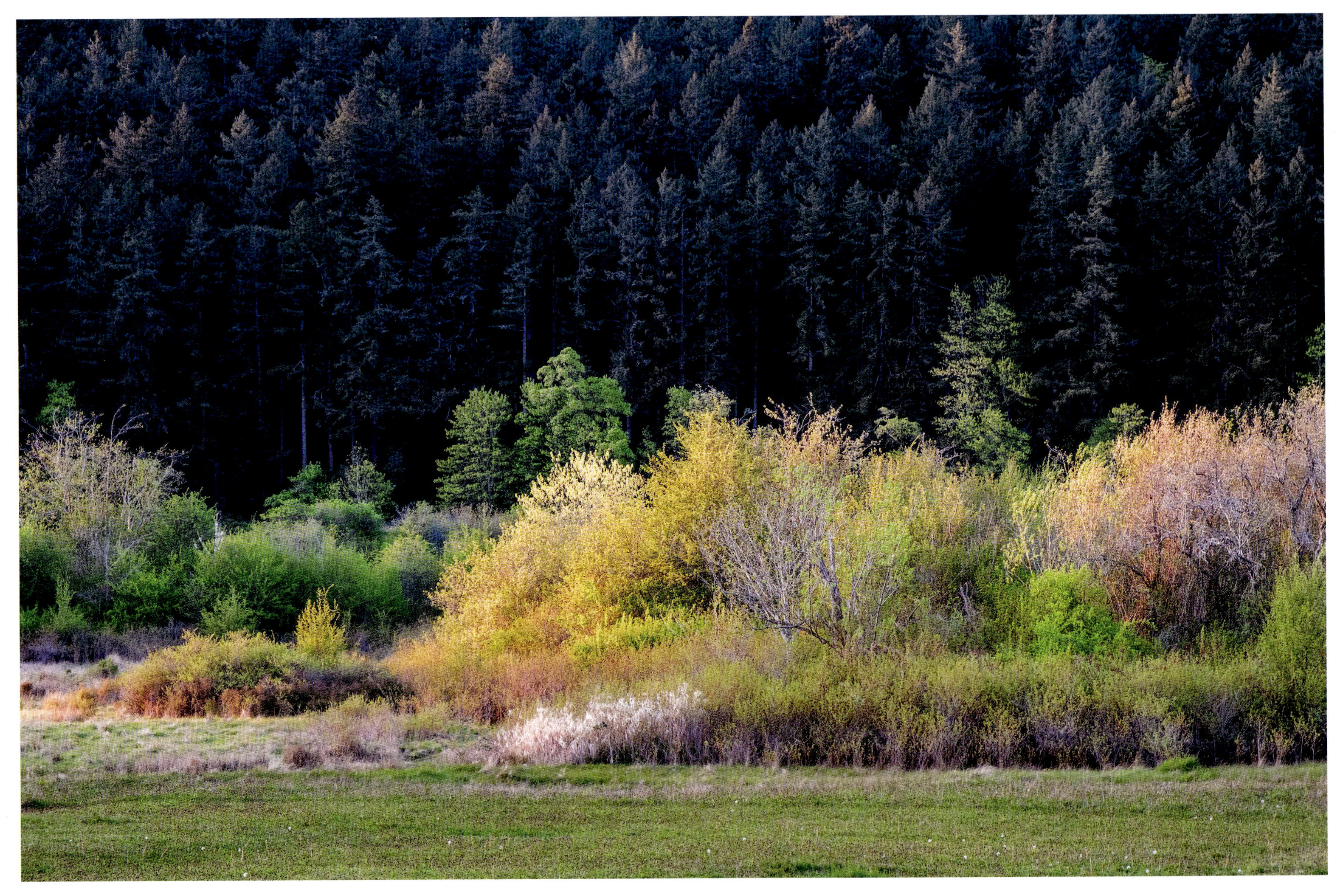

April in Burgoyne Bay Provincial Park.

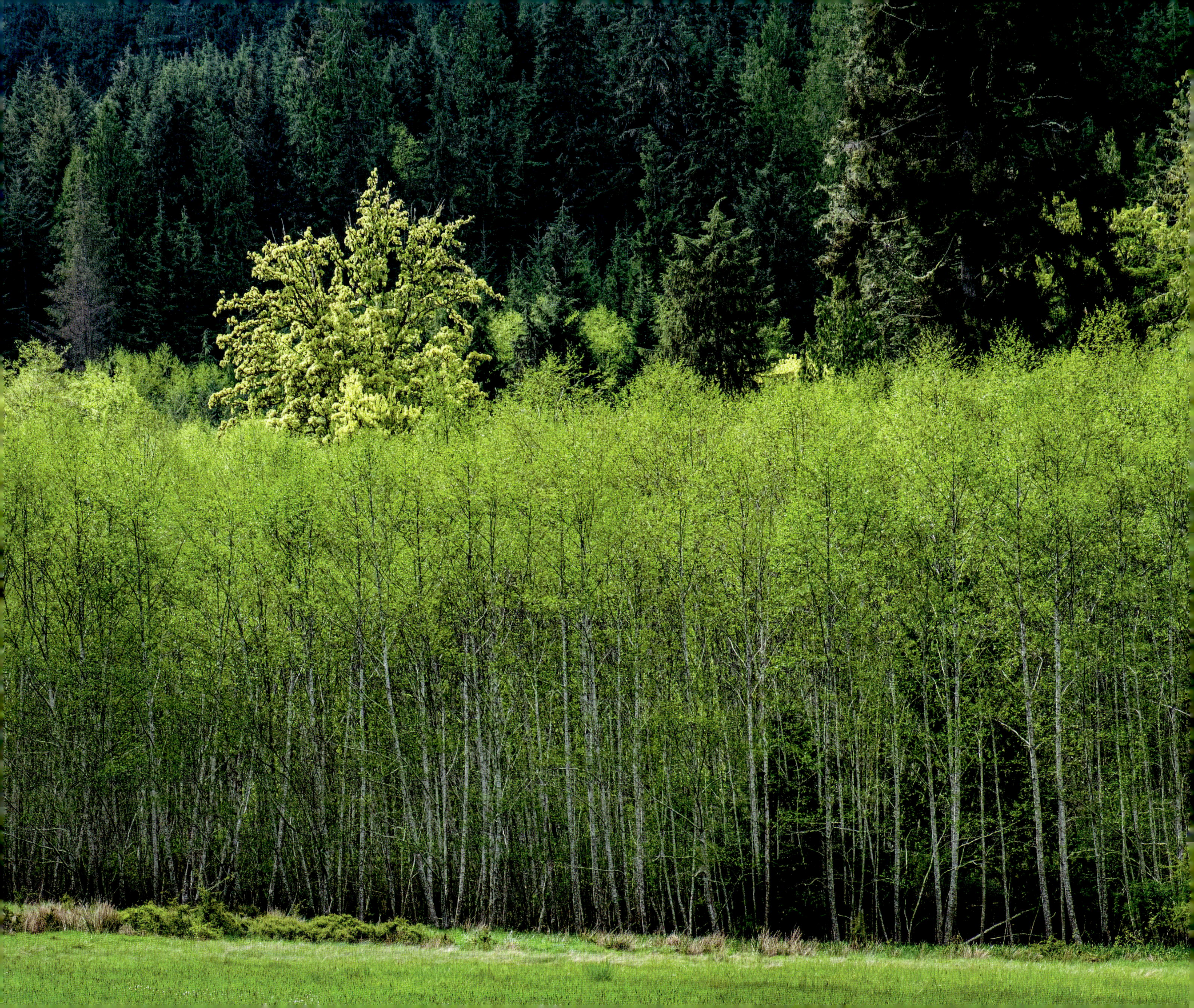

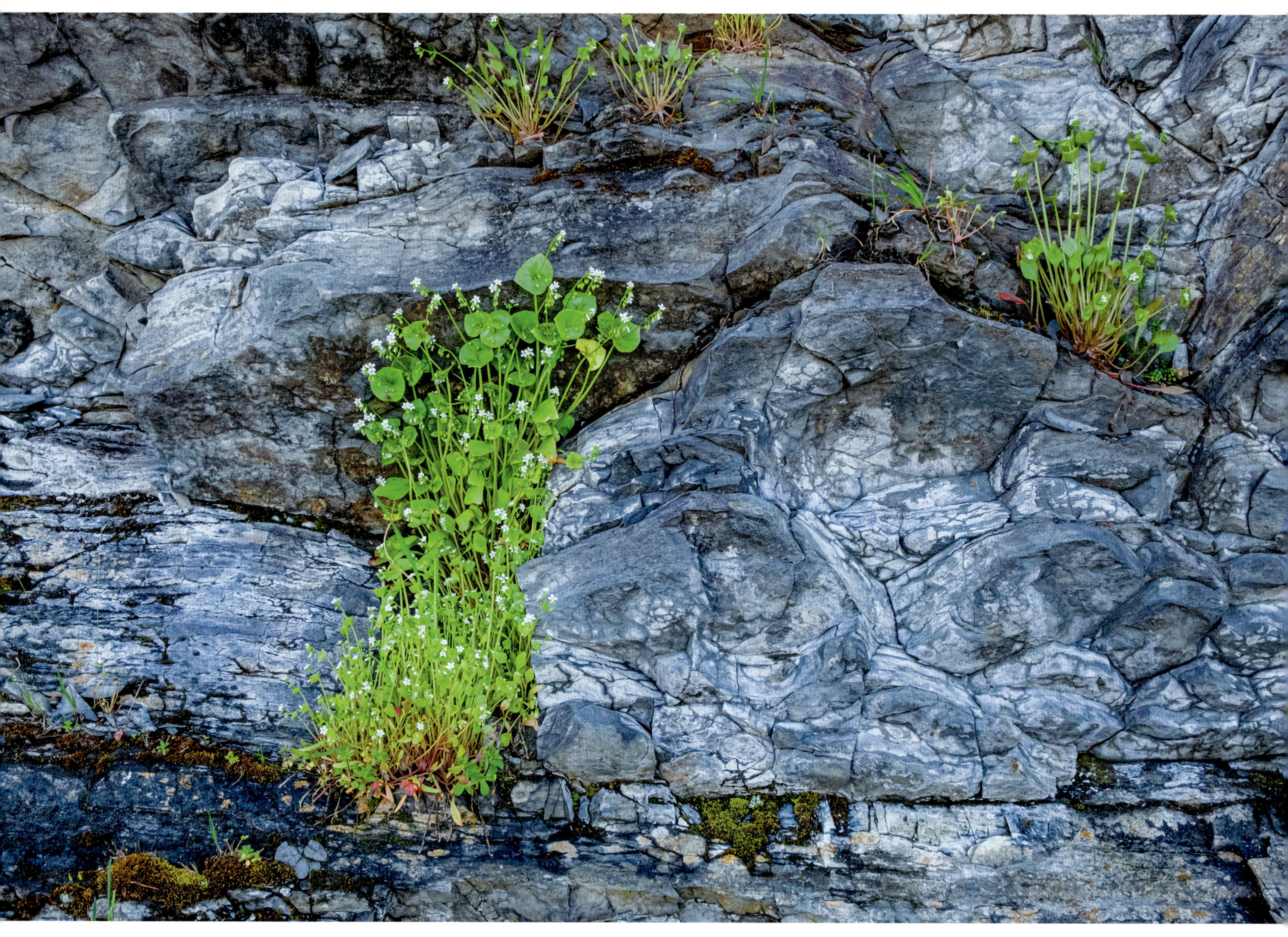

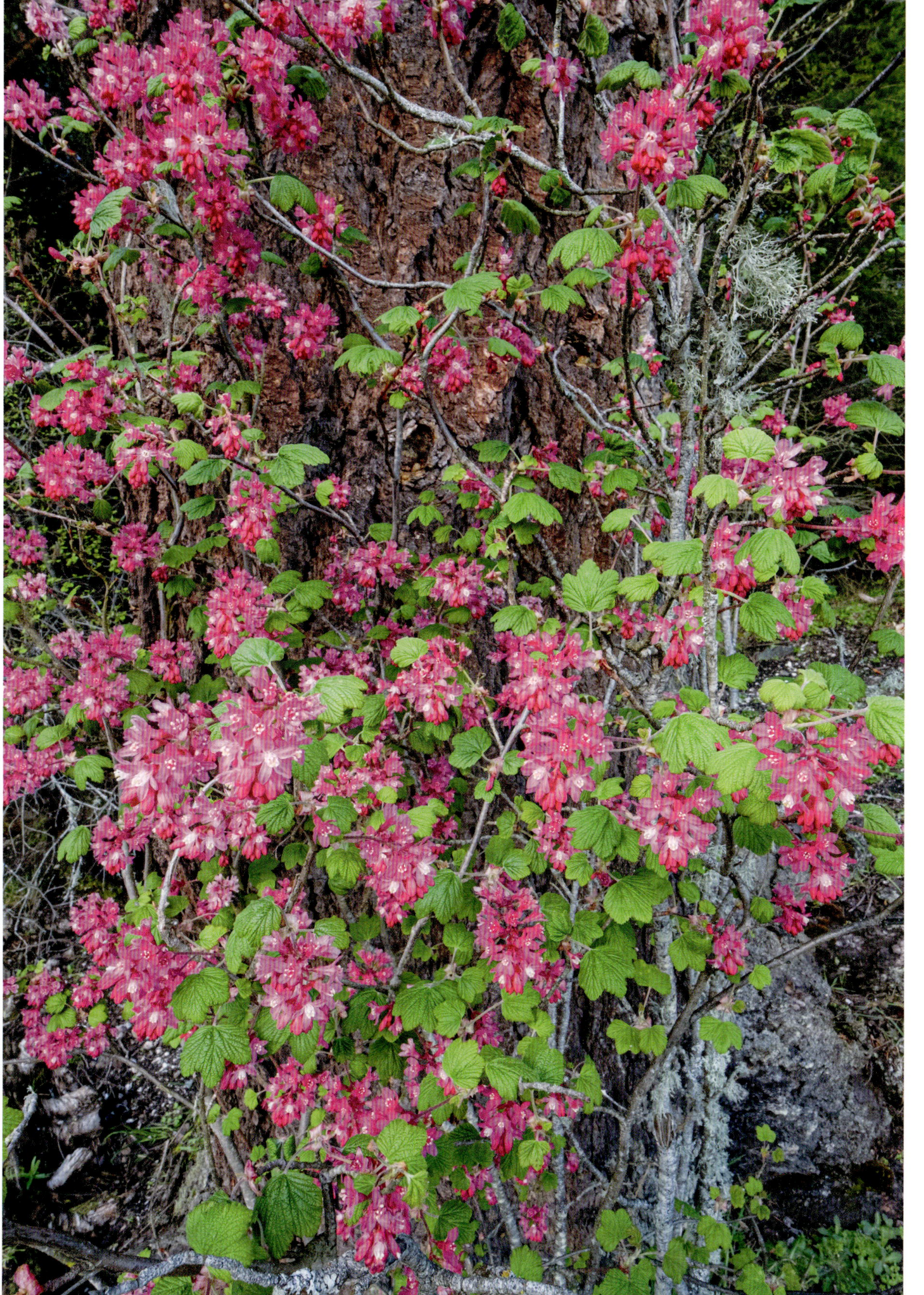

Miner's lettuce in shoreline rocks at Fernwood Point in April (far left).

Red-flowering currant in March (left).

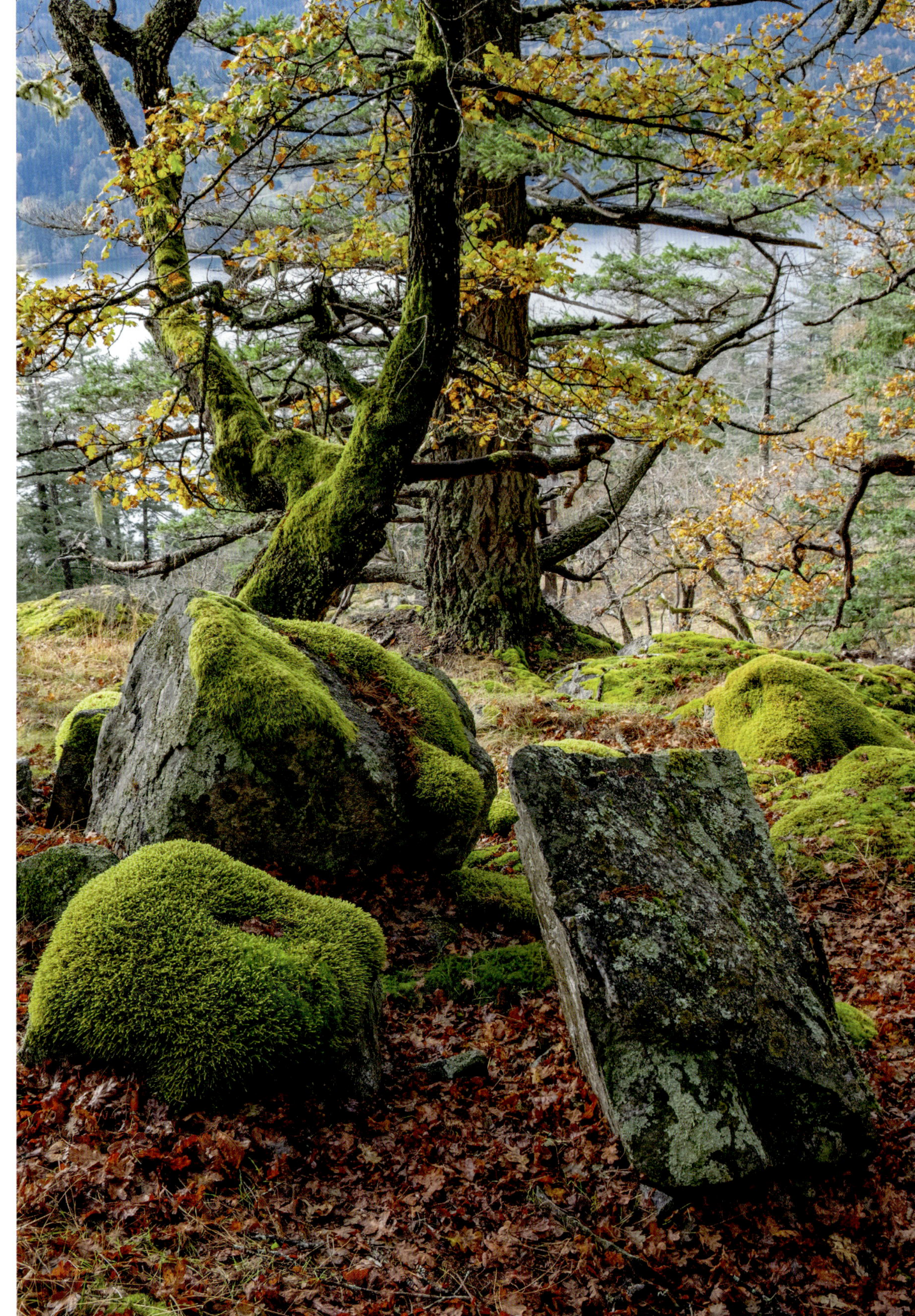

Moss is abundant in the rocky, rugged terrain and deep forests of the island, and especially verdant in the wetter months, here in November (right).

Fall colour in Fulford Valley in mid-October (far right).

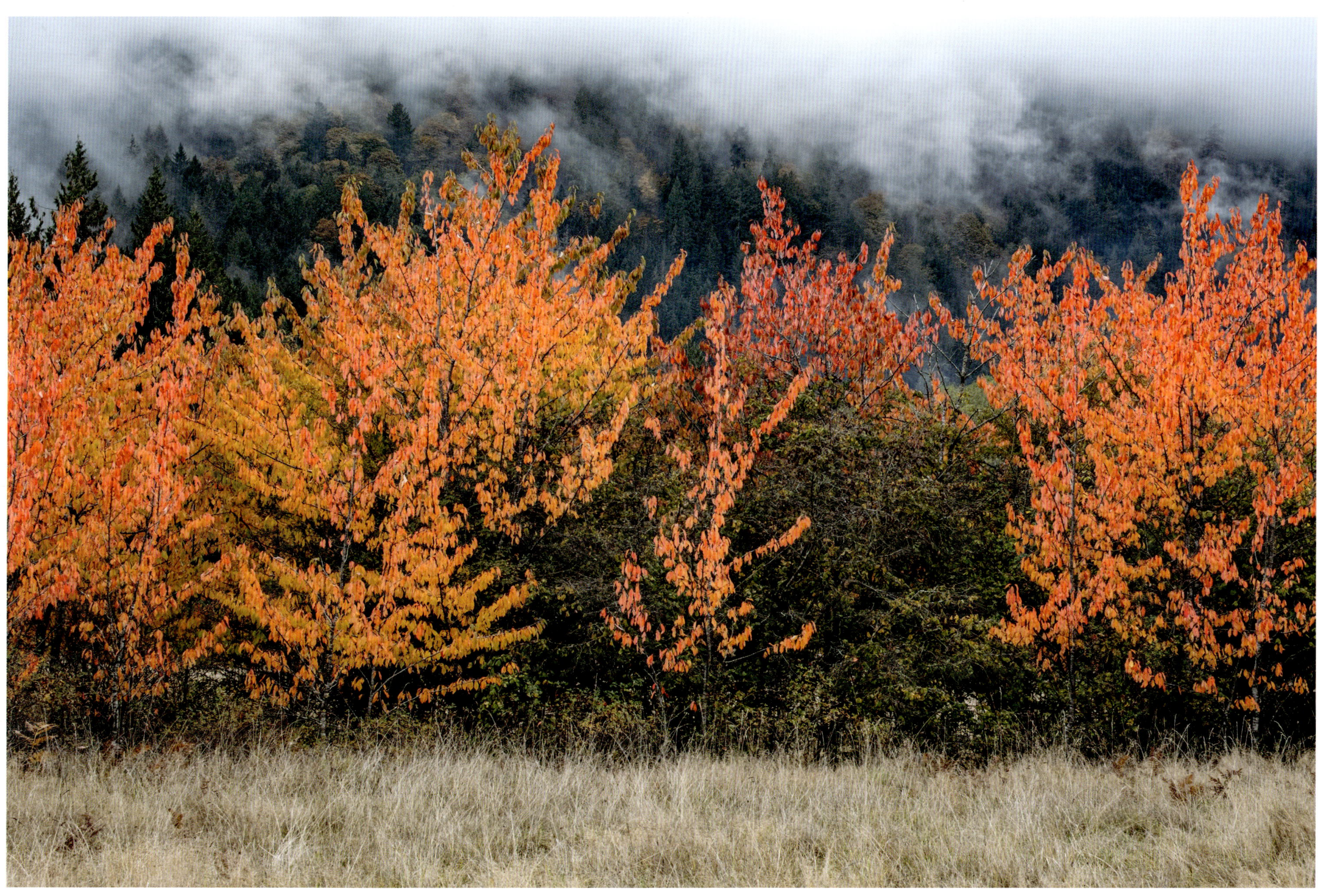

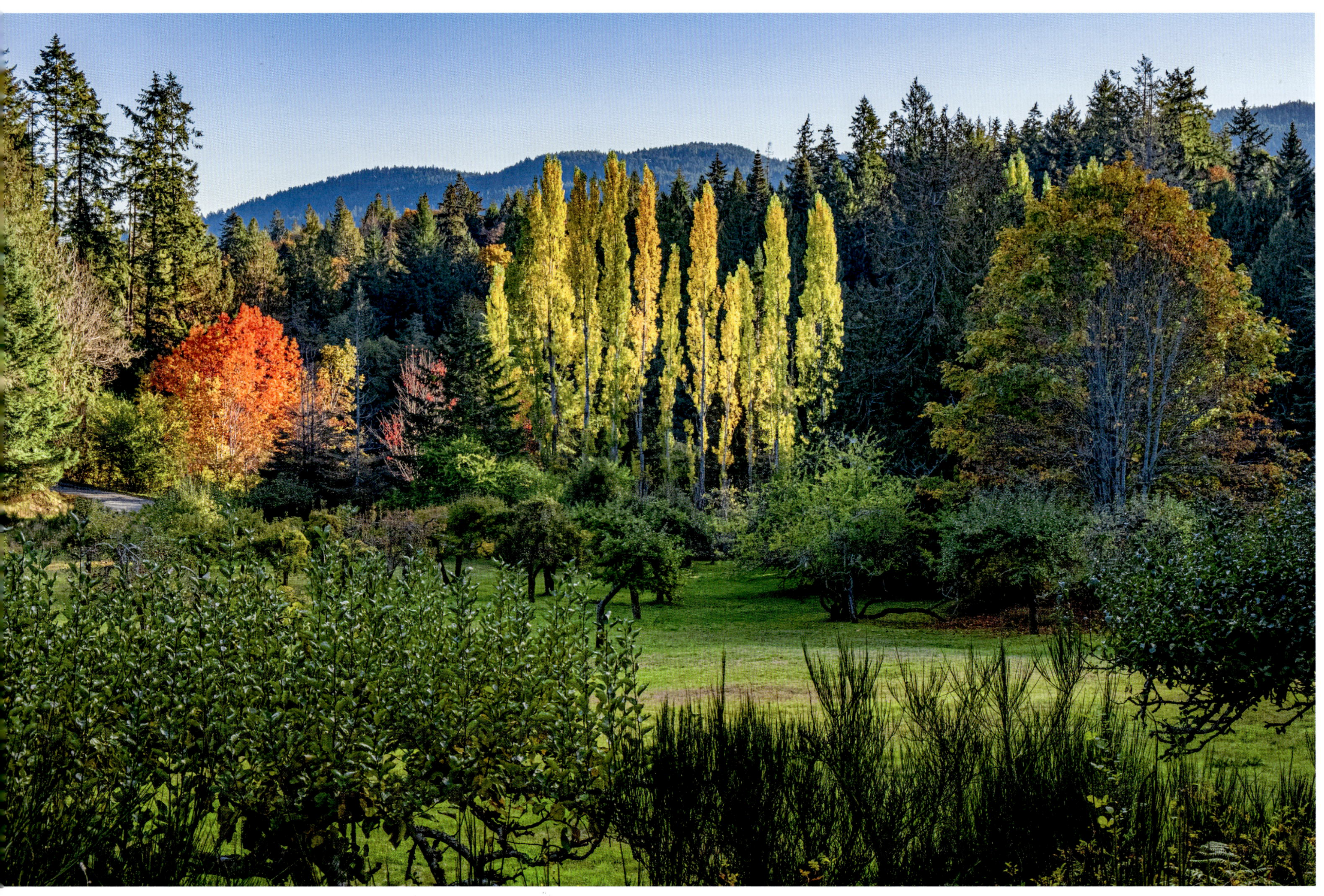

A small orchard and tall poplars in October along Upper Ganges Road at Highwood Place.

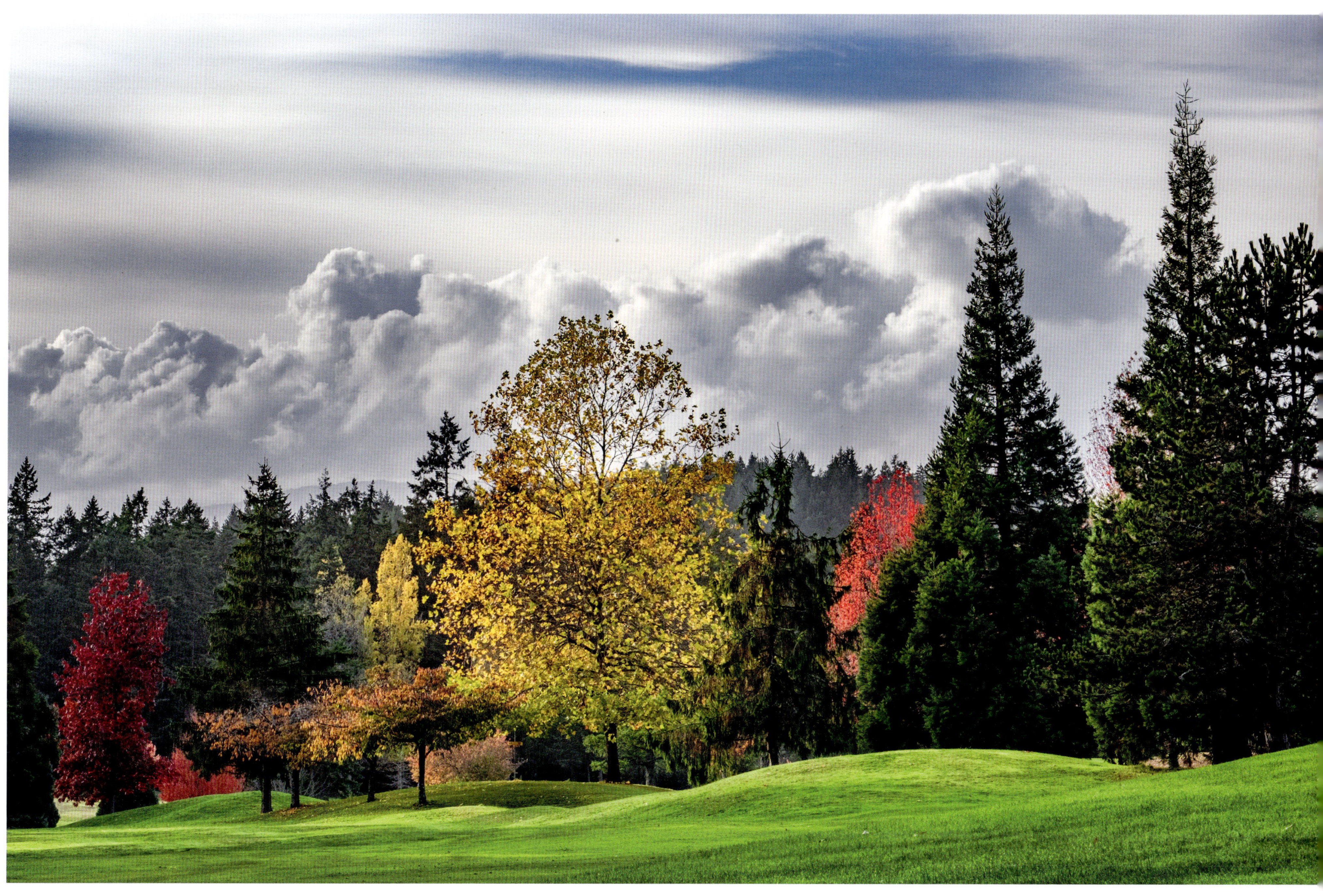

Fall colours and fall weather at the Salt Spring golf course.

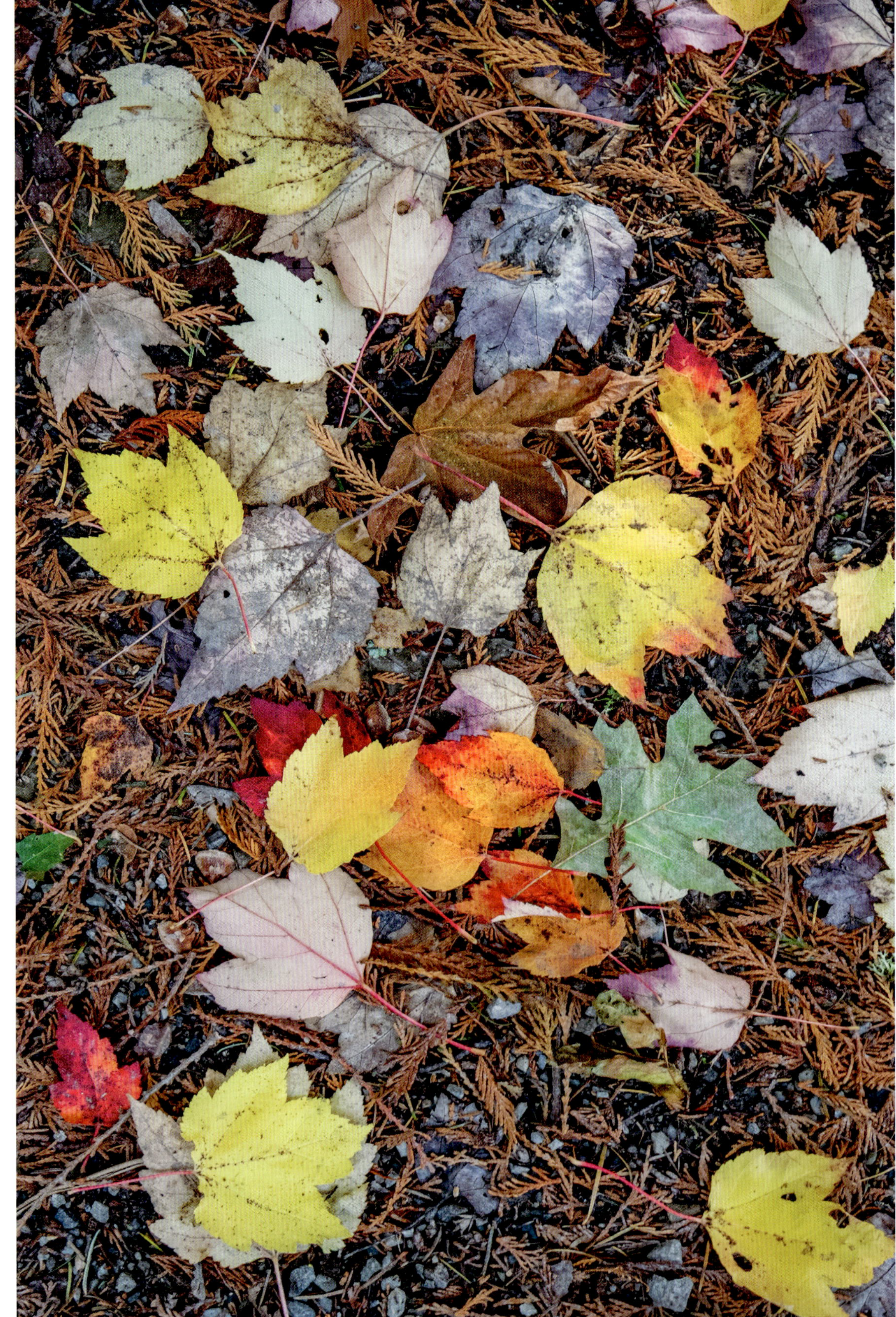

Autumn leaves on the ground, early November.

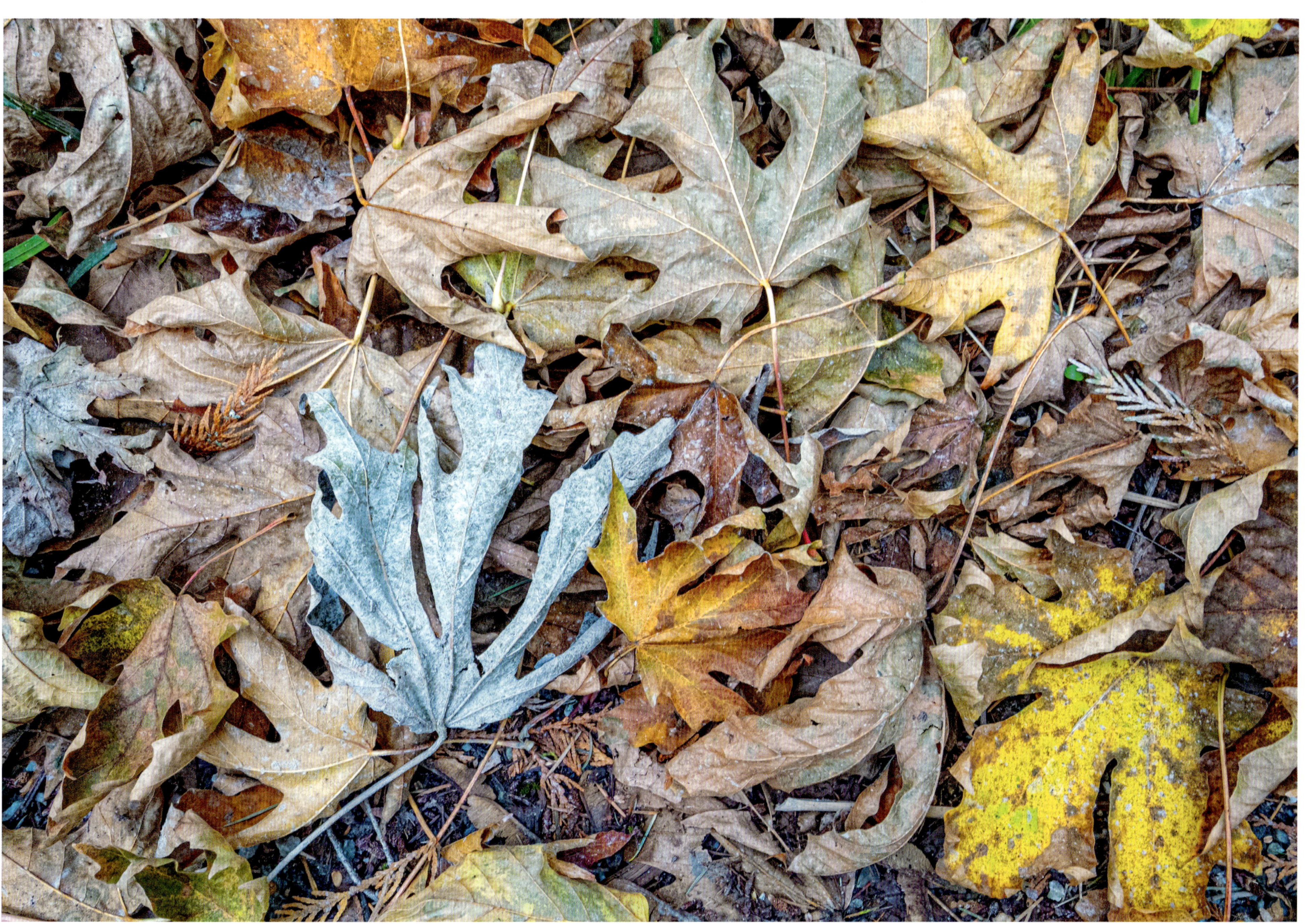

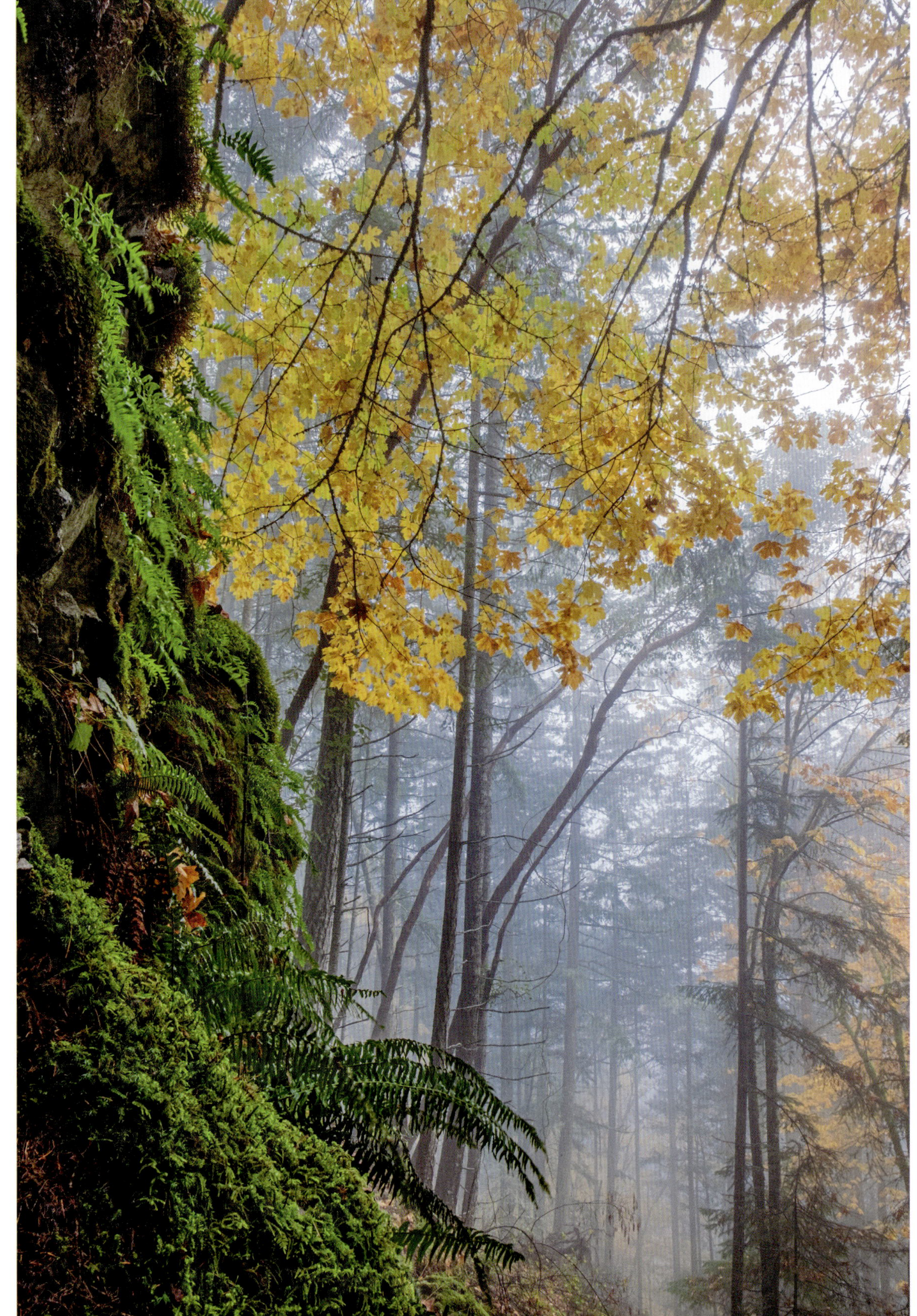

November fog on Reginald Hill drifts behind ferns and bigleaf maples (right); huckleberry, salal and moss nurtured by stumps left over from logging in the 1940s (far right).

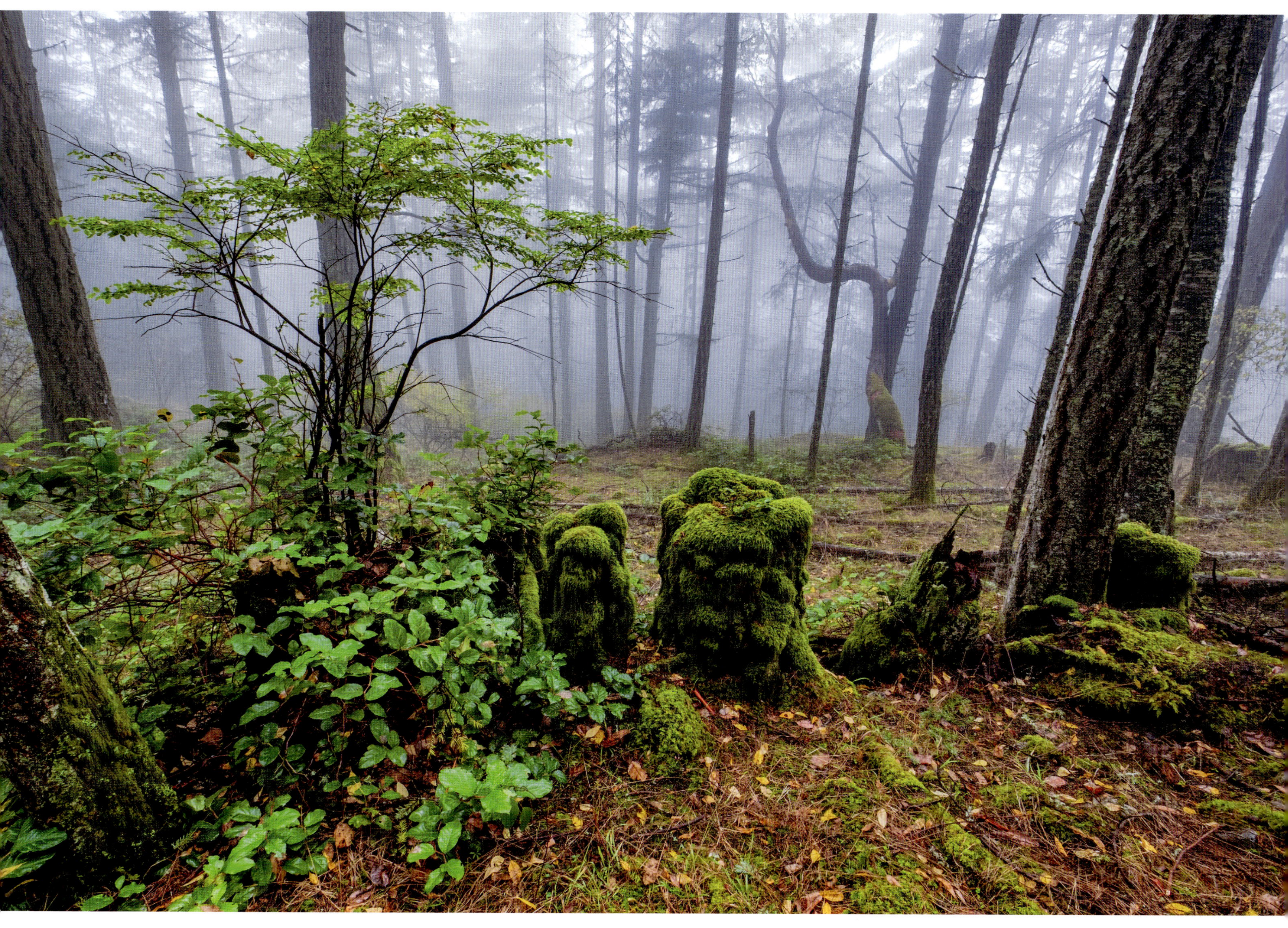

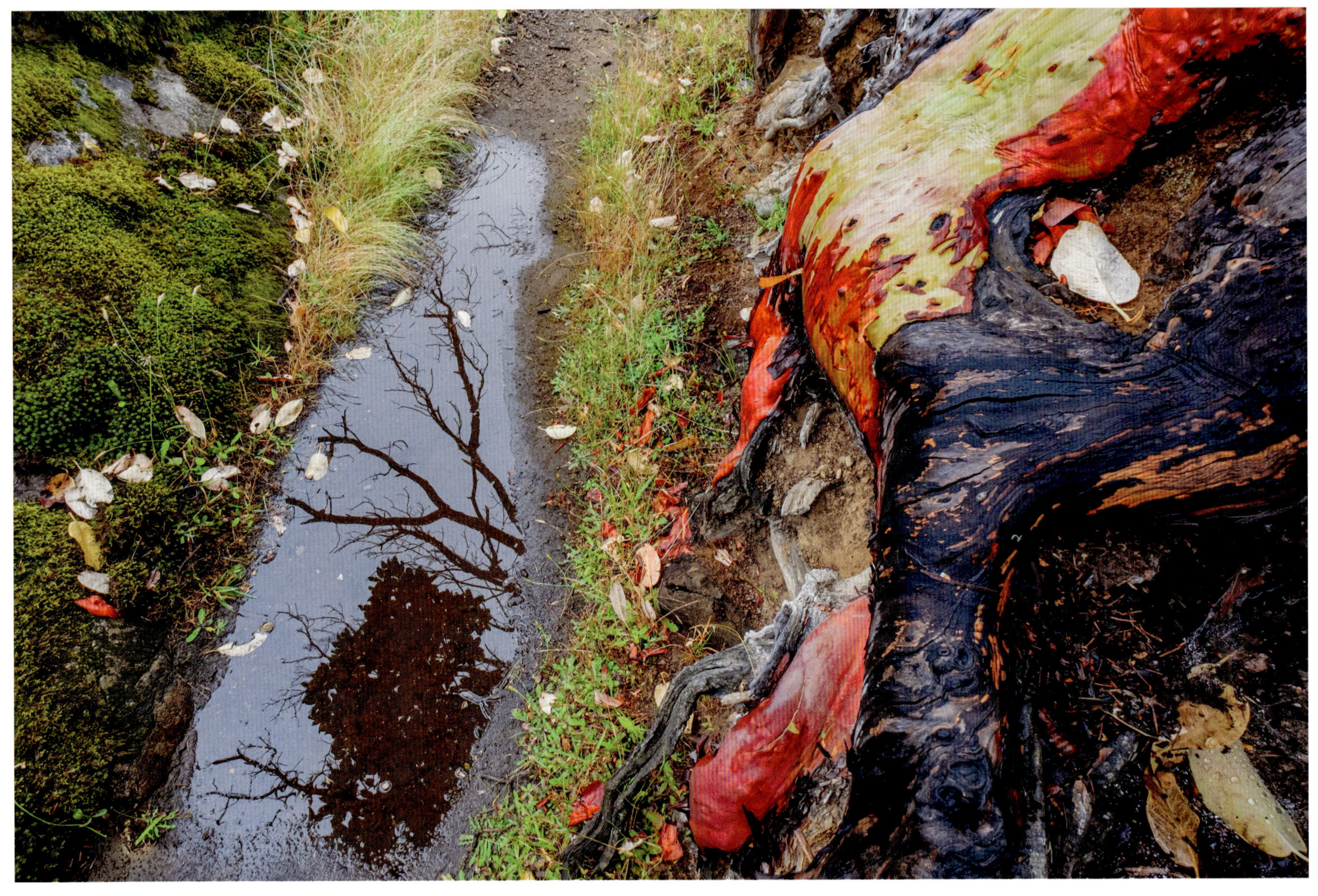

Two different intimate views of the same arbutus tree.

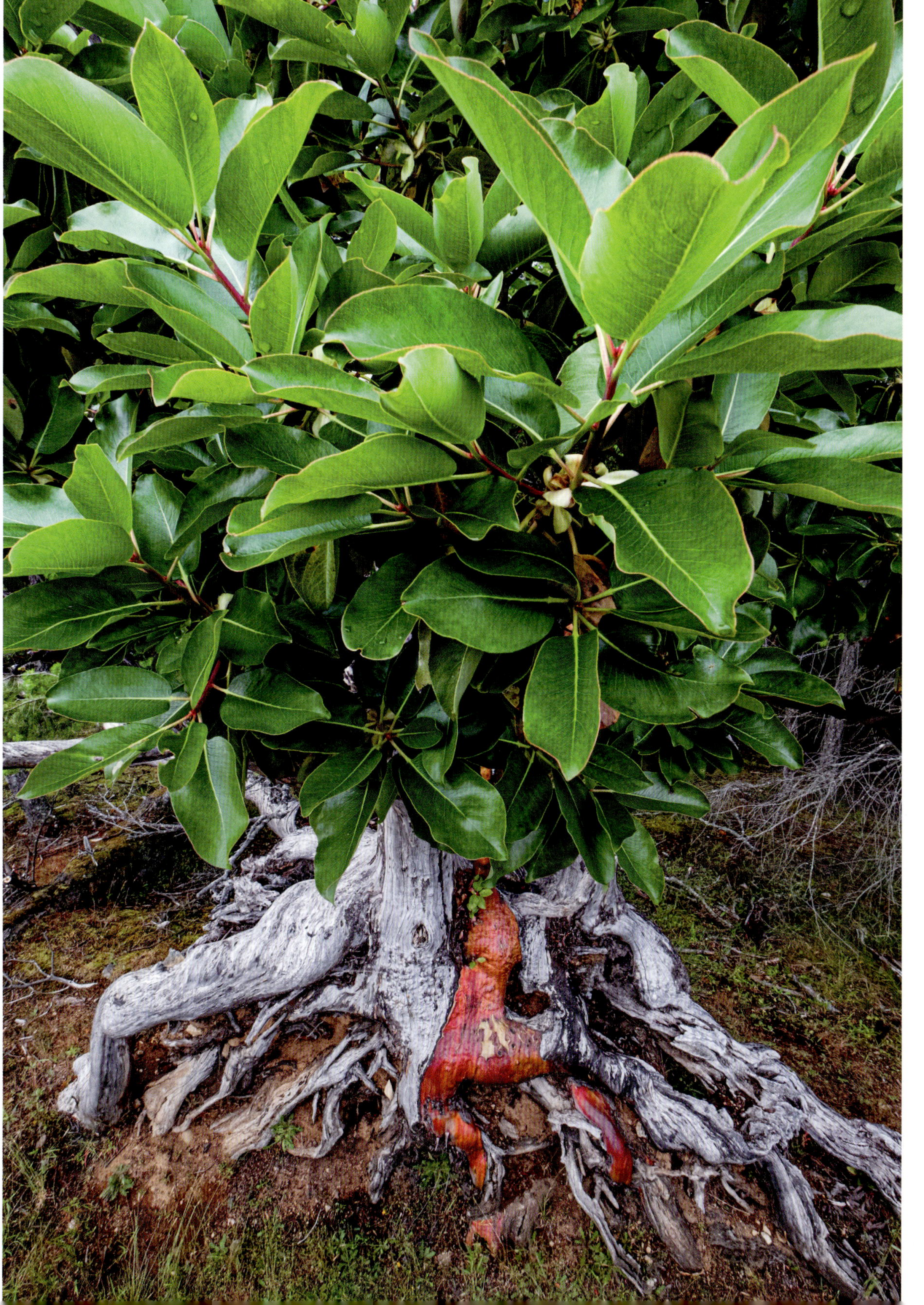

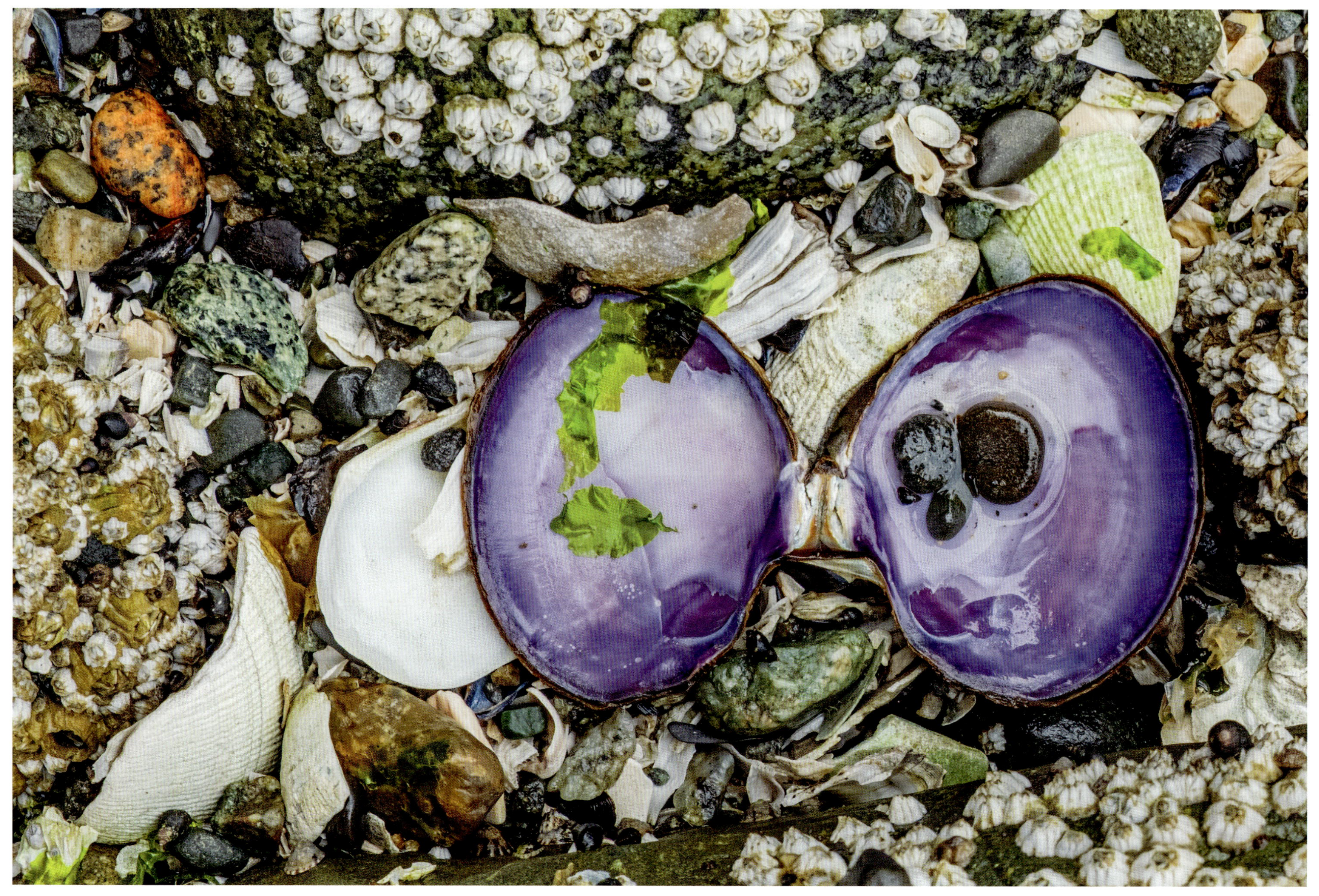

A purple varnish clam (above) and red rock crab (right) at low tide.

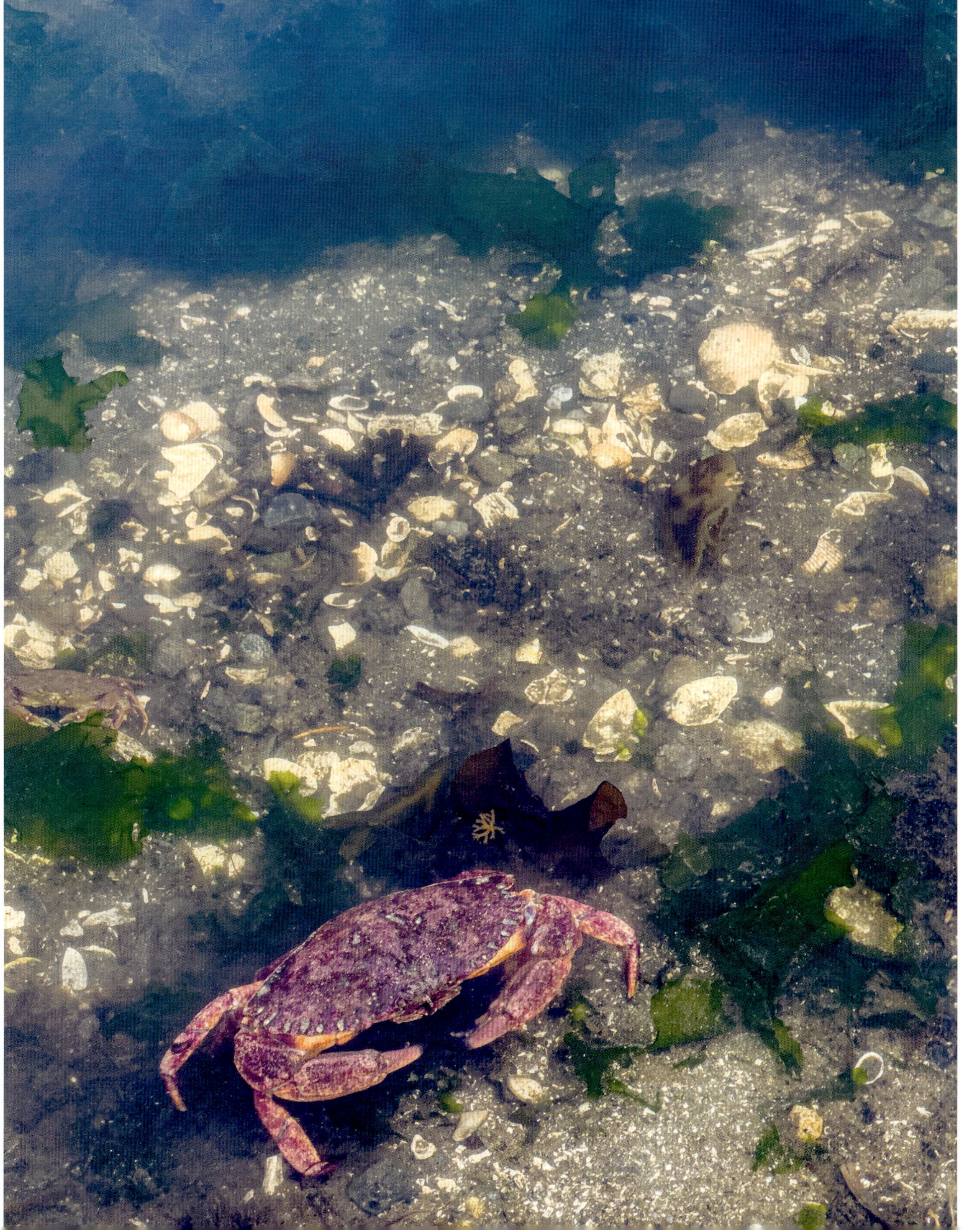

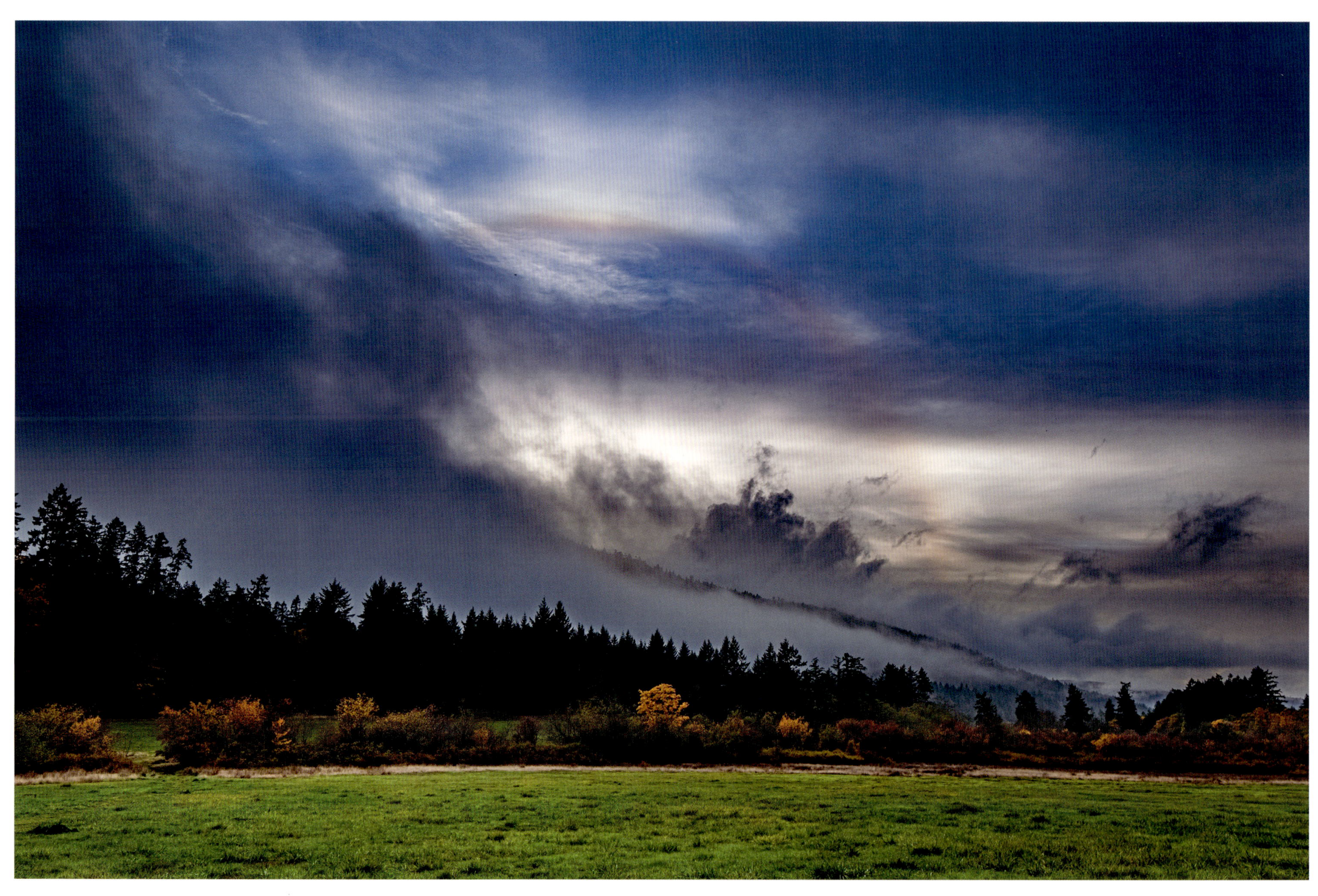

A 22° halo around the sun appears during clearing weather in Burgoyne Bay Provincial Park in October.

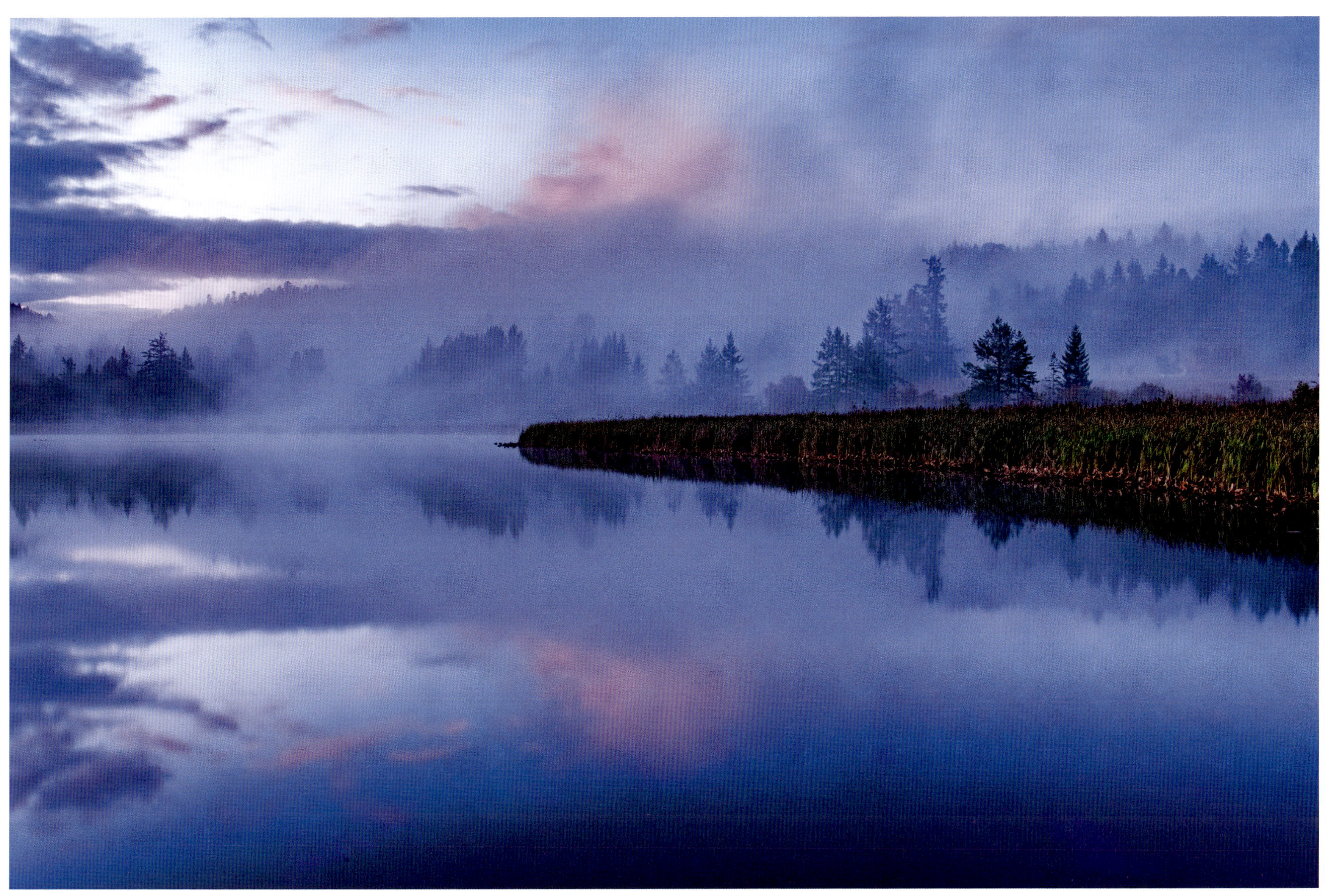

Dusk at Blackburn Lake in October.

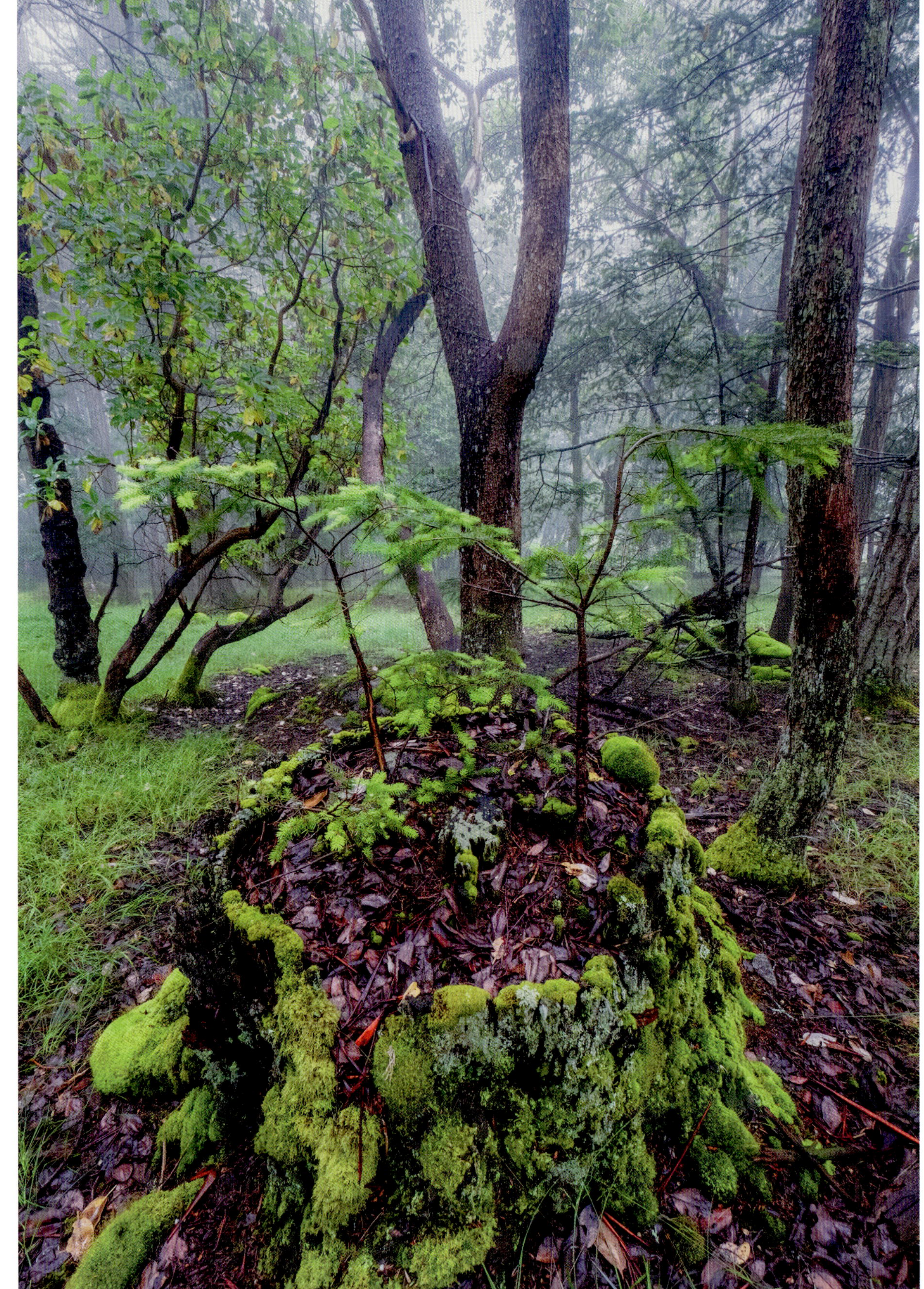

Fir saplings in June, nursed in the stump of a tree logged many decades ago.

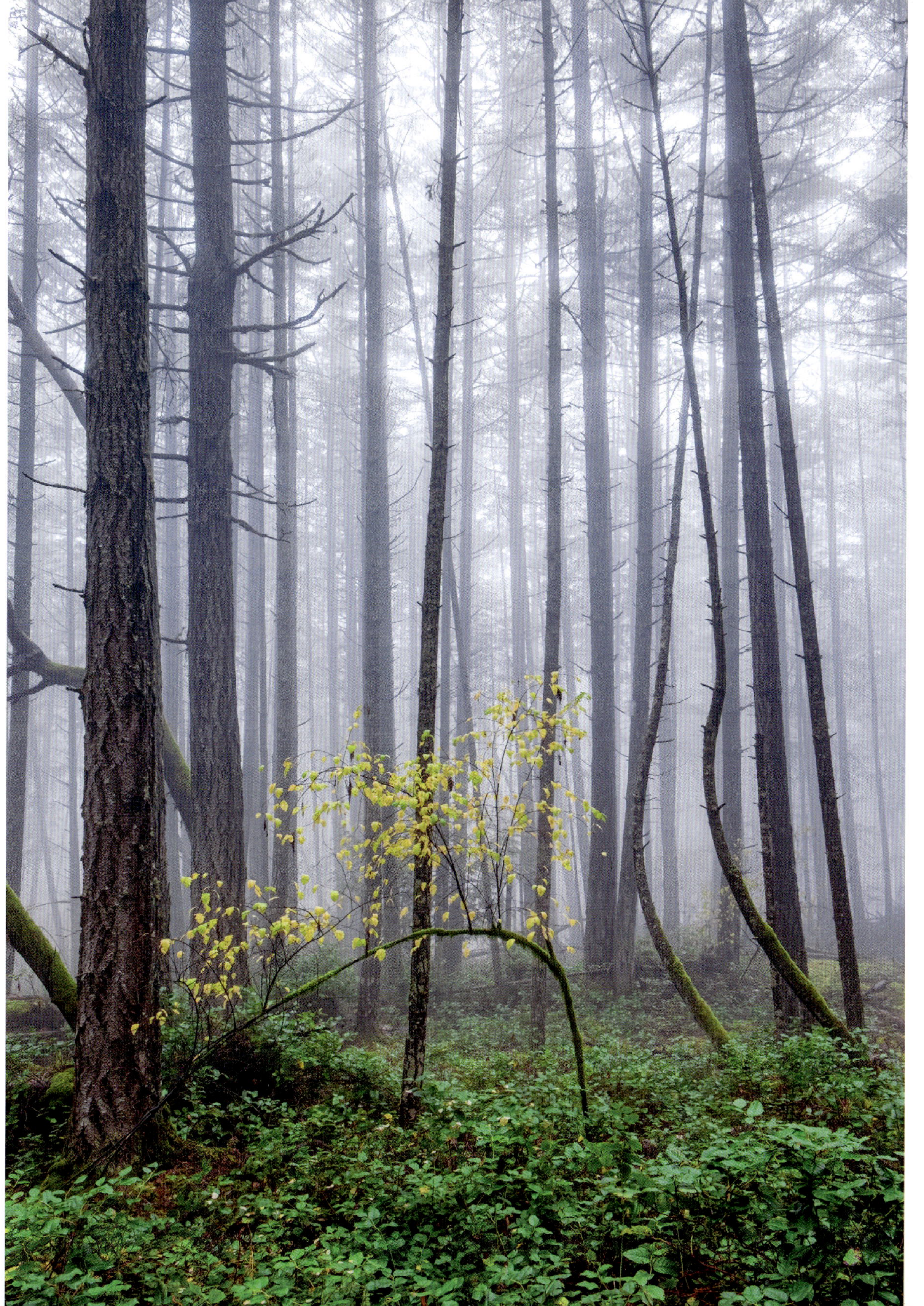

An oceanspray shrub with yellow autumn leaves amidst columns of fir and hemlock on a fogbound day in early November.

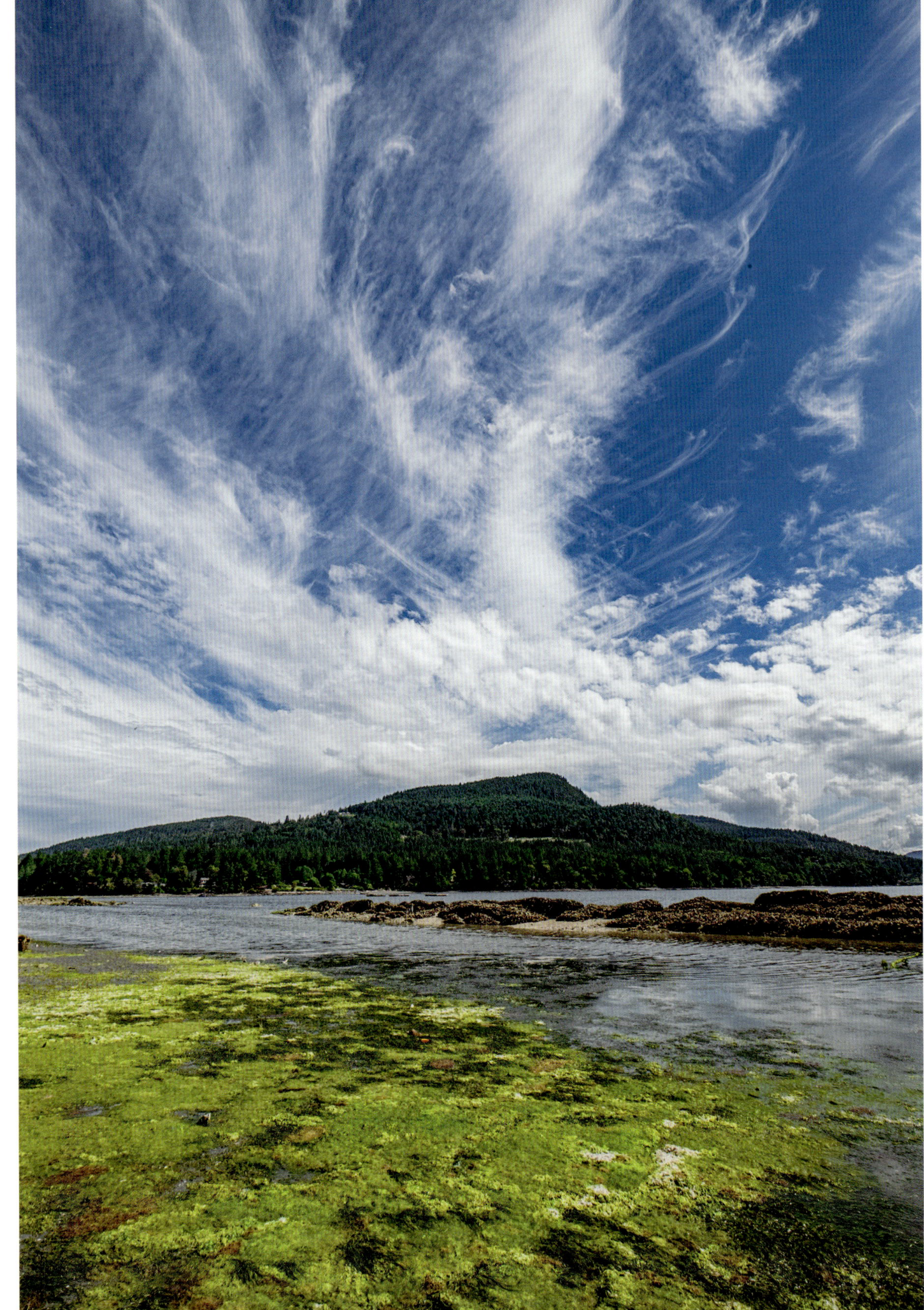

A mid-June sky over Mount Erskine from seaweed-covered tidal flats in Booth Bay.

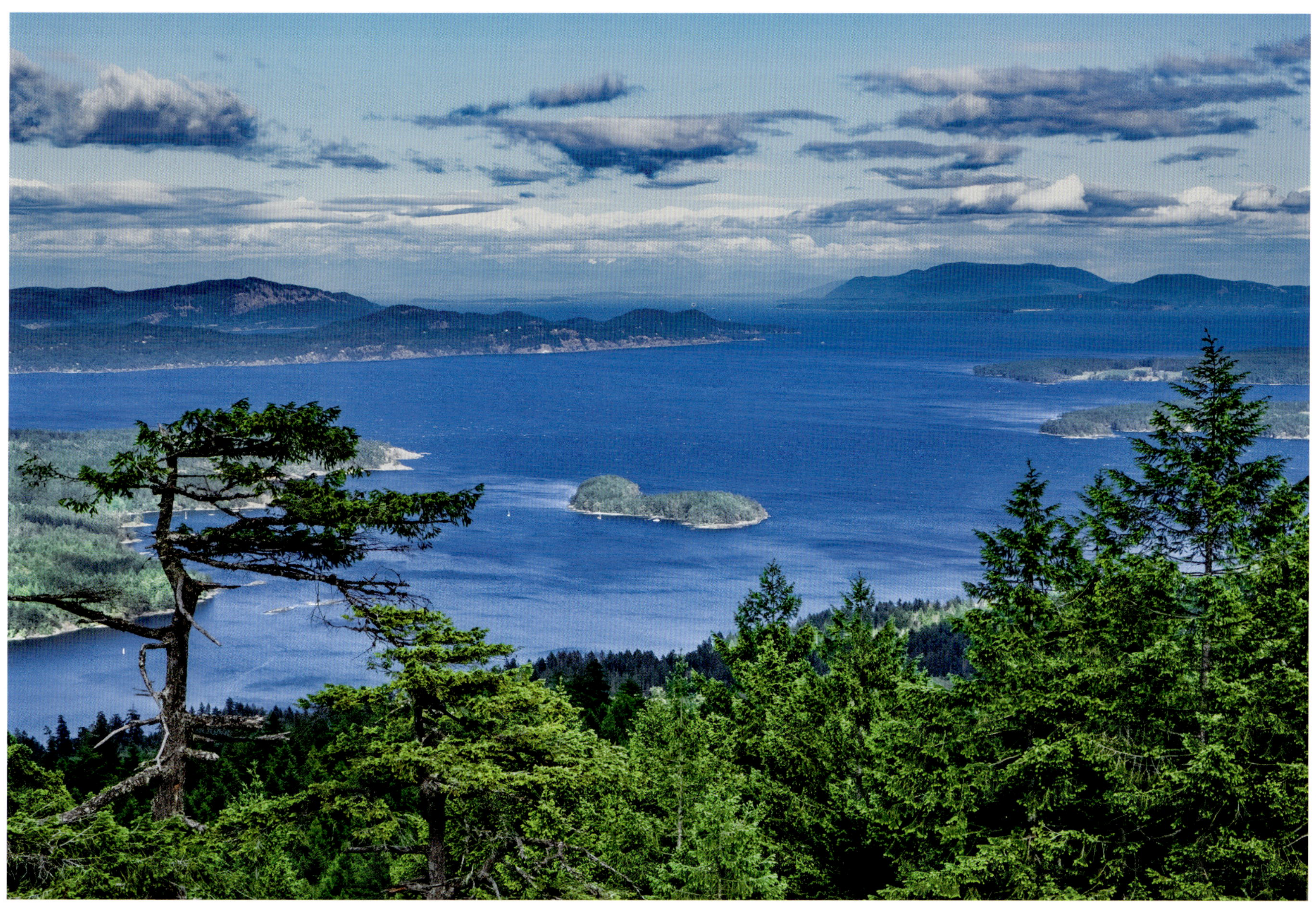

Russell Island from a trail on Hope Hill in June.

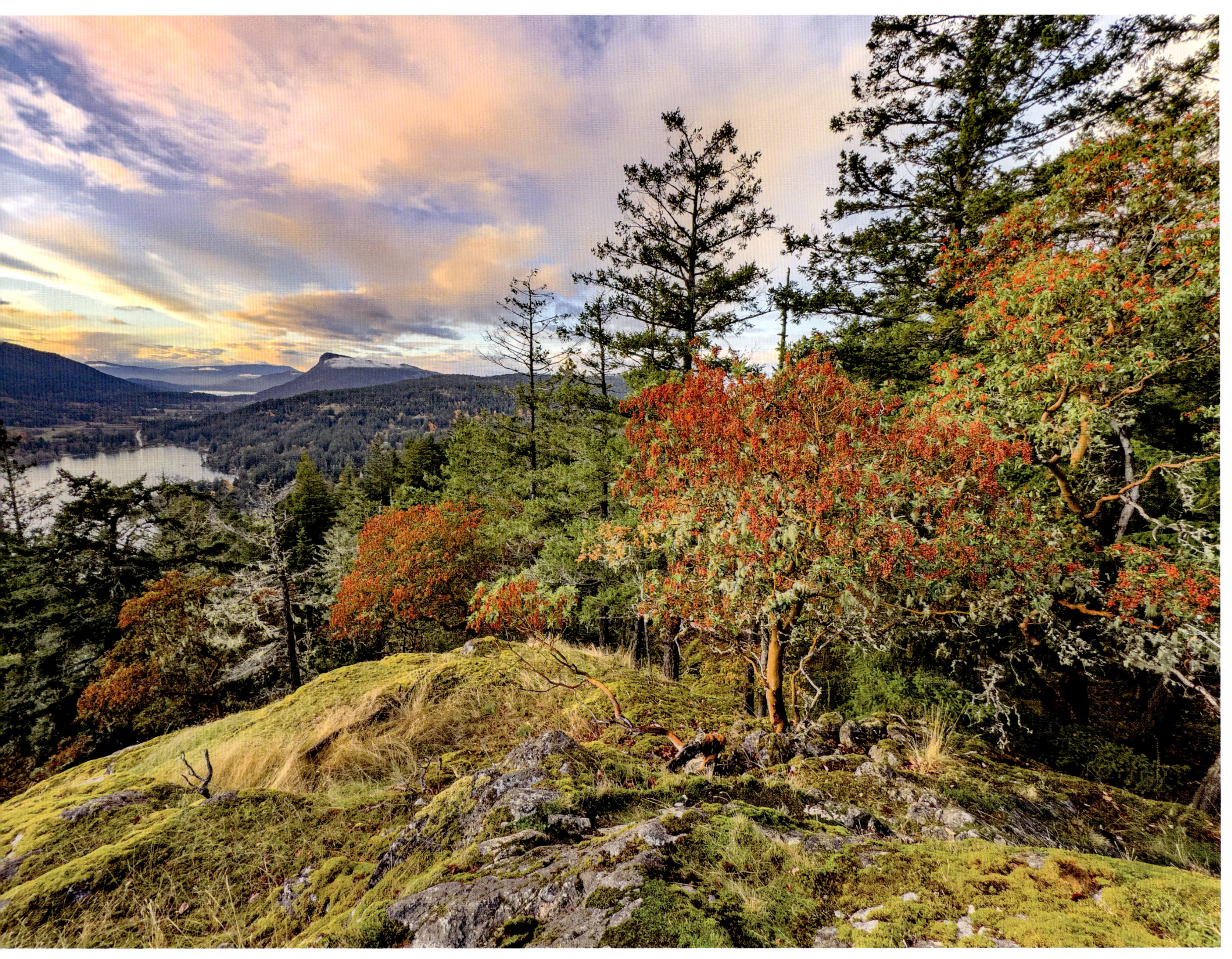

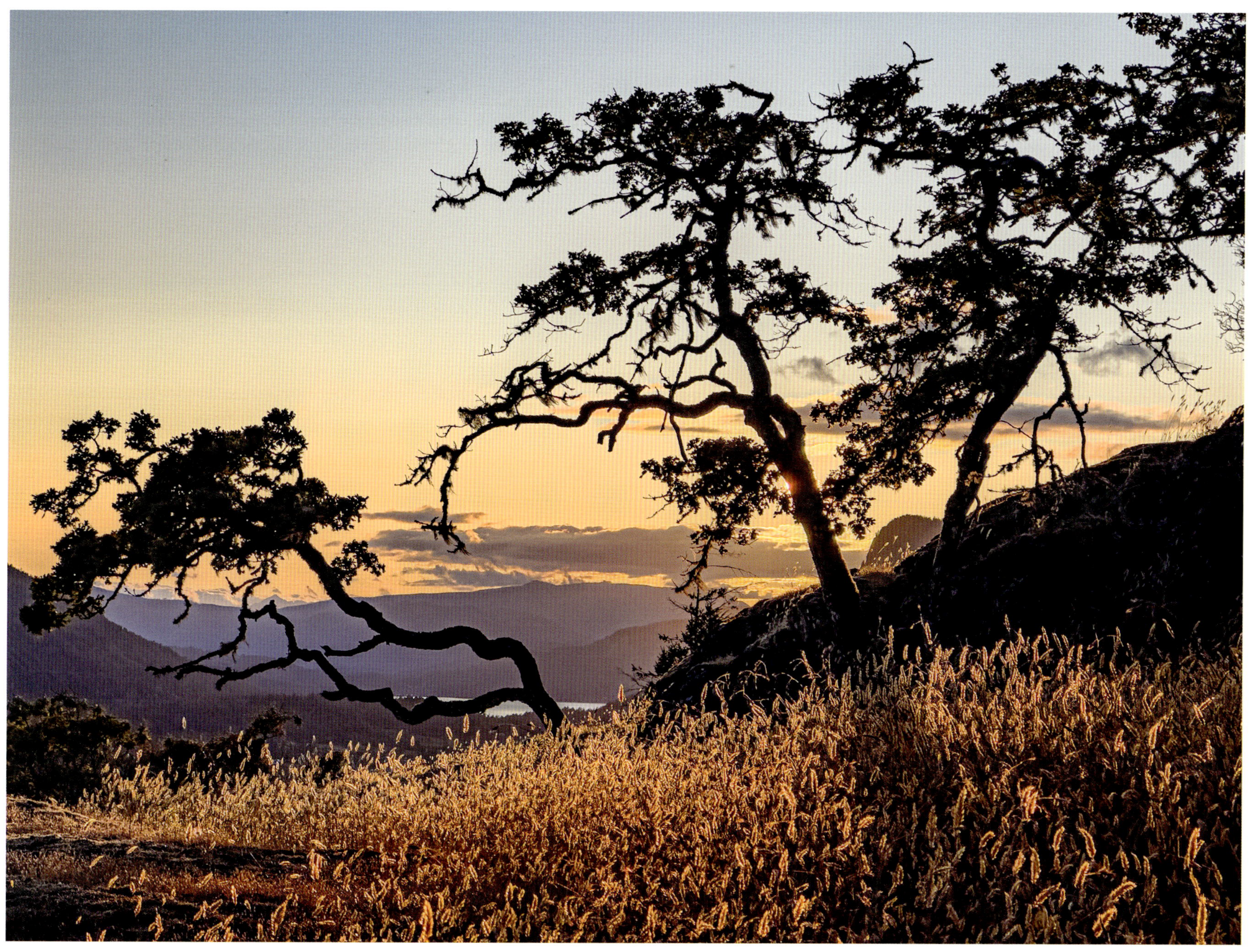

Scarlet arbutus berries in October brighten the view from Reginald Hill towards Mount Maxwell on the horizon (left).

A view in the same direction past the silhouettes of Garry oaks in mid-June (above).

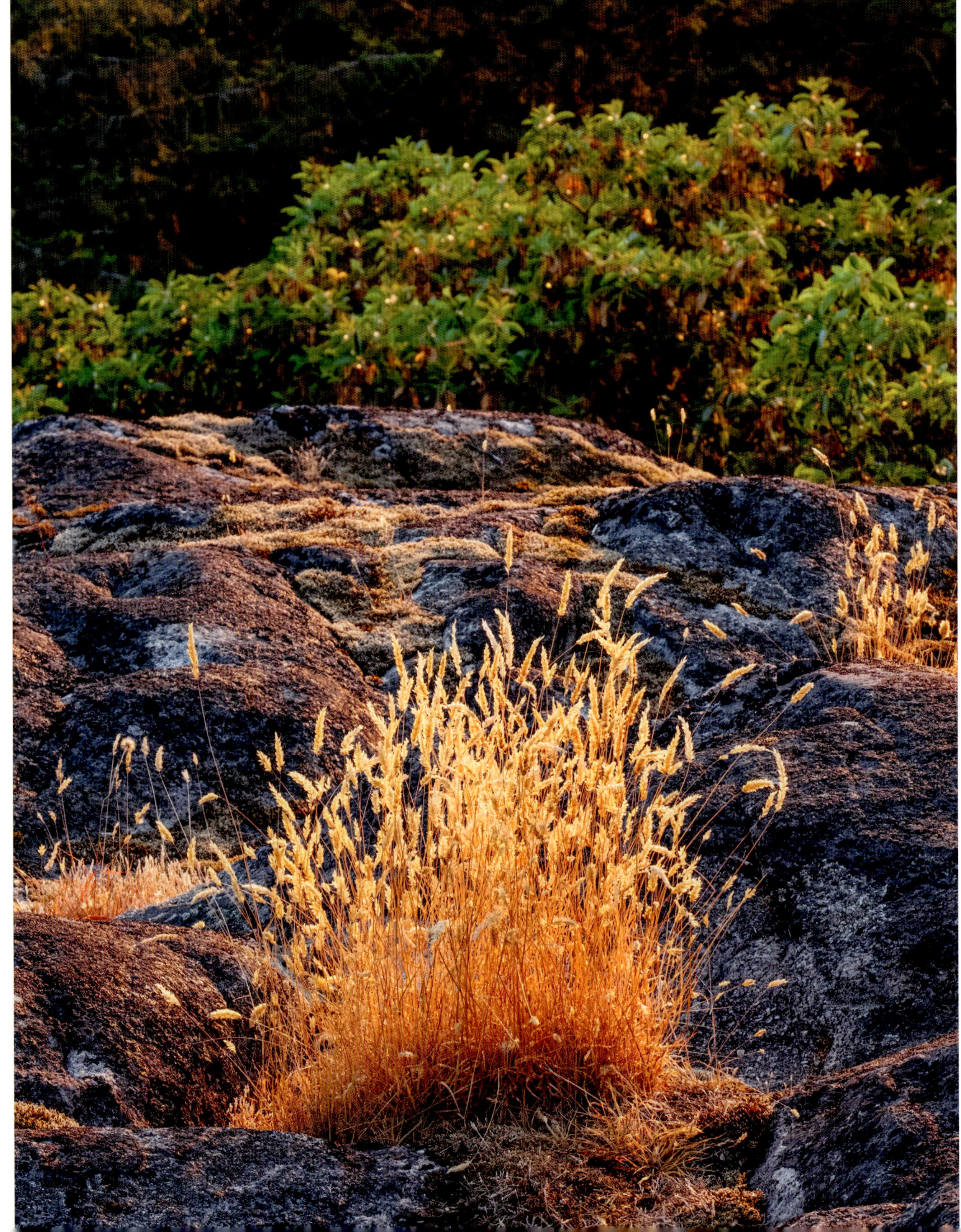

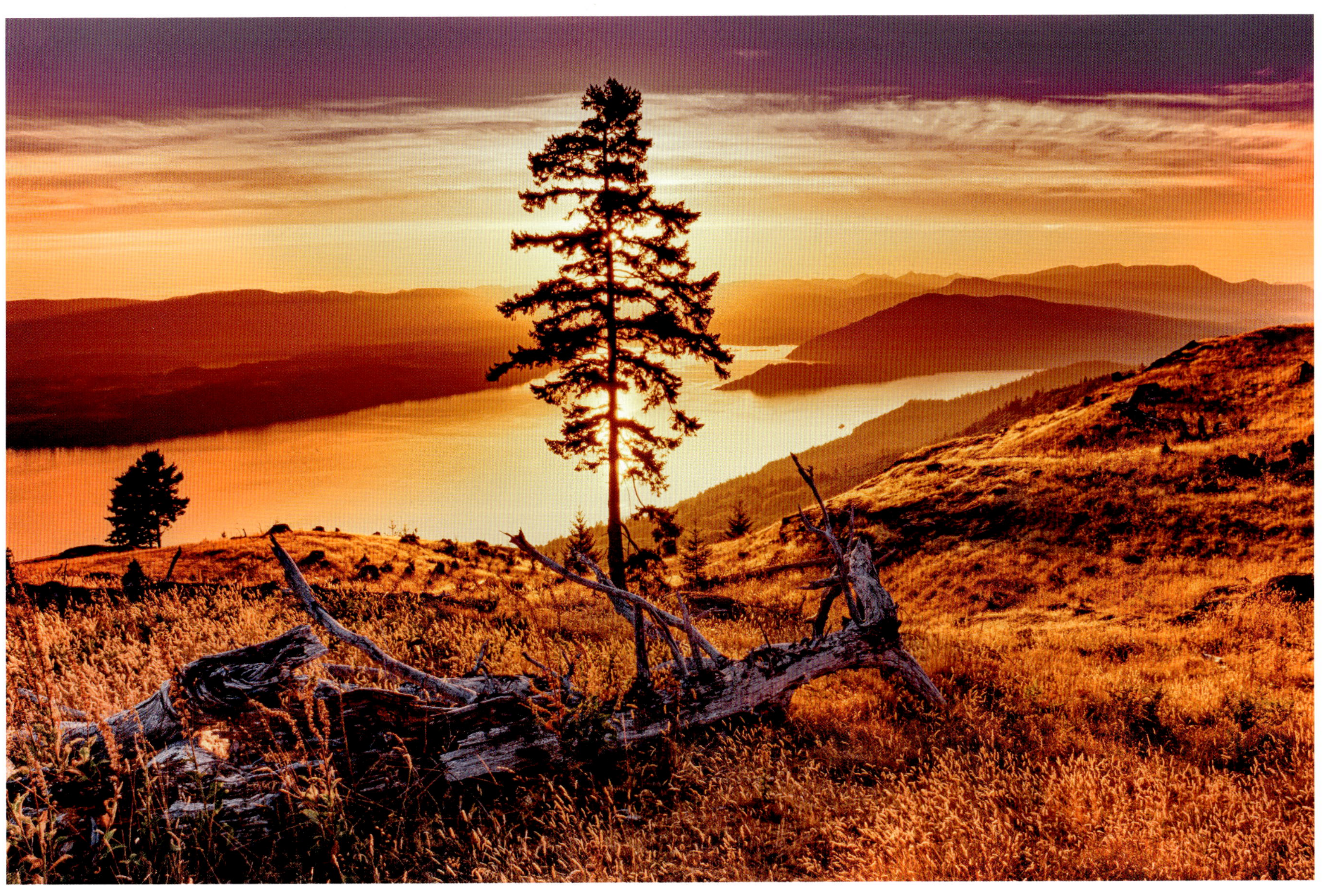

Dried grasses illuminated by the setting sun in late July (left).

The view from the summit of Mount Tuam towards Cowichan Bay and Vancouver Island at sunset (above).

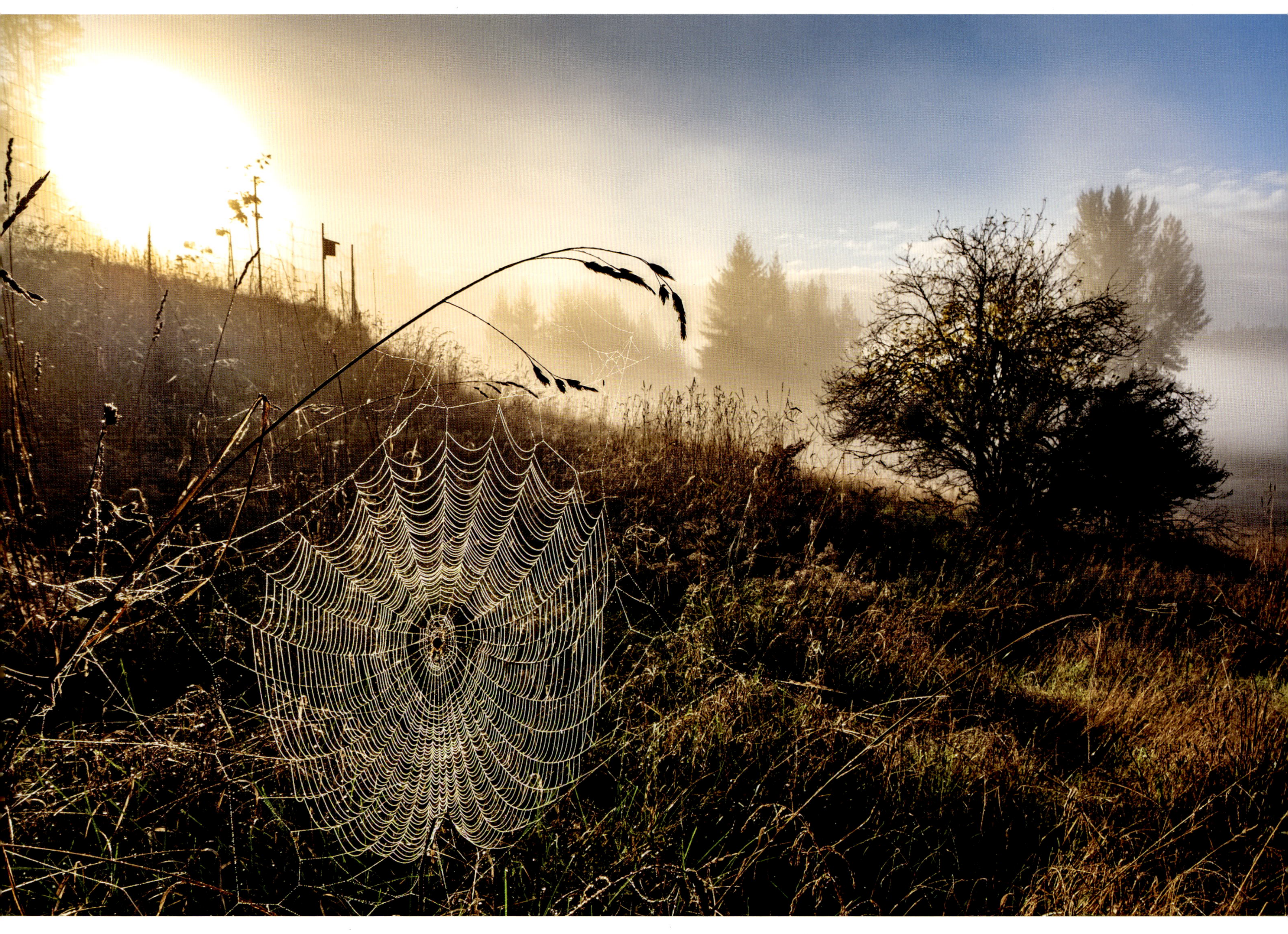

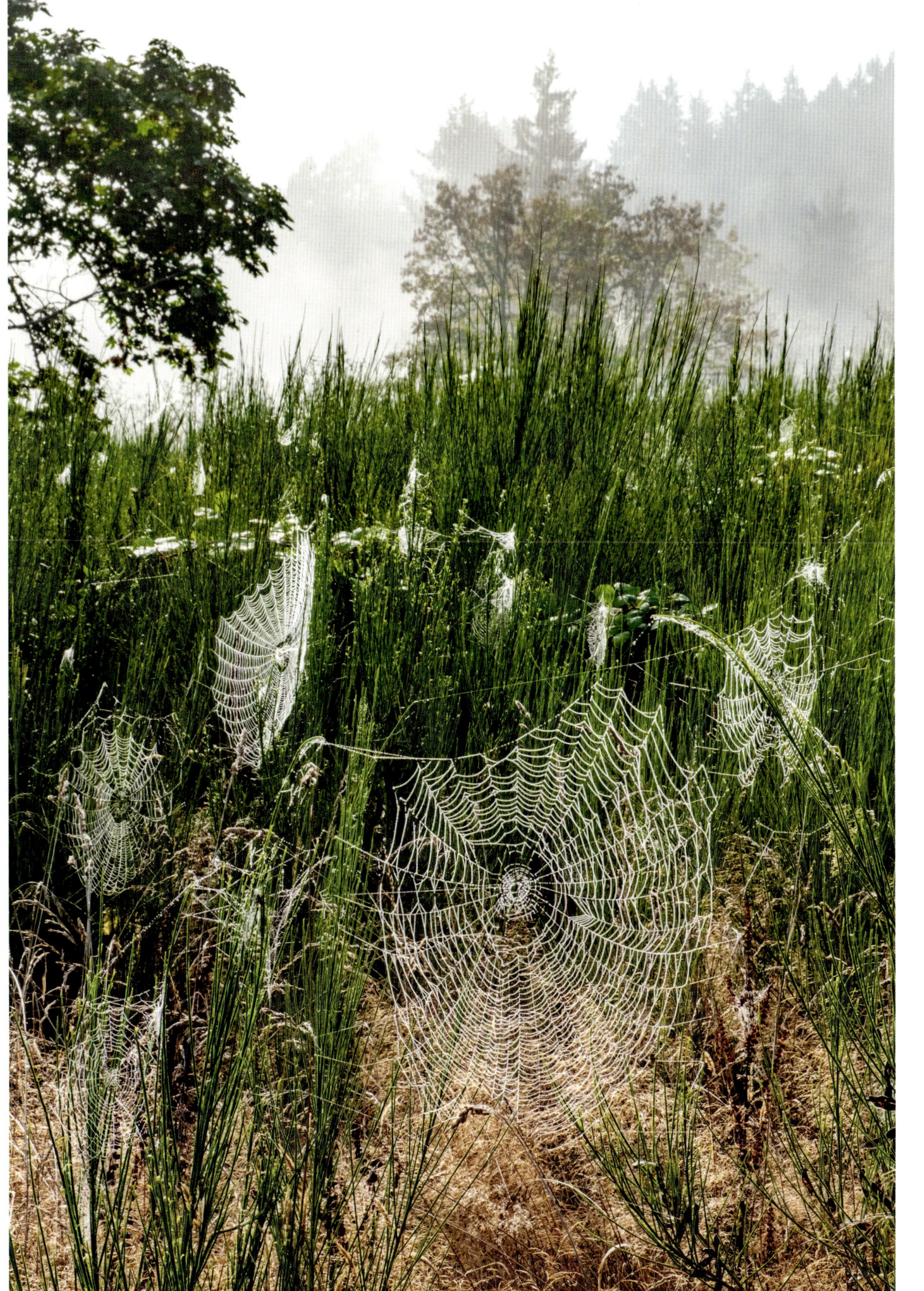

October brings an abundance of spider webs on dewy mornings at Blackburn Lake Nature Reserve (far left) and near Musgrave Road (left).

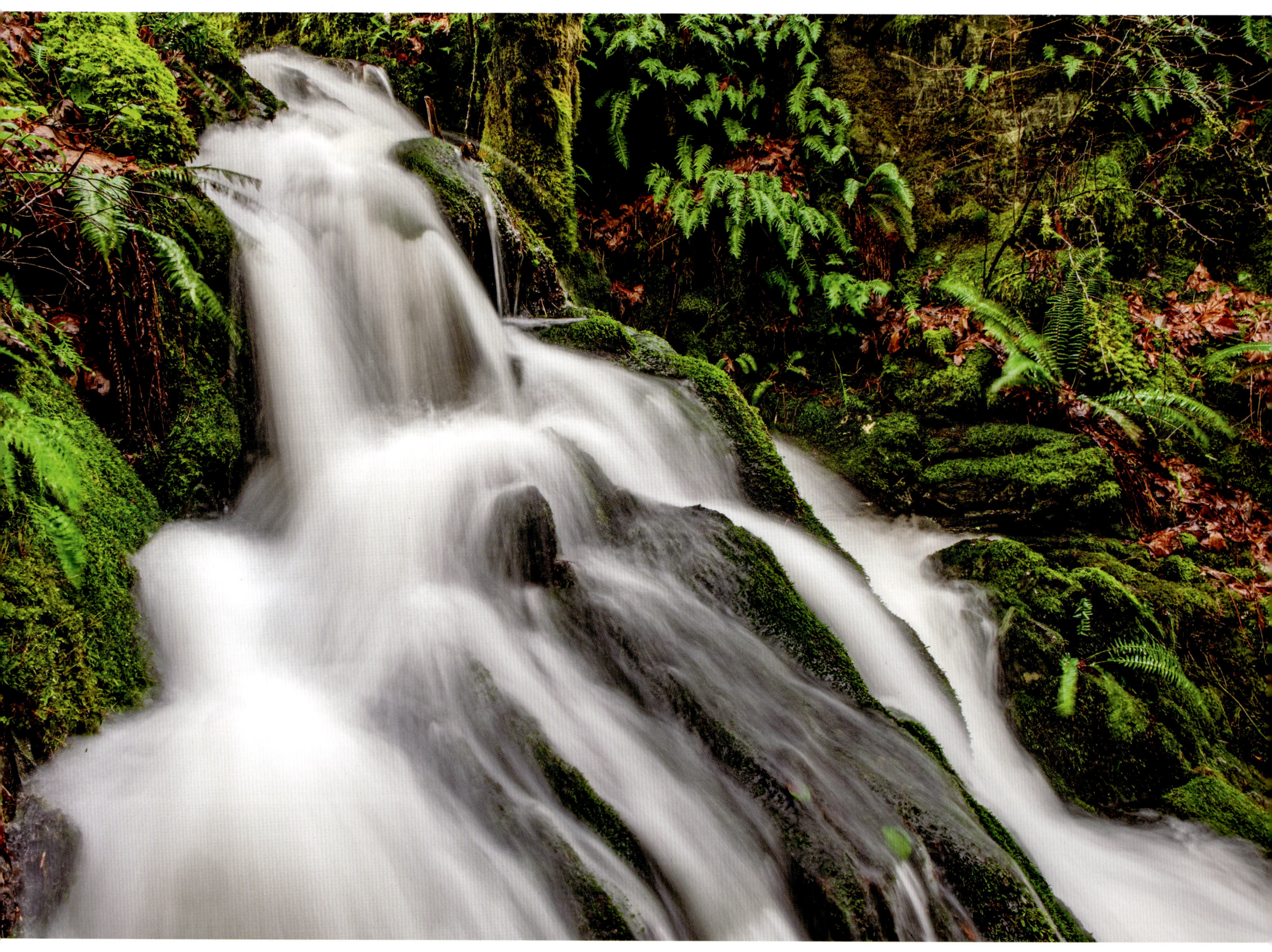

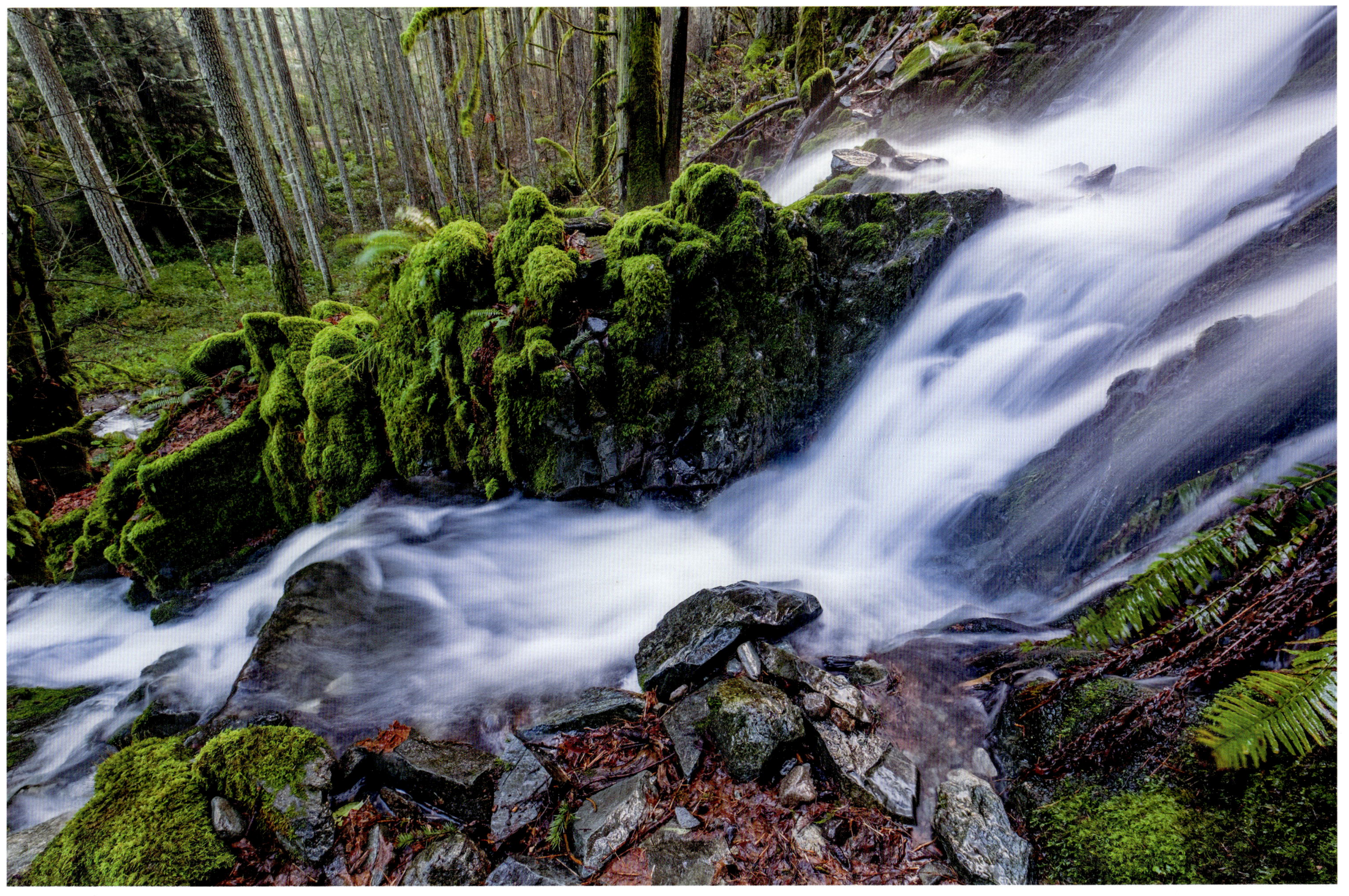

Two waterfalls above and below Mountain Road are some of the numerous cascades in Mount Tuam Nature Reserve during the rainy months, January in this instance.

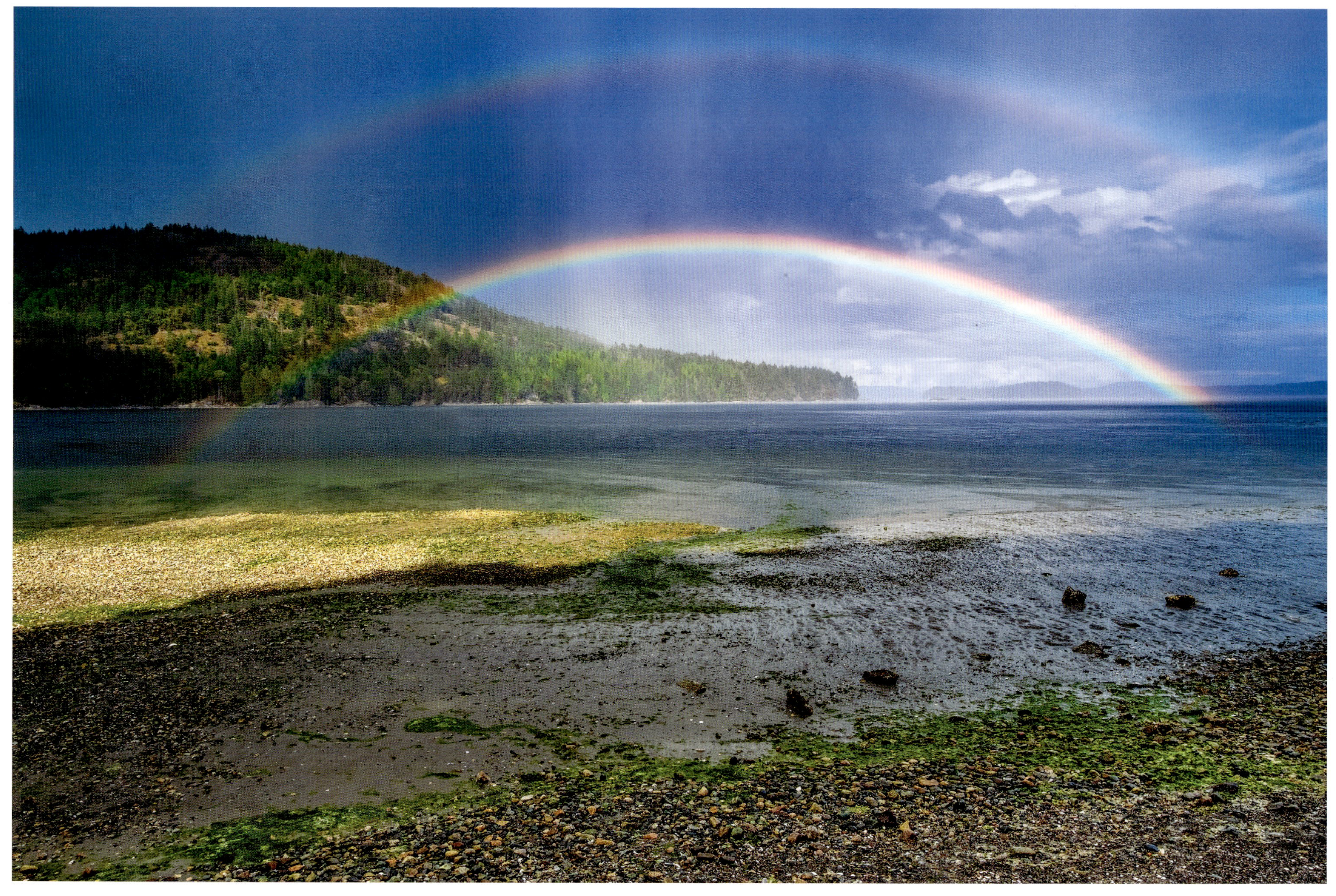

A rainbow frames the Tsawout Reserve across Fulford Harbour from Isabella Point Road in June (above).

A December full moon breaks through the clouds (right).

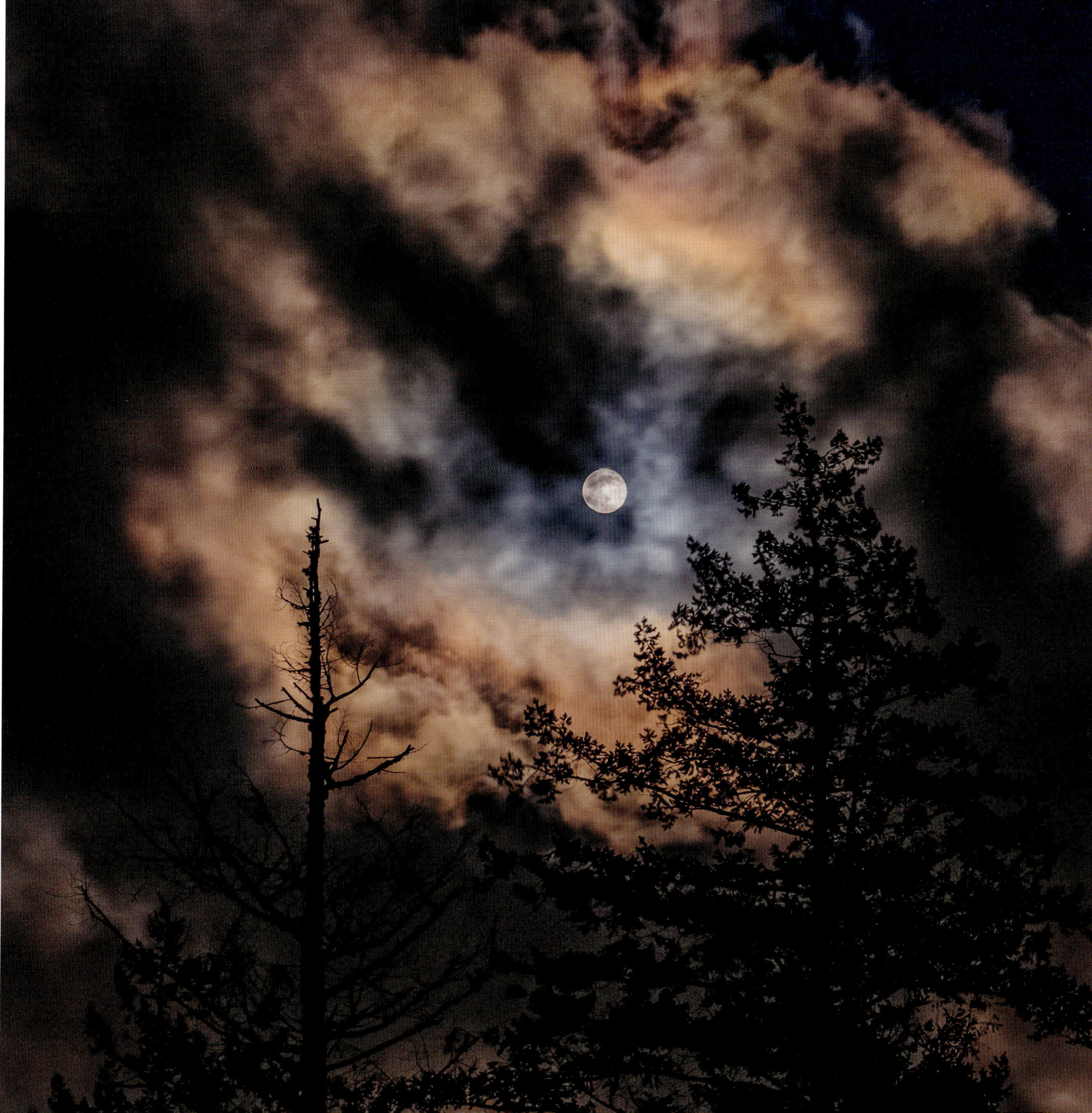

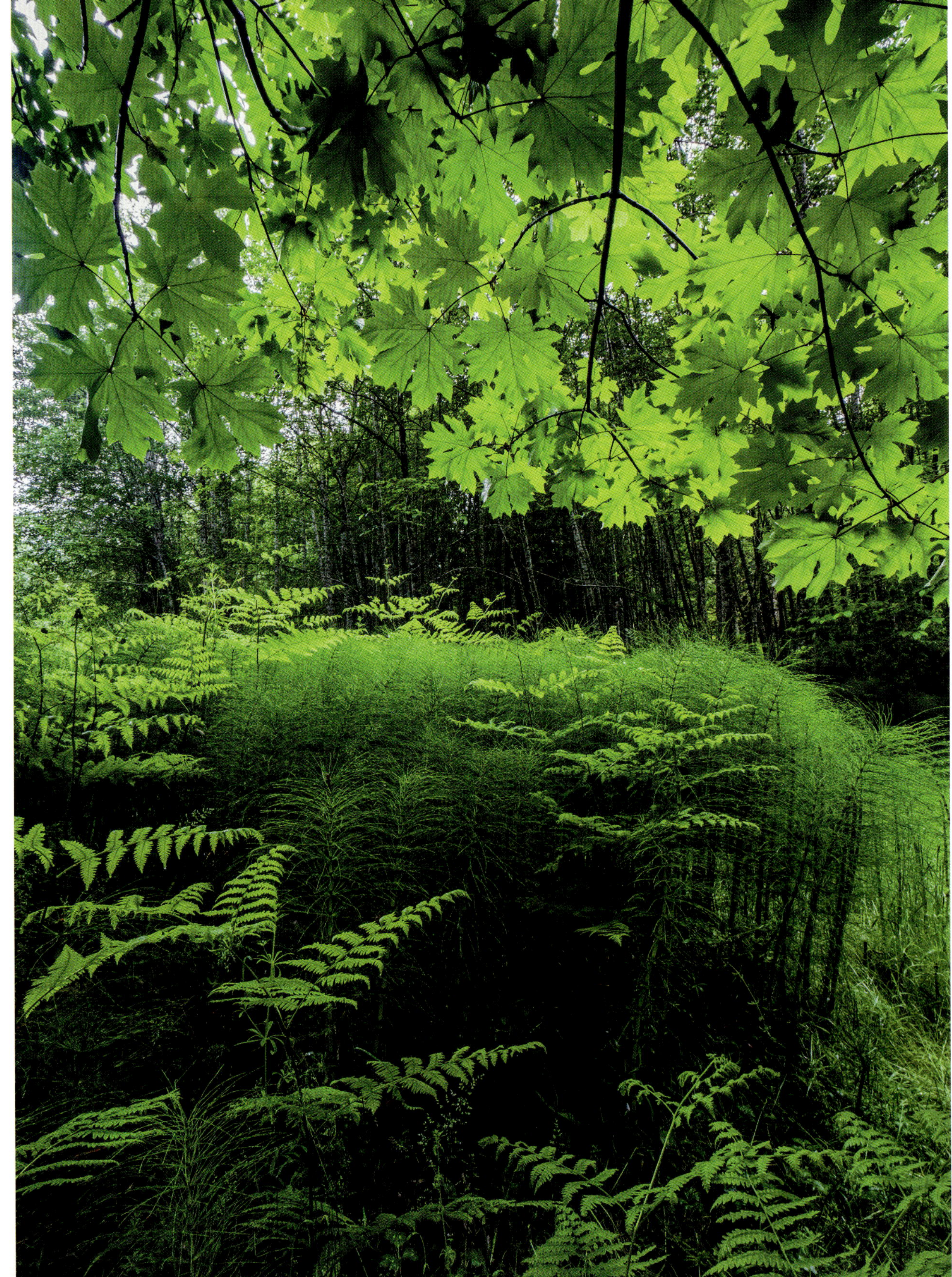

Ferns, *equisetum* and bigleaf maple (right), and bigleaf maple seed samaras (far right) in June.

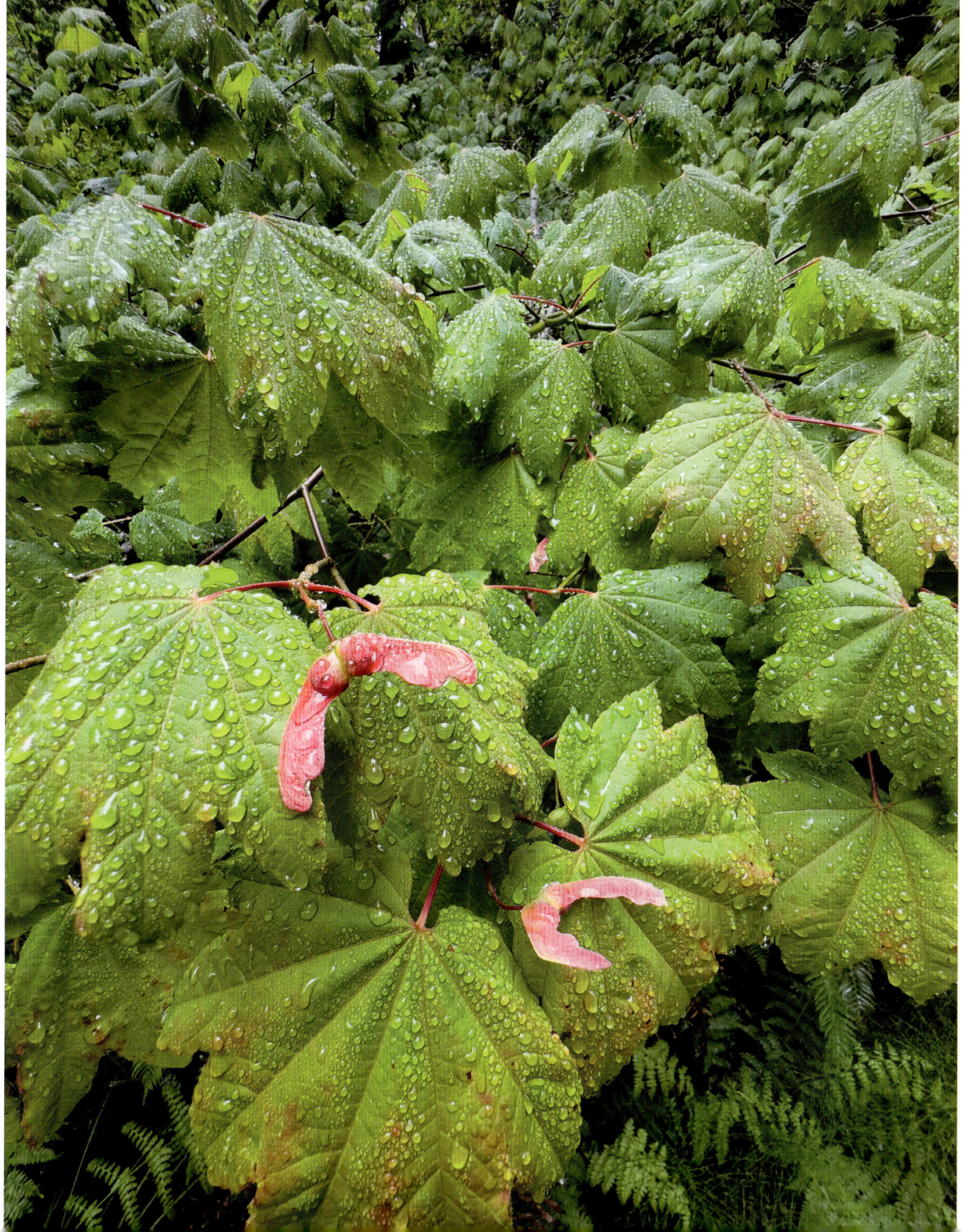

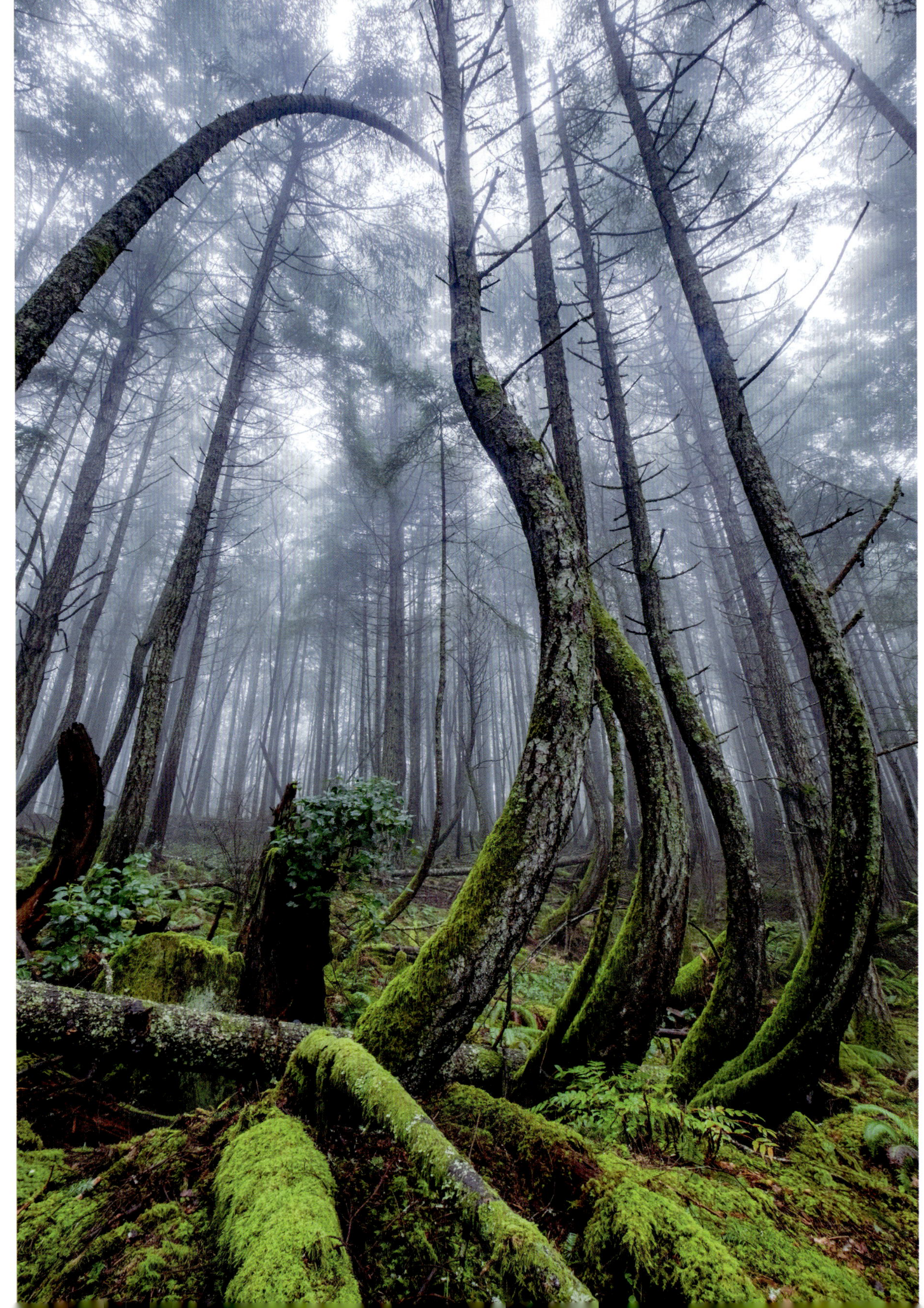

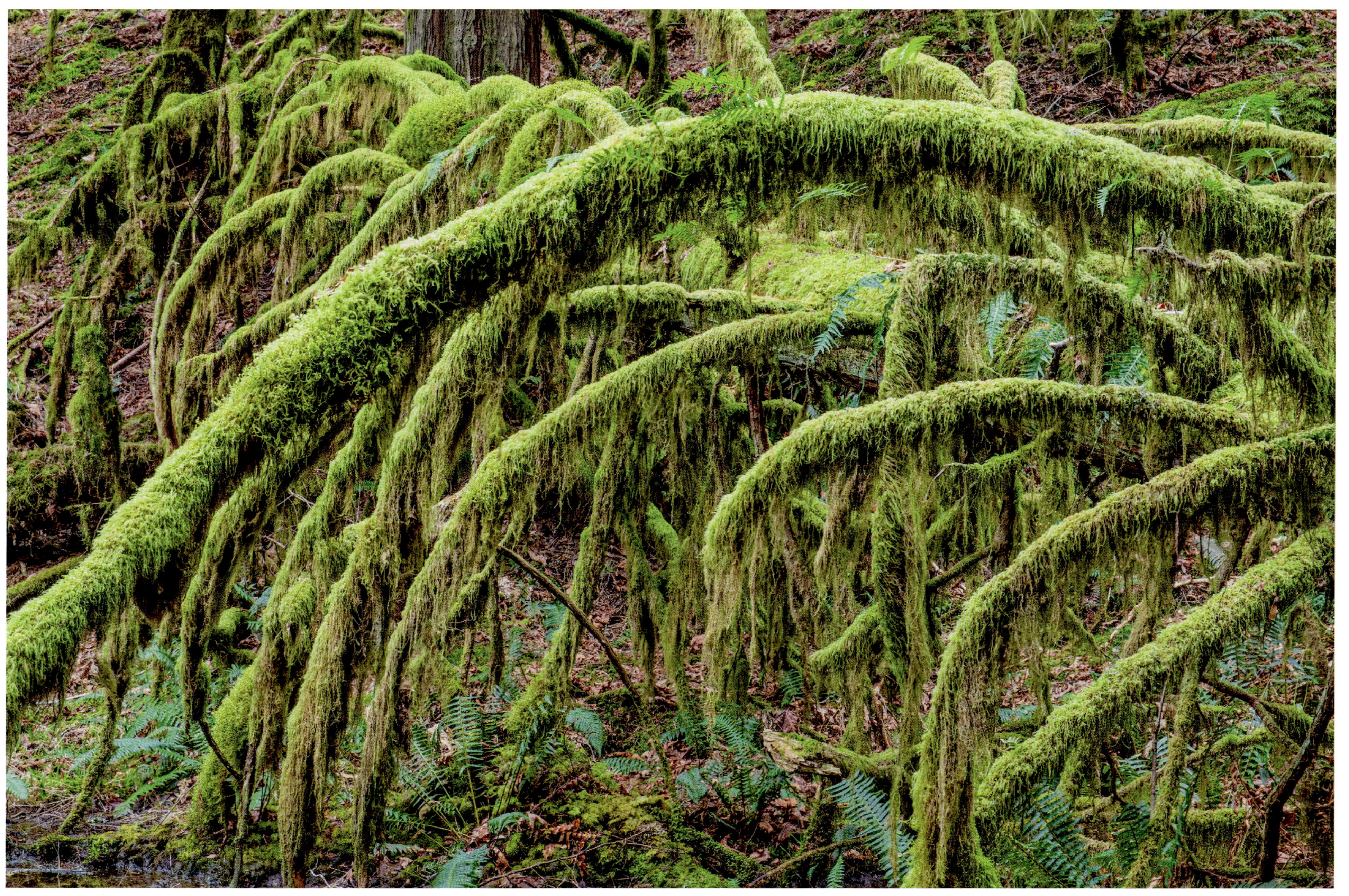

Soil creep on part of a slope has caused the curved growth in the trunks of these trees beside a trail on Channel Ridge (left).

Moss hangs from the branches of a fallen fir along the Chris Hatfield Trail in March (above).

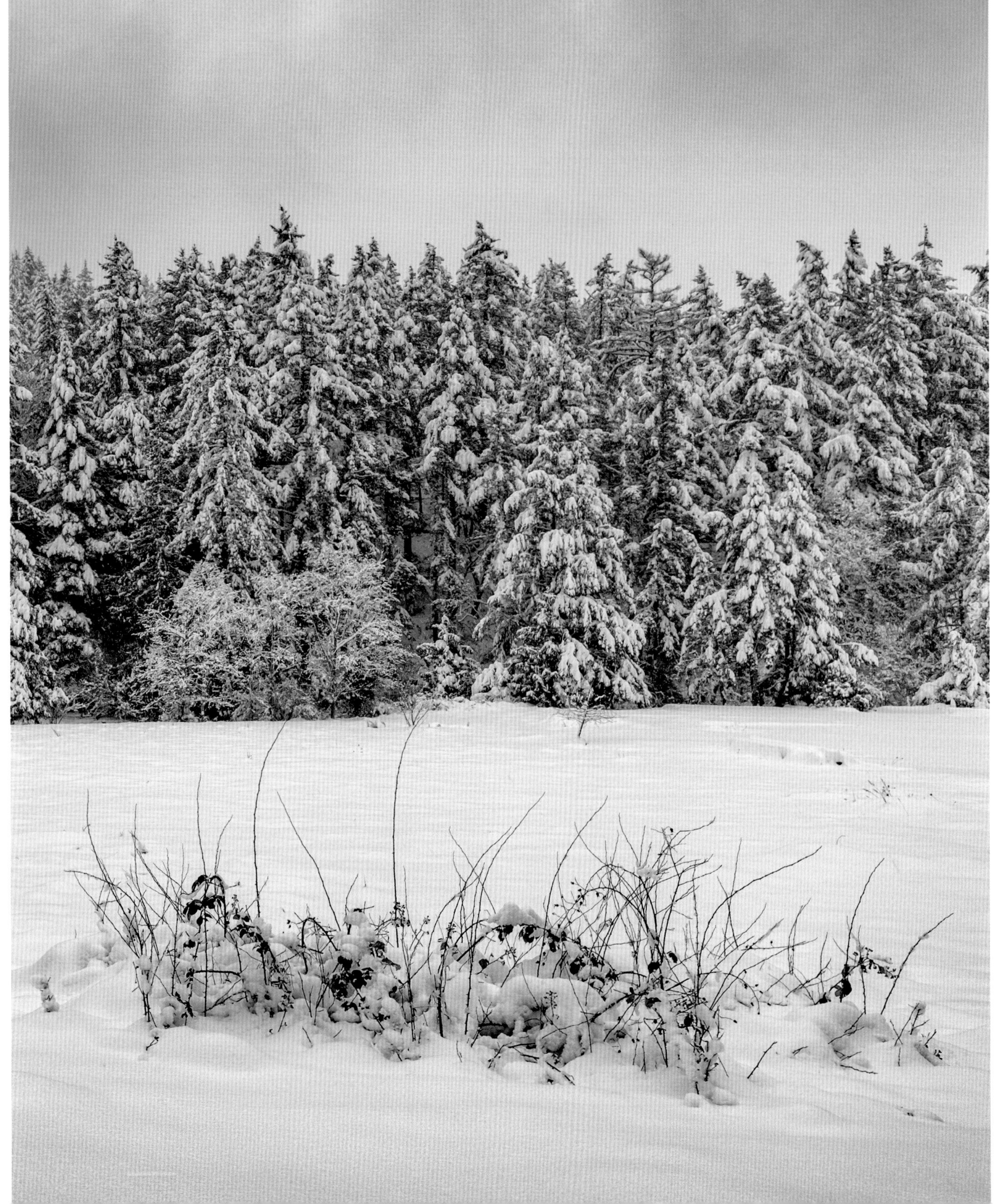

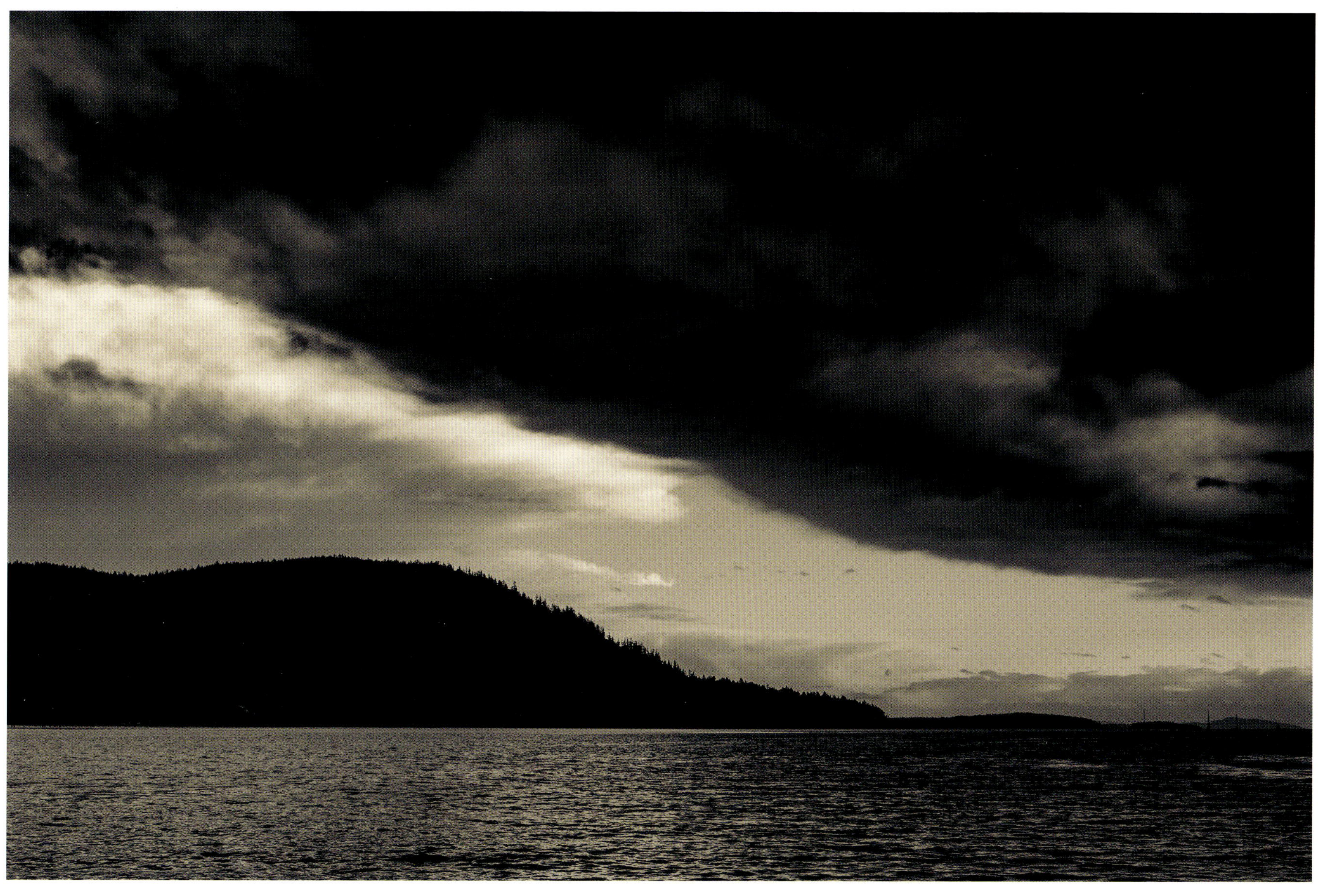

A February snowfall blankets the landscape near the mouth of Fulford Creek (left).

Stormy weather in October arcs over Reginald Hill, seen across Fulford Harbour (above).

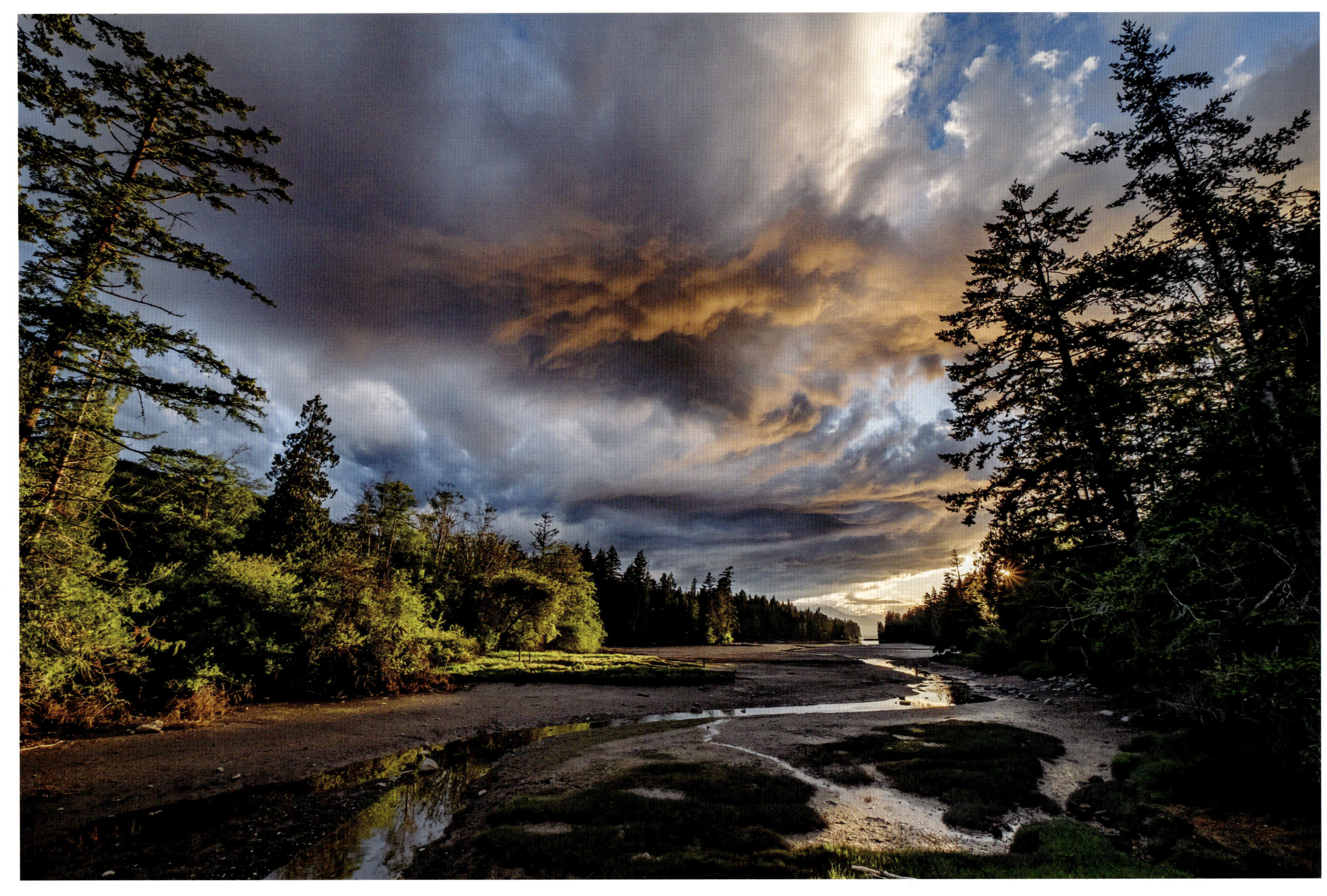

A summer solstice sunset at Booth Inlet during low tide.

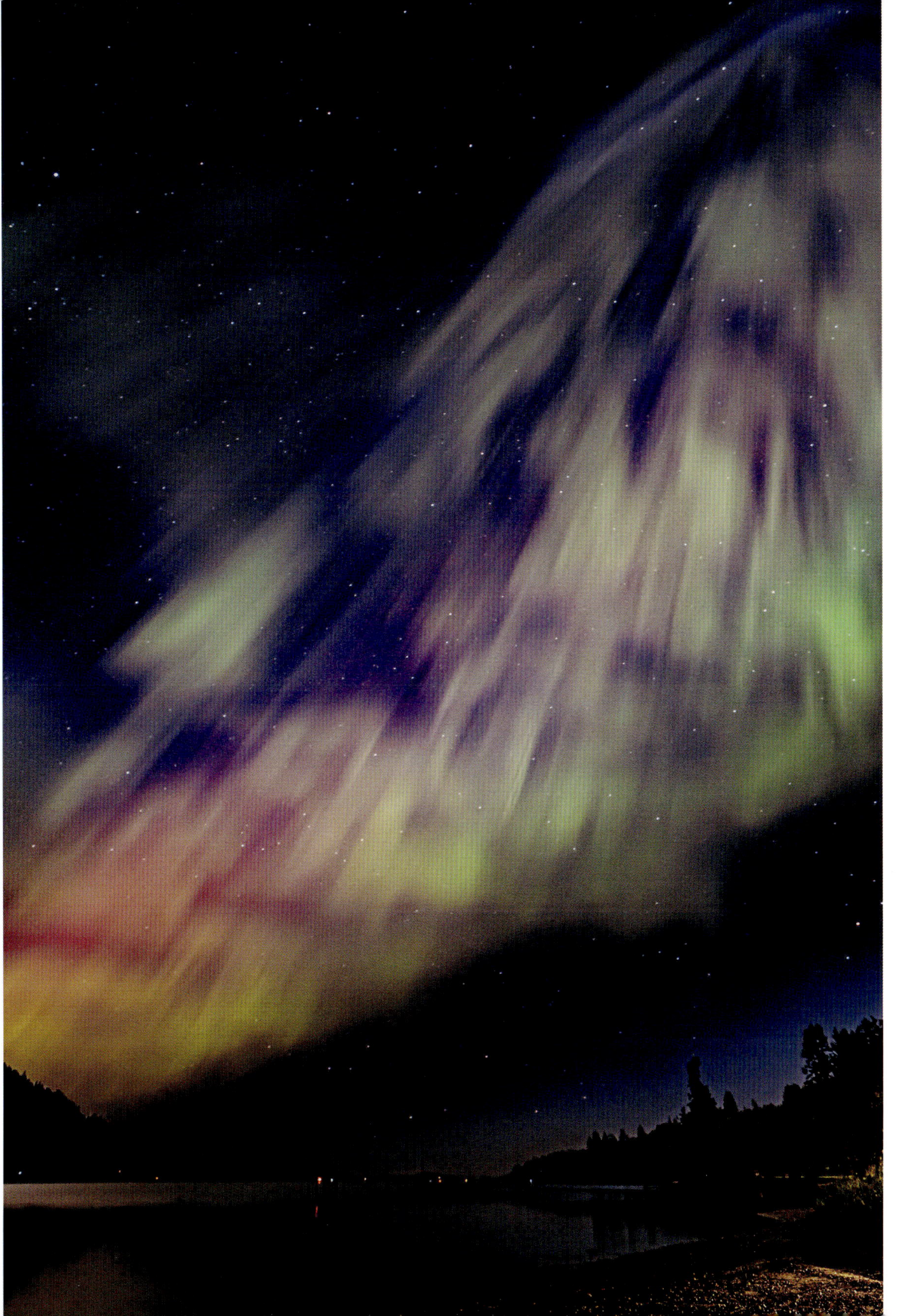

The aurora borealis on May 11, 2024 at Drummond Park.

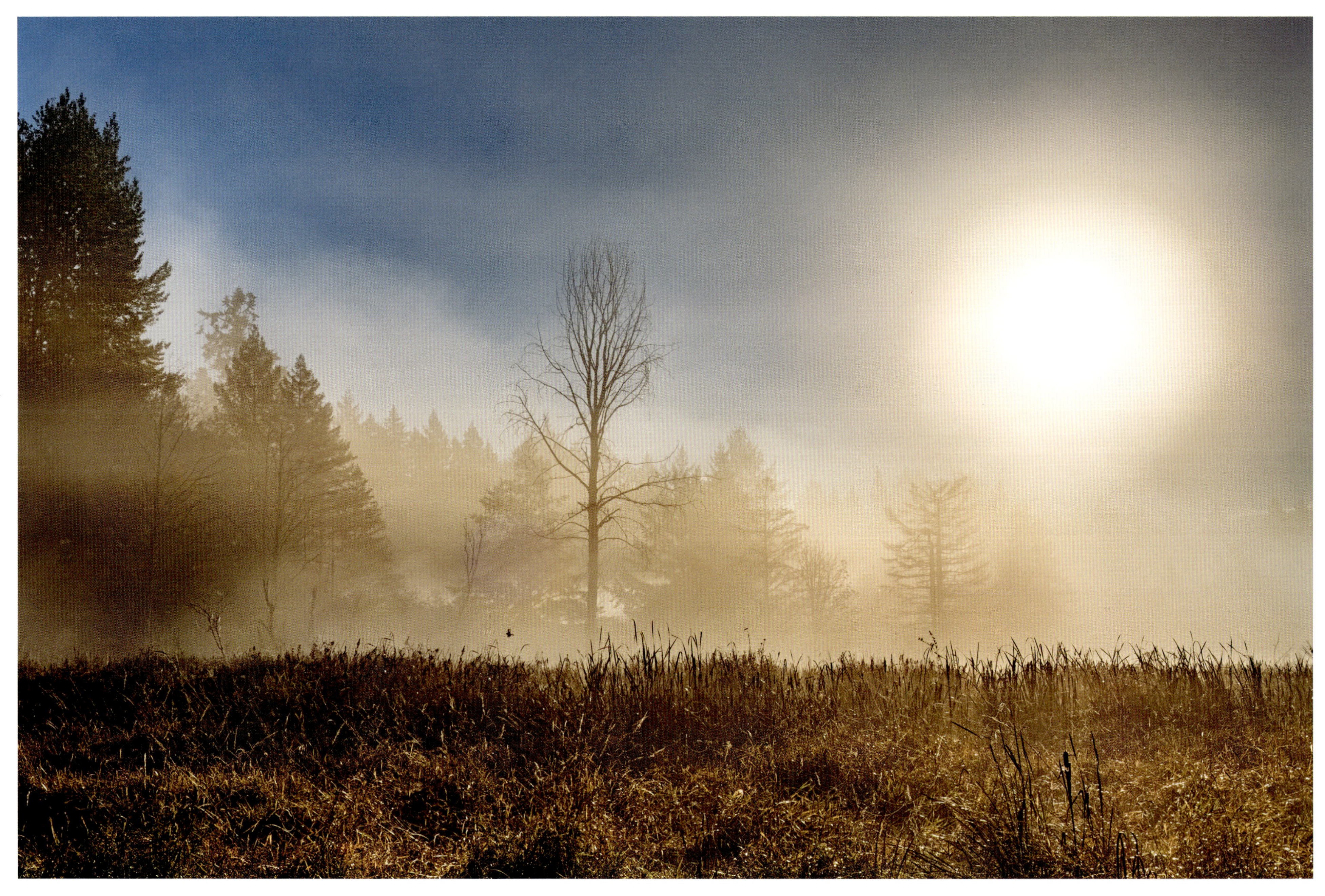

October sunrise at Blackburn Lake Nature Reserve.

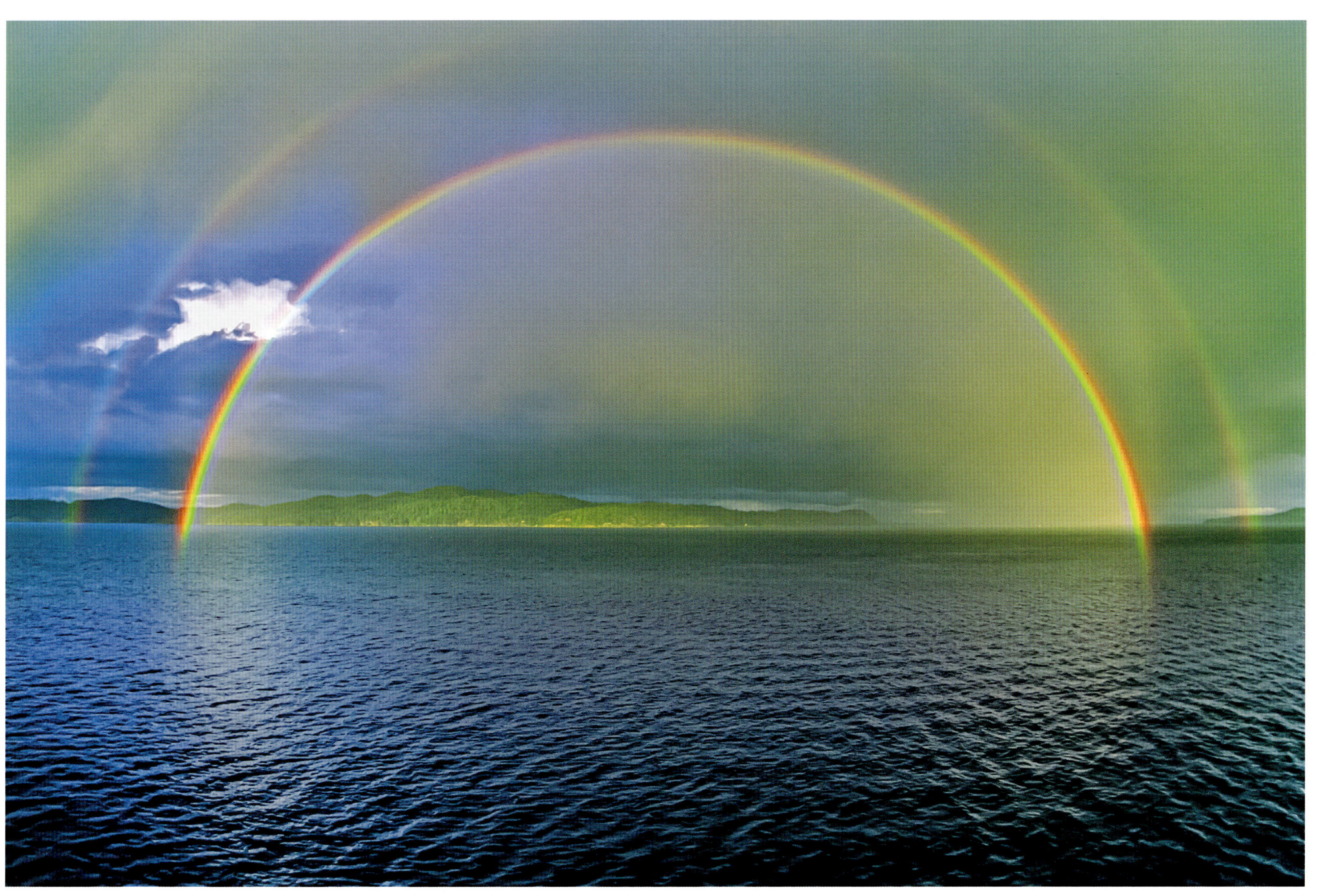

A double rainbow from the waters off Beaver Point, looking towards Pender Island.

LAST WORD

Every book is a summary of many intersecting journeys, not all of them made by the author.

I trace my journey to Salt Spring back to my birth in 1949 in Stockholm, Sweden, to which my Latvian parents had fled to escape the brutal invasion and occupation of their country by the Soviet Union at the close of WWII.

I was not yet two years old when my family arrived in Canada. My earliest and best memories of childhood are the summers spent in the countryside north of Montreal picking berries, catching (and releasing) frogs, collecting rocks and learning about different flowers, mushrooms and trees. These summers primed me for a lifelong love of exploring the natural world. As an adult, the high mountain ranges and the wild Pacific coast drew me back repeatedly to the west.

After earning three degrees in science and architecture at McGill University, I was offered the opportunity to supply the photography for my first book, Alpine Canada in 1978, with text by Andy Russell. Little did I know that what I expected would be a welcome, but short, break from all-nighters spent in design work would, instead, lead to a full-time career in photography sustained mainly by commercial stock photo licensing, magazine work, calendars and more book contracts.

This book owes its existence directly and indirectly to far more people than I can properly acknowledge. The path to it follows from my association with several publishers, to whom I remain very grateful. I am especially indebted to the late Mel Hurtig, along with Anna Porter and Lionel Koffler. Mel published my first books, among them *The Islands of Canada* with Marian Engel which initially brought me to Salt Spring to photograph in 1980. More recently Lionel commissioned me to produce three successive books on the Canadian landscape.

Those books in turn inspired me to pursue this one. When I began work I wondered if the landscapes and natural details on Salt Spring could yield enough diversity and beauty to match what I had been able to find and capture when I had the entire vast country of

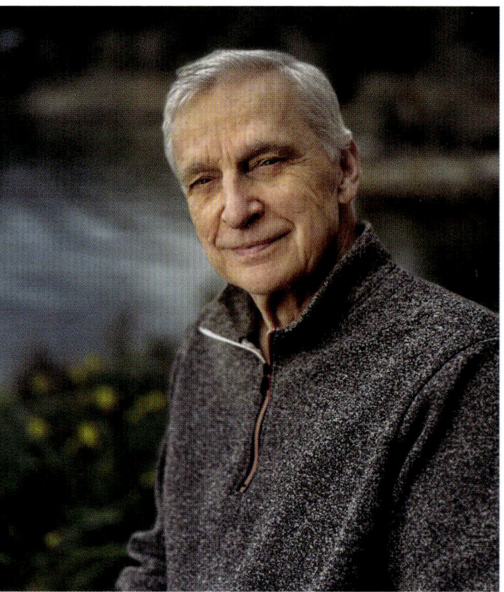

Photo courtesy of Bob Anderson

Canada for my subject matter. Fortunately, I discovered that finding beauty and diversity on Salt Spring was no challenge at all.

Family and friends have provided me with encouragement throughout. It is through the initiative of my late wife, Linda Kuttis, that we came to live on Salt Spring in the first place. Our kids, now adults, Anna and Theo, and my son-in-law Kal have been regular companions on the trails around the island and a constant source of help.

Like all islands, Salt Spring is effectively a self-contained world of its own and, as such, it invites reflection on the vulnerability and limits of one's environment. So, it is no accident that this island is home to First Nations custodians and a particularly large community of social and environmental activists, of artists, agriculturalists, foresters, naturalists, conservationists, land donors, and others who care deeply for the land. Most of their names I do not know, but for their stewardship and care of the places photographed herein I express my gratitude.

JAK

All the author royalties on this book are donated directly to environmental causes on Salt Spring Island.